TEACHING LIFETIME OUTDOOR PURSUITS

In Loving Memory of
James A. Wilkerson III
Adventurer and Gentleman

TEACHING LIFETIME OUTDOOR PURSUITS

Jeff Steffen, PhD

University of Wisconsin-La Crosse

Jim Stiehl, PhD

University of Northern Colorado

Editors

Human Kinetics

Library of Congress Cataloging-in-Publication Data

Teaching lifetime outdoor pursuits / Jeff Steffen, Jim Stiehl, editors.
      p. cm.
   Includes bibliographical references.
   ISBN-13: 978-0-7360-7999-0 (soft cover)
   ISBN-10: 0-7360-7999-8 (soft cover)
   1. Exercise. 2. Physical fitness. 3. Outdoor recreation. I. Steffen, Jeff.
II. Stiehl, Jim.
   GV481.T43 2010
   613.7'1--dc22

                              2010009745

ISBN-10: 0-7360-7999-8 (print)
ISBN-13: 978-0-7360-7999-0 (print)

The Web addresses cited in this text were current as of April 2010, unless otherwise noted.

Acquisitions Editor: Gayle Kassing, PhD; **Developmental Editor:** Melissa Feld; **Assistant Editor:** Rachel Brito; **Copyeditor:** Jocelyn Engman; **Permission Manager:** Dalene Reeder; **Graphic Designer:** Joe Buck; **Graphic Artist:** Dawn Sills; **Cover Designer:** Keith Blomberg; **Photographer (cover):** Paul Harris/Stone/Getty Images; **Photographer (interior):** Jim Stiehl (pp. 1, 9, and 37 [left column]); philippe Devanne/fotolia.com (p. 17); Daniel L. Chase (p. 21); Brand X Pictures (p. 33); Ryan Hammes (pp. 45, 46, 47, 48, 49, 50, 52, 53, 54, 55, 56, 57, 58, 59, 60, 61, 62, 63, and 64); John and Karen Hollingsworth/USFWS (p. 67); Mark H. Zmudy (pp. 93 and 95); Michael Odberg (pp. 107 [upper photo] and 113); Kristen Csiacsek (pp. 125, 132, 137, and 139); vigorin/fotolia.com (p. 143); Alan Bonds (p. 144); Matt Howie (pp. 146, 148, 149, 150, and 151); Gay L. Timken (pp. 157, 158, 163, 164, 165, 166, 167, 171, 173, and 174); Photodisc/Getty Images (p. 179); John Saunders (pp. 181 and 186); Tim P. Taylor (pp. 207, 209, 211, 212, 213, and 214); all other photos © Human Kinetics; **Photo Asset Manager:** Jason Allen; **Art Manager:** Kelly Hendren; **Associate Art Manager:** Alan L. Wilborn; **Printer:** Versa Press

Printed in the United States of America   10   9   8   7   6   5   4   3   2   1

The paper in this book is certified under a sustainable forestry program.

Human Kinetics
Web site: www.HumanKinetics.com

United States: Human Kinetics
P.O. Box 5076
Champaign, IL 61825-5076
800-747-4457
e-mail: humank@hkusa.com

Canada: Human Kinetics
475 Devonshire Road Unit 100
Windsor, ON N8Y 2L5
800-465-7301 (in Canada only)
e-mail: info@hkcanada.com

Europe: Human Kinetics
107 Bradford Road
Stanningley
Leeds LS28 6AT, United Kingdom
+44 (0) 113 255 5665
e-mail: hk@hkeurope.com

Australia: Human Kinetics
57A Price Avenue
Lower Mitcham, South Australia 5062
08 8372 0999
e-mail: info@hkaustralia.com

New Zealand: Human Kinetics
P.O. Box 80
Torrens Park, South Australia 5062
0800 222 062
e-mail: info@hknewzealand.com

E4712

Contents

Chapter 10 Cycling   157
Gay L. Timken and Amy Lutz

Chapter 11 Snowshoeing   179
John T. Saunders

Chapter 12   Nordic Walking   191

Malin Svensson

Chapter 13   Knot Tying   207

Tim P. Taylor

CD-ROM Contents

Preface

In the gym we seldom confront discomforts such as developing a blister on a difficult hike, getting soaked in the rain, being exhausted and dirty at the end of a strenuous day, or dealing with bothersome insects. Since most of us don't deliberately seek uncomfortable situations, why should we take kids into the outdoors where surprise changes in the weather or unexpected obstacles might impose physical and emotional demands? Moreover, in an age when many adults are trying to protect children from every conceivable disappointment and inconvenience (see Malone, 2007, regarding the bubble wrap concept), why should we assume the added responsibility of dealing with anxieties that being outdoors creates for some kids?

First, outdoor activities don't automatically entail discomfort. Students who know how to stay warm and dry, for example, can be comfy and content in a cold environment. Second, the rewards and pleasures usually far outweigh the frustrations and demands of an outdoor experience. Outdoor experiences can provide excellent opportunities to learn about resilience and patience. They also offer a sense of satisfaction and accomplishment when newly acquired skills are used to solve a tough problem or to surmount an obstacle. In short, students may occasionally feel discomfort, but in doing so they discover how to deal with problems while also feeling competent and good about themselves. They may even have a great time as well.

Each author in this book has used the outdoors to create noncompetitive opportunities for students to challenge themselves and to spend time with their teacher outside of the traditional classroom. We do not view outdoor pursuits as an escape from the gym but as a limitless classroom and an integral part of a student's educational experience. It is one thing for students to learn kayaking from a hired guide, but it is quite another thing for students to go kayaking on coastal waters with their physical education teacher—and the same goes for climbing or snowshoeing. The shared adventure and perspective can create a profoundly different student–teacher relationship.

In searching for a useful instructional text, we could not locate anything devoted solely to outdoor pursuits. There is no resource that is widely available or extensive enough or useful enough to help teachers initiate outdoor pursuits in a physical education setting. Some books mix outdoor pursuits with other outdoor activities such as cooking and sanitation. Other books present teaching strategies in some chapters while omitting them in others. Still other books assume extensive background training and experience in teaching outdoor activities. And few offer any suggestions about assessment.

In writing this book, we assumed the following: *Teachers want to know what to teach and how to teach it as well as how to determine whether learning occurs.* Thus, we solicited chapters from physical education instructors who have successfully incorporated outdoor pursuits into their traditional physical education programs. Our contributors know the ropes, so to speak. Each chapter follows a similar format and includes both content and pedagogy for a particular outdoor pursuit. In the accompanying CD-ROM, our authors provide samples of unit plans, lessons, and assessments (unit plans are also found at the end of chapters 2-12). We also include information about knots that are used frequently in various outdoor settings in the final chapter.

When used by university and college educators, this book can be adopted for a single course or can be used across several courses. We have included a reasonable number and breadth of activities that, regardless of geographic location, can be incorporated into a school physical education program. For instance, the chapter on snowshoeing may be irrelevant to someone in the southwest, but the chapters on hiking, bouldering, rock climbing, canoeing, geocaching, and so on should be relevant to that area.

This book is also written for the physical education teacher who has a keen interest in outdoor pursuits but may have minimal knowledge and experience, a modest budget, and questionable planning time yet required accountability. We hope you will join the increasing number of teachers who are adding outdoor pursuits to their physical education programs. Days can be long and strenuous. Cuts, bruises, and poison ivy may appear. All are part of the joy of being outside with students.

REFERENCE

Malone, K. (2007). The bubble-wrap generation: Children growing up in walled gardens. *Environmental Education Research, 13*(4), 513-527.

chapter 1

Introduction to Outdoor Pursuits

Jeff Steffen

Jim Stiehl

Modern life and education tend to be moving farther away from experiences close to nature.
Julian Smith

During the past decade, adventure education and outdoor pursuits have been increasingly incorporated into physical education curricula (Wurdinger & Steffen, 2003). Although outdoor and adventure programs have existed for almost a century (Neill, 2004; Outward Bound, 2006), recognition and support by the National Association for Sport and Physical Education (NASPE) has brought about a new era for adventure and outdoor teaching.

During the unfolding of this new era, it has become common for public schools to feature climbing walls, ropes courses, and other equipment for outdoor pursuits. The days of viewing activities such as snowshoeing and rock climbing as alternative or high risk are dwindling. At the same time, distinctions between adventure education and outdoor pursuits have become blurred. Terms such as *adventure programming, outdoor education, outdoor activities, adventure education, outdoor adventures,* and *outdoor pursuits* are often used synonymously. While there may be similarities among these terms (e.g., reference to a type of curriculum or units of instruction or professional associations), there are some important differences worth noting, especially with respect to the concepts of adventure and outdoor pursuits, since the latter is the focus of this book.

OUTDOOR PURSUITS DEFINED

Adventure education often takes place in developed, facility-based areas (e.g., gymnasiums, playgrounds, nearby athletic fields) and involves activities geared toward increasing personal confidence and mutual support within a group (Miles & Priest, 1999). Many adventure programs include acquaintance activities (activities for getting to know other group members), disinhibition games and icebreakers (movement for fun and laughter), communication tasks (activities for decision making and conflict resolution), and problem-solving and trust-building activities (Rohnke & Butler, 1995). Low and high ropes course challenges may also be included (see Association for Challenge Course Technology, 2008).

Outdoor pursuits take place in natural settings and involve skills for traveling from one place to another without using motorized transportation (Ford, Blanchard, & Blanchard, 1993). In contemporary physical education programs, outdoor pursuits have been associated with lifetime activities (National Association for Sport and Physical Education, 2004) and may include rock climbing, hiking, backpacking, canoeing, biking, kayaking, camping, snowshoeing, scuba diving, surfing, skiing, and snowboarding. Not considered among outdoor pursuits are activities such as paragliding, cliff parachuting, skydiving, and bungee jumping. Although these intense sports are marching into the recreational mainstream, their purpose (thrill seeking) and dangers (potential injury and death) do not align with the goals of physical education.

In addition to their differences in settings and activities, adventure education and outdoor pursuits possess two important distinctions that have implications for the curriculum and instruction ideas given in this book. First, with its orientation toward personal and interpersonal growth, adventure education tends to be heavily weighted in the affective domain. Although conducted in a movement context, it requires little in the way of psychomotor skills. Outdoor pursuits, on the other hand, place greater emphasis on the psychomotor and cognitive domains because of the requirements for traveling in the outdoors. Explicit skills and knowledge are necessary for a specific outdoor pursuits activity (e.g., caving or canoeing). Thus, while students at all skill levels can enjoy outdoor pursuits, these pursuits involve greater knowledge and skill acquisition than that required by adventure education.

The second distinction between adventure education and outdoor pursuits involves their risk or potential for physical or emotional harm. Both carry risks and both require proper policies and procedures for risk management. But in adventure-based programs there is a large contrast between the perceived risk and the actual risk. Much of the risk taking in an adventure setting is related to the disequilibrium that occurs from people participating in an experience that is beyond their comfort zone. Unfamiliar and unexpected activities are presented in a novel setting. As a consequence, students experience anxiety and perceptions of risk.

In outdoor pursuits there is less contrast between perceived risk and actual risk simply because these activities take place in natural settings. The outdoors present real risks in the form of wildlife, insect bites, adverse weather, contaminated drinking water, avalanches, and a host of other possible hazards. Certainly adventure activities and outdoor pursuits can provoke emotional anxiety, but potential physical risks are more real in the outdoors than in the adventure setting.

BENEFITS OF OUTDOOR PURSUITS

Several reasons account for the increased popularity of outdoor pursuits in physical education programs. First, for some young people the most appealing physical activities are those that provide excitement, challenge, and a degree of risk while minimizing the importance of winning and losing (Stiehl, 2000). Second, more physical education teachers are recognizing the many benefits that students can derive from outdoor pursuits and are considering these benefits when preparing objectives and activities. These benefits include the following:

• **Self-confidence.** Having self-confidence can lead to a greater willingness to handle challenges and to learn from and admit to mistakes. Many students with limited physical skills experience a swift success in outdoor pursuits that leads them to believe in their ability to succeed. Learning how to read a map, for example, can help a student plan a travel route that is efficient and enjoyable for everyone. More specifically, by understanding a map's contours, the student can not only avoid potential hazards (e.g., moving water, exposure to lightning) but also conserve energy by avoiding unnecessary elevation gain or loss. By matching the difficulty of the route to the abilities of the group, the student supports the group while also experiencing a sense of accomplishment. Acquiring a new technical skill empowers and encourages continued involvement in an activity. Students are better poised to take on new challenges when they feel genuinely capable as a result of gaining new proficiencies.

• **Mutual support.** Group efforts sometimes fail because of conflict among group members. Therefore, an important aspect of successful outdoor pursuits programs is the emphasis on working together and respecting others. This necessitates a combination of interpersonal skills and appropriate communication. Rock climbing, for example, involves cohesiveness and trust between climber and belayer. Good belayers provide climbers with the reassurance to push their physical limits by giving them the knowledge that they can do so without worry. Another aspect of mutual support is the need to belong, which is a strong motivator. When students feel connected to others and safe enough to try new things, their willingness to persevere at a task increases. But they also must understand that conflicts may arise and must know how to resolve potential conflicts. Outdoor pursuits develop enthusiastic and contributing group members who view their roles as an important component of an effective team.

• **Fitness.** Different outdoor pursuits involve different types of fitness. For instance, some activities can be vigorous, requiring cardiorespiratory endurance. Cycling up a steep incline provides the steady, sustained exercise recommended for health and weight control. Bouldering, on the other hand, demands power, agility, and flexibility. Any outdoor activity can provide opportunities for people of all fitness levels to be challenged and included. Cycling can be adapted to individual fitness levels, and bouldering involves certain skills that can compensate for insufficient power (e.g., relying more on the legs than the arms or using techniques for shifting weight and resting). Consequently, students can experience early success with accompanying increases in fitness.

• **Excitement and fun.** An element of risk, whether perceived or real, adds to the excitement of outdoor experiences. And as students cope successfully with risks, many of them learn to be more autonomous and self-sufficient. There is also a sense of excitement associated with trying something new. For instance, caving often includes squeezing through cramped, shadowy passages that may be steep or slippery. This task can be a daunting, even threatening, proposition, especially for students who are claustrophobic, afraid of the dark, or concerned about spiders, bats, and other mysterious cave-dwelling critters. But it also can help students learn how to cope with fears and anxieties. Furthermore, the fun of outdoor pursuits cannot be overemphasized. If an activity isn't enjoyable, students will not willingly experience more of it. According to Karl Rohnke, "Rediscovering the capacity for play can be an extremely powerful experience" (Rohnke & Grout, 1998, p. 11) and can lead to a more resilient, playful spirit.

• **Wonder of nature.** In his popular book, *Last Child in the Woods*, Richard Louv (2006) suggests that too many young people today have what he terms a *nature-deficit disorder.* According to Louv, a broken bond with natural surroundings reduces not only the richness of our human experience but also our mental, physical, and spiritual health, which all depend on such a bond. Nature offers something that the street, gated community, or computer game cannot. Moreover, using our own power to arrive at a destination unexplainably adds to our appreciation of beauty. Although climbing high peaks presents important challenges, an equally valuable experience may be sitting still in a quiet place away from the usual distractions and listening to the breeze or observing a vast landscape or delicate flower. As Texas Bix Bender says, "See the heavens, smell the air. . . . On a good day, that's all you need. On a bad day, that's all you need" (Bender, 1997, p. 39). Finally, of considerable value is the possibility of an increased sensitivity to taking care of the surrounding environment. As we often remind our students, it isn't about how long you're in a place—it's about what you do while you're there. Did you leave it a better place for being there? Although having more immediate significance in an outdoor setting, this important lesson also applies to students' schools and neighborhoods.

WHY SO MUCH INACTIVITY?

Despite the known benefits of participating in physical activities such as those enjoyed in outdoor pursuits, why is there so little participation? Lack of physical activity, as well as its causes and consequences, is much discussed. Consider these interesting facts:

- In the United States, the fourth leading cause of coronary heart disease is physical inactivity.
- The number one predictor of exercise adherence is enjoyment and self-satisfaction.
- Less than 6% of U.S. residents participate in organized sports after high school.
- One in six children in the United States is obese; many of these children will face a lifetime of chronic illness. According to the Centers for Disease Control and Prevention, this problem would cure itself if children engaged in the informal outdoor activities that used to be the norm.

Taken together, these facts suggest that despite the harmful effects of inactivity, too few of today's students participate in physical activities that could provide pleasure and good health throughout life. Why is this so? Some reasons may be financial, such as the high monetary costs associated with playing certain sports. More often, reasons are either internal or external.

Internal Reasons for Inactivity

- **Lack of skill.** The willingness of students to participate in physical activity relates to their competence—more specifically, it relates not to their *feelings* about their competence but to their *actual degree of skillfulness* (Stodden & Langendorfer, 2008). When they discover their lack of skill, they stop participating for fear of public embarrassment.
- **Physical self-consciousness.** Some students are uncomfortable with their body shape or function. Children who are overweight are particularly vulnerable to bias by peers. They report that they experience teasing, rejection, and bullying because of their weight or other physical differences.
- **Fear of injury.** Whether the body is moving or is controlling moving objects, there always exists the prospect of injury.
- **No interest in competition.** As mentioned earlier, some students prefer not to participate in competitive activities. Their many reasons for avoiding such activities include an emphasis on winning and losing, a pressure to perform, an emphasis on violence in some contact sports and a need for eye–hand coordination in others, an importance of size and speed, the type of conditioning required, too

little downtime and too much specialization to participate, and an overemphasis on team rather than individual functioning.

External Reasons for Inactivity

- **Geography.** Rather than promoting walking and bike riding, suburbs often necessitate chauffeuring.
- **Safety.** Afraid of abductions and unsafe streets and playgrounds, parents discourage kids from leaving home to play.
- **Soccer myth.** Parents believe organized youth teams provide enough exercise, even though many kids are left on the sideline waiting their turn.
- **High-stakes testing.** A national obsession with improving standardized test scores has shifted resources and class time away from physical education and recess and toward preparing for standardized tests.
- **Technology.** Cable, digital, and high-definition television coupled with video games and the Internet has resulted in a generation of screen-addicted children who sit and click. In recent decades the amount of time people in the United States spend in activities that remove them from physical activity and the outdoors (watching television, listening to MP3 players, playing video games, visiting Web sites) has doubled to 8 hours each day (Sigman, 2009).
- **Improper practices.** Despite countless examples of excellent physical education programs run by competent teachers, there is persistent criticism of the improper practices that continue to exist in physical education in the United States. Baumgartner (2004) summarized these criticisms as "questionable practices in which children have few opportunities to learn and often lead to negative outcomes" (p. 4). He argues that despite well-publicized best practices, many programs still do not focus on health and wellness, do not offer enough options that appeal to a larger student audience, and are not taught by individuals whose first priority is teaching physical education.

NASPE SUPPORT

Each of the aforementioned reasons for physical inactivity among today's youths has implications for physical education. But improper practices is the issue that we can address most directly through curriculum and instruction. Fortunately, the NASPE (2004) offers guidance through national content standards that define what a student should know and be able to do as result of a quality physical education program. The standards provide a framework for developing realistic and achievable expectations for student performance at every grade level.

Some physical education instructors are surprised to learn that outdoor pursuits were added to NASPE standards more than 15 years ago. According to the NASPE (1991) benchmarks, students at the eighth grade level shall "explore introductory outdoor pursuit skills (e.g., backpacking, rock climbing, hiking, canoeing, cycling)" (p. 7). An accompanying teaching objective is that "students will be able to demonstrate basic competence in physical activities from each of the following categories: aquatics, self-defense, individual, dual, and team activities and sports; and outdoor pursuits" (p. 8). As noted earlier, rather than being considered an alternative or progressive offering, outdoor pursuits are recognized to play a proper role in regular physical education.

Any motivated physical education teacher can teach at least some of the outdoor pursuits presented in this book. In cases in which a teacher may need justification for introducing an outdoor pursuit (beyond the benefits already stated in this chapter), the NASPE standards can be helpful. All of the outdoor pursuits in this book lend themselves to addressing the six NASPE standards summarized in the sidebar. Since the activities described throughout the following chapters may focus on specific NASPE standards, each lesson plan in this book identifies the standards a given activity addresses.

Bouldering, for example, provides opportunities to learn new motor skills (edging and smearing), apply new knowledge and conceptual skills (maximizing steadiness and conserving energy), enjoy a sense of involvement in a new sport, enhance health-related fitness (strength, flexibility), practice personal and social as well as environmental responsibility (learning how to fall, spotting, caring for a fragile environment), and gain appreciation and enthusiasm for the various joys available in bouldering (challenges, competitive and expressive forms of play, personal meaning).

The importance of standard 6, appreciation, cannot be overstated. Certainly we can justify the use of outdoor pursuits toward pragmatic (e.g., fitness), intellectual (e.g., concepts and principles), and affective (e.g., fun and enjoyment) ends. However, as Daryl Siedentop states, "We do not have to *use* our activities. . . . There

---

National Association for Sport and Physical Education Standards for Physical Education

Standard 1: *Motor skills*—demonstrates competency in motor skills and movement patterns needed to perform a variety of physical activities.

Standard 2: *Conceptual skills*—demonstrates understanding of movement concepts, principles, strategies, and tactics as they apply to the learning and performance of physical activities.

Standard 3: *Involvement*—participates regularly in physical activity.

Standard 4: *Fitness*—achieves and maintains a health-enhancing level of physical fitness.

Standard 5: *Responsibility*—exhibits responsible personal and social behavior that respects self and others in physical activity settings.

Standard 6: *Appreciation*—values physical activity for health, enjoyment, challenge, self-expression, and social interaction.

From *Moving Into the Future: National Standards for Physical Education,* 2nd ed., 2004 (Reston, VA: National Association for Sport and Physical Education), 11.

---

is no doubt that they can be used, and often for quite legitimate and noble purposes . . ." (1980, p. 259). Rather, the activities are "valuable *in and of themselves*" (1990, p. 80).

WHAT TO EXPECT FROM THIS BOOK

To avoid unnecessary redundancy, the next few sections of this chapter address shared topics that cut across all outdoor pursuits, such as general risk management, trip planning, and Leave No Trace. The subsequent chapters then focus on particular types of outdoor pursuits, each following a similar format in order to provide ease of presentation and a basis of comparison among chapters. For example, how might safety considerations for rock climbing differ from those for mountain biking? Unit plans, lesson plans, and assessments for each chapter are included on the accompanying CD-ROM. A sample lesson plan is included at the end of this chapter.

Bear in mind that these chapters are not written for outdoor education teachers with extensive training and background experience in outdoor pursuits. Rather, they provide essential information for introducing a group of physical education students to new experiences in ways that maximize enjoyment and minimize risk. The following is the general format used for each outdoor pursuits chapter:

- **Introduction.** The introduction includes a general description of the activity and, when helpful, background information on its history or development. Benefits specific to that activity, such as the social aspects of certain orienteering activities or the cognitive challenge of solving a bouldering problem, might also be included.

- **Equipment.** After the activity is introduced, the basic equipment required is identified and explained. This should assist in determining the type and extent of resources required for the activity.

- **Basic skills and technique.** This section describes the agreed-upon educational goals and basic content suggestions for each activity. Popular teaching techniques and terminology unique to the activity may also be included.

- **Safety considerations.** Although a number of principles apply to all outdoor pursuits, specific activities might involve specific risks. In rock climbing, for example, complacency when tying into a harness may lead to an unwelcome and serious mishap. This section discusses these risks and how to manage them. Also included are recommendations for how to treat the outdoor environment responsibly when participating in the various physical activities.

- **References and recommended readings.** This book should be viewed as a springboard from which physical education teachers can enhance their effectiveness. Eventually many teachers will want to fine-tune their curriculum and look for new ways to teach it. The accompanying resources should serve as a starting point for obtaining additional information and support.

- **Unit plans.** To aid the reader, unit plans that match those on the CD-ROM are included at the end of each chapter.

In addition, each chapter provides Teaching Tips. These are hints and suggestions to help physical education teachers integrate a given outdoor pursuit into their programs.

SHARED TOPICS

To avoid redundancy across the outdoor pursuits chapters, this chapter covers topics that apply to all outdoor pursuits. Later chapters may include more specifics on each topic.

Risk Management

No activity can be guaranteed as safe and nothing we do in life is risk free. However, maintaining a reasonable margin of safety can minimize the dangers inherent in outdoor pursuits. As a physical education teacher, you have the responsibility to manage the risks you encounter and to help your students learn to do the same. Furthermore, you can enhance your risk management by consciously considering the effects that your teaching (through role modeling and instilling good practices in students) has on safety.

Although it is impossible to address the particulars of every situation and activity, it is possible to summarize some sensible considerations for ensuring the safety of students as they venture into natural settings. A frequently mentioned formula for accidents is *environmental hazards + human factors = accident potential*. When these two areas interact, the likelihood of an accident increases. For example, if the weather deteriorates (environmental hazard) and fatigue causes error in judgment (human factor), the potential for an accident escalates. Once you gain an understanding of environmental hazards and human factors, you can take action to reduce risks or avoid them altogether.

1. *Environmental hazards.* Environmental hazards must be anticipated and evaluated in light of the dangers they present to students. An extensive inventory might include deep or moving water, slippery terrain, potentially dangerous animals and insects, poor weather, loose rock, fallen and falling trees, and illness. Venturing into the outdoors requires a degree of risk. If you or your students are uncomfortable with a certain hazard, it may be best to avoid it. If you don't know how to cross a river, find a different route. Stay away from moose country if they are rutting in the fall. If you anticipate possible bear encounters, learn how to contend with them (e.g., by avoiding them on the trail and discouraging them in camp).

2. *Human factors.* Potential errors in judgment resulting in unsafe acts are often overlooked as hazards, yet some people consider human mistakes to be the cause of most accidents. The following are just some of the more common judgment errors: lack of respect for an objective hazard, poor communication, inadequate conflict resolution, and carelessness. Heading the list of unsafe acts is being unprepared; a properly planned program or activity is less prone to mistakes. Other potentially unsafe acts include slips and falls, exceeding personal abilities, failure to follow instructions, inadequate supervision, and inappropriate role modeling.

As a physical education teacher, you must become familiar with environmental and human factors that might jeopardize your students' well-being. In addition, your students must understand that careless, thoughtless behavior can be dangerous to themselves as well as to the group. Emphasize that watching for and avoiding hazards are everyone's responsibility. In addition, recognize that students will observe and emulate your positive as well as your negative role modeling and will often lack the experience to recognize the latter.

Not only physical safety but also emotional safety is of paramount importance. For some students, merely venturing into the outdoors is intimidating. The thought of being in the great outdoors can summon fears of everything from getting lost to starving to death. Some students may harbor intense fantasies such as being attacked by wolves, killer ants, monsters jumping out of the undergrowth, or strange winged creatures that eat children. It is no wonder that many students are nervous when they walk through the woods. And for students who initially were unperturbed, new sounds (owls, coyotes, thunder) and sights (shadows, lightning flashes) might provoke anxiety. Few books on outdoor pursuits address the important issue of emotional safety, and yet it is essential that you do not discount students' worries. Validate whatever emotions they are expressing and be reassuring rather than dismissive. After all, walking in the dark is scary.

Trip Planning

Planning an outdoor pursuits trip can be time consuming for any physical education teacher. You must consider the budget, prepare for risk management, and plan for logistics such as transportation, reservations, and equipment. All this background work must be done in order to gain approval from supervisors. Obviously, some planning tasks are the sole responsibility of the teacher, but student involvement in planning should receive strong consideration. Students of any age are quite capable of making important decisions if the areas of concern are brought to their attention. Initially, students may work in small groups to plan menu items, equipment needs, activity schedules, tenting groups, and so on. As the groups share their information with the entire class and decisions are finalized, the students become increasingly committed to the trip logistics and to the cooperation demanded of them as members of the class. The following are a few of the crucial things to consider ahead of time, but keep in mind that each trip will introduce its own specific considerations.

Route and Location

Where will you go (state or national park, national forest, scenic river way, trail) and what kind of area will you visit (desert, mountains, rivers and lakes; someplace thick with insects, crowded, or with weather conditions such as sudden afternoon storms)? Check with the most competent weather information service within 24 hours of the trip. Call ahead and watch or read national weather forecasts to get probable weather conditions. Plan for possible extremes to prevent emergency situations, and have a contingency plan.

Find out what facilities are available, what fees are charged, what permits are required, and what arrangements must be made in advance, such as reservations for campsites. Inquire about any special regulations such as those regarding bear camping, raptors, fire restrictions, restoration areas, equipment requirements, and limits on group size. Review guidebooks, trail guides, and maps, all of which can suggest points of interest such as amazing rock formations or petroglyphs. To learn more about your destination, ask knowledgeable people such as park rangers and public land managers, and supplement your research with Web searches (e.g., www.recreation.gov).

Determine the distances to the target location and of the route (2 mi or 3 km versus 20 mi or 32 km) as well as the difficulty of terrain (rocky, flat, sandy, hilly, wet, or high altitude). Also note the potential hazards. Is the area susceptible to flash floods? Are there wildlife that pose a threat, such as rattlesnakes, mountain lions, bears, and scorpions? Will you encounter toxic plants such as poison ivy?

Skills and Physical Condition

Your students need to be adequately prepared for an outdoor experience. For example, do they have camping skills such as pitching a tent, lighting a stove, canoeing, and so on? Also, are the general health and physical condition of everyone adequate for the demands of the trip? You must be aware of any medical restrictions, allergies, physical limitations, and special medications your students may have. Will there be adult leaders who have the experience and the skills needed to support you, and are they aware of their specific responsibilities?

Transportation, Meals, and Travel Itinerary

Will transportation be provided by the school because of liability? If so, schedule the bus, or assign students to specific cars if a bus is not available. Arrange for a car shuttle if needed, as in the case of a canoe trip. File with the principal and other appropriate authorities a list of all students making the trip. Include anticipated rest stops or fuel and food stops in your itinerary. Include dates and locations if possible.

When preparing menus, keep in mind personal tastes, cost, weight, ease of preparation, and allergies. Make sure you have adequate cooking supplies, such as stoves, pots, spatulas, spoons, and tools for building fires; cleanup materials such as dishpans and pans to heat water; storage containers such as ice chests and water jugs; and eating supplies such as plates, cups, and spoons.

Equipment

What to wear and carry depend largely on the particular outdoor pursuit. Clothing and shelter should accommodate anticipated weather. While snowshoes and polypro underwear might be necessary for a winter trip, shorts and climbing hardware might be more appropriate for rock climbing in warmer weather. Typically, students might be required to bring, wear, or carry the following when traveling in warmer weather:

- Day pack
- Water (minimum 1 qt or 1 L)
- Snack food (high energy)
- Rain gear and wind gear
- Long-sleeved shirt (and sweater or fleece depending on weather conditions)
- Shorts or long pants (depending on weather conditions)
- Sturdy footgear and an extra pair of socks
- Journal and pen

- Spare medications (including a bee-sting allergy kit)
- Other items such as whistles, water treatment pills, insect repellent, nylon cords, toilet paper, plastic bags (for trash or waterproofing), spare glasses or contacts, binoculars, cameras (with extra film or memory cards), cell phones (fully charged), and walking sticks

It is useful for students to learn about and carry special items that they may need in the event of an outdoor emergency. The *10 essentials*, a term first made popular by The Mountaineers (an organization dedicated to exploring, preserving, and enjoying outdoor areas), is a list of items that help serve as an insurance policy against the unexpected. While these items will not be used on every trip, at some point students may be glad to have them along. The items can be placed in a ziplock plastic bag or other suitable lightweight container that is easily accessible. Over time several different lists have been developed, so you may wish to modify the list included here to suit your own program. The list of 10 essentials includes the following (but does not include the items already identified as required to bring on a trip):

1. Waterproof matches (lighter or other fire starter)
2. Map and compass
3. Pocketknife
4. Rain gear (poncho or large trash bag)
5. Extra layers of clothing (possibly including a space blanket)
6. Extra food and water
7. Sun protection (sunglasses, sunscreen, hat)
8. Flashlight (or headlamp, with spare batteries and bulb)
9. First aid kit
10. Common sense

Although not on some lists, the most important essential is common sense, which isn't all that common. Most often, it isn't a person's equipment that makes the difference in an unexpected situation. It is the person's experience and good judgment. Conversely, it is generally inexperience and lack of good judgment that lead to trouble.

Although your group should leave with gear in good condition, it is helpful to carry a basic field repair kit. A

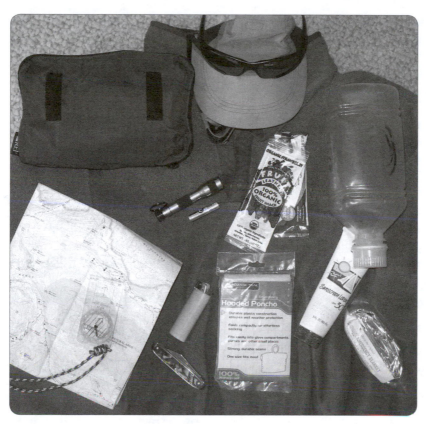

The 10 essentials to bring on a trip.

field repair kit increases self-sufficiency, which is especially necessary on longer, more remote trips, and contains essentials for repairing equipment in the outdoors. Depending on the length and remoteness of your trip, the basic contents of the kit might include duct tape, a large needle and thick nylon thread (or dental floss), a multitool, and safety pins or bailing wire. It may also include items specific to your trip activity (e.g., tools and patch kit for a biking trip or a tent pole sleeve and stove repair kit for camping overnight).

Outdoor Itinerary and Emergency Resources

In addition to developing the travel itinerary as discussed earlier, you must leave a full written outdoor itinerary with school authorities and other responsible individuals (see appendix for sample itinerary). When developing, sharing, and implementing the itinerary, consider the following items:

- Explain each day's trip plans and stick to your plans as much as possible.

- Map out destinations and distances to be traveled, locations of intended campsites, expected water locations, potentially hazardous areas, and emergency and alternative routes; include days and dates.

- Set time deadlines of when you will return or when you will call, and leave information concerning any special medical needs.

- Carry a list of the parents' home and work telephone numbers.

- Check into and out of any wilderness areas with park rangers or other authorities.

- Know the location of the nearest medical facility and the person who handles rescues in the trip area (e.g., sheriff, park ranger).

- Carry a list of emergency contacts (phone and address of medical facilities, park ranger, sheriff or police).

- Specify, for the case of a medical emergency, who will go with a patient and who will stay with the group.

A detailed discussion of wilderness first aid is beyond the scope of this book. While the majority of injuries you will see on your trip will be minor scrapes, bruises, or blisters, serious injuries can worsen during an outdoor trip. Investigate one of the many good wilderness first aid books available for people who plan to spend time in the outdoors, and, more importantly, take some type of backcountry first aid course. Accidents happen, and essential to any outdoor activity is an appropriately equipped first aid kit. Know what is in each kit, where each item is packed, and how to use all the kit items. Be mindful, however, that kits aren't always enough. A fully equipped first aid kit is a supplement, not a substitution, for proper outdoor medical care. The kit that helps a hurt or sick person "rarely comes from a bag but, instead, from a brain packed with medical expertise" (Tilton, 1998, p. 289). Although you can compile your own first aid kit, there are many commercial first aid kits available that often contain necessary items for less than what you would spend if you assembled a kit yourself. In addition to quality, considerations for purchasing a first aid kit include the number of students in the group, the duration of stay in the outdoors, and the probability of getting to a medical facility within 8 to 12 hours.

Knowledge of first aid for young people may be more important than knowledge of first aid for adults. Children gain core heat faster than adults do, and thus children may need more time to acclimatize to heat. Encourage your students to drink lots of water. Since young people dehydrate faster than adults do, fluid loss, especially through diarrhea, can be more serious for children. Teach students to check their urine output to ensure appropriate color and volume (clear and copious). Carry a mild antidiarrheal medication in your first aid kit to treat diarrhea when it occurs. To treat dehydration (from diarrhea, vomiting, or heat), use oral rehydration salts instead of plain water. Children also sunburn more easily than adults do. Even though sun damage may not show up for decades, it is important to prevent sunburn (with clothing, hat, and sunscreen). Reapply sunscreen often, especially during swimming. Start treatment for sunburn immediately with cool compresses, moisturizing lotions, and acetaminophen for pain; students experiencing sunburn should also drink lots of water. Finally, kids make up the great majority of patients who have ingested poison. Check outdoor areas carefully for poisonous plants and teach students how to identify and avoid them. Learn about what to do and what not to do when a student has been exposed to (through skin contact or suspected ingestion) different poisons (plant poisons, insect poisons, or corrosive products) and may be experiencing certain reactions (rash, seizures, vomiting).

Leave No Trace

When students venture into the outdoors, they should understand how to avoid degrading the outdoor experience for themselves and others. Students would not disrespect a friend's home by carving on the walls, littering, or dirtying the drinking water. They should show no less consideration when visiting the backcountry (outdoor areas, nature areas, and wilderness areas). Leave No Trace is a national program that promotes the protection of wildlands in the United States. By using minimum-effect practices, students can have an enjoyable adventure while allowing others the same experience.

At the heart of Leave No Trace is a set of principles that can be applied to any natural setting. In-depth information can be obtained through your local land manager or local office of the U.S. Bureau of Land Management, Forest Service, National Park Service, or Fish and Wildlife Service. You can also contact Leave No Trace directly at 800-332-4100 or visit Leave No Trace on the Internet at www.lnt.org. The seven principles of Leave No Trace are the following:

1. *Plan ahead and prepare.* Know the terrain and any regulations applicable to the area you're planning to visit, and be prepared for extreme weather, hazards, or other emergencies. This will enhance your enjoyment and ensure that you've chosen an appropriate destination. Small groups have less of an effect on resources and the experiences of other backcountry visitors. Consider splitting larger groups into smaller ones. Use a map and compass (and GPS device) to eliminate the use of marking paint, rock cairns, or flagging. Proper planning ensures enjoyable outdoor experiences because the outing matches the skill level of the students.

2. *Travel and camp on durable surfaces.* Travel and camp on established trails and campsites, rock, gravel, sand, compacted soil, dry grasses, or snow. In popular areas, walk single file in the middle of the trail, even when wet or muddy. In pristine areas, take different paths to avoid creating new trails that cause erosion. When camping in these same pristine areas, disperse tents and cooking activities and move camp daily to avoid creating permanent-looking campsites. Good campsites are found, not made; altering a site is not necessary. Camp at least 200 ft (about 61 m or 80-100 strides for a youth) from lakes and streams, and focus activities on areas where vegetation is absent.

3. *Dispose of waste properly.* Pack it in, pack it out. Inspect your camp for trash or food scraps. Deposit solid human waste in cat holes that are dug 6 to 8 in. (15-20 cm) and located at least 200 ft (61 m) from water, camp, and trails; cover and disguise the cat hole when finished. Pack out toilet paper and hygiene products. To wash yourself or your dishes, carry water 200 ft (61 m) away from streams or lakes and use small amounts of biodegradable soap. Scatter strained dishwater.

4. *Leave what you find.* Natural objects such as plants or rocks should be left as found. Examine but do not touch cultural or historic artifacts; it may be illegal to remove artifacts. Do not build furniture or other structures or dig trenches. Also, do not hack at trees with hatchets or saws, and replace surface rocks or twigs that you cleared from a campsite.

5. *Minimize campfire impacts.* Campfires can have lasting effects in the backcountry. Cook on a stove, and enjoy a candle lantern instead of a fire. Use established fire rings, fire pans, or mound fires. If a campfire is built, keep it small and use dead sticks found on the ground. Burn all wood and coals to ash, put out campfires completely, and then scatter the cool ashes.

6. *Respect wildlife.* Observe wildlife from a distance. Do not follow, approach, or feed the animals. Feeding them damages their health, alters their natural behav-iors, and exposes them to predators and other dangers. Protect wildlife from your food by storing rations and trash securely. Avoid wildlife during sensitive times, such as when animals are mating, nesting, raising young, or surviving the winter.

7. *Be considerate of other visitors.* Be courteous, respect the quality of other visitors' backcountry experiences, and let the sounds of nature prevail (i.e., avoid loud voices and noises and leave radios at home). Make sure the colors of clothing and gear blend with the environment. Yield to other users on the trail, and take breaks and camp away from trails and other visitors. Respect private property and leave gates (open or closed) as found.

Following Leave No Trace principles and combining them with personal judgment and experience help to protect precious natural resources and preserve the outdoor experience for students and for future visitors. In order to teach young people about Leave No Trace in a fun and engaging way, the Leave No Trace Center for Outdoor Ethics created a program called *Promoting Environmental Awareness in Kids,* or *PEAK.* You can access PEAK at www.lnt.org/programs/peak.php.

Finally, to help your students remember the seven principles of Leave No Trace, consider teaching them the song in figure 1.1. It originated from an outing with

LEAVE NO TRACE

(Sung to the tune of "Take Me Out to the Ball Game")

Lyrics	**Seven principles**
Plan your trips to the mountain	Plan ahead and prepare
Pack out what you pack in	Dispose of waste properly
Kindly dispose of the other stuff	
Hike, camp, and cook on a surface that's tough	Travel and camp on durable surfaces
And to keep our wild places natural	Minimize campfire impacts
Watch fires, and leave things in place	Leave what you find
And respect *all* wildlife out there	Respect wildlife
That's called Leave No Trace	Be considerate of other visitors

Figure 1.1 The Leave No Trace song is one way to help students remember the seven Leave No Trace principles.

an elementary school group, during which the kids composed and sang it (incessantly!).

Teaching Considerations

Teaching in the outdoors can be a physically and mentally challenging experience for students and instructors alike. This book cannot contain everything you need to know about teaching effectively in an outside setting. However, this book does attempt to identify several key considerations as well as a few popular teaching techniques. Although there is no right way to teach in the outdoors, Jay Roberts (2007), Hammerman and colleagues (Hammerman, Hammerman, & Hammerman, 2001), and others have provided a few suggestions that might help along the way.

- **Setting.** The outdoors is not a nice, organized classroom environment. Intense sunlight, difficult weather, loud noise, wind, critters, and exposure are a few of the many conditions that can affect student learning. Are your students facing the sun? Is it too windy? Are mosquitoes unbearable? Do the students need a snack or meal? Despite your best intentions, your students can be distracted by these and other factors such as homesickness. In order to maximize student learning, you should anticipate and minimize as many distractions as possible when teaching in the outdoors.

- **Timing and brevity.** Generally speaking, thinking activities are more effective in the morning, hands-on activities are best in the afternoon, and discussions are more productive in the evening. Roberts (2007) refers to this sequence as "AM-Brain, PM-Body, and Evening-Heart" (p. 1). Given the many factors that might influence a student's attention span, consider breaking up lessons into brief manageable chunks that are short and to the point. During longer lessons, intersperse active movement with reflection. Remember that unlike the traditional classroom setting, the outdoors provides boundless firsthand learning opportunities.

- **Preparation.** Do your homework. Develop strong lessons, write them down, and then be flexible in the face of distracting conditions. Use effective teaching progressions and choose activities and instruction that match the abilities and interests of your group. Try to accommodate various learning styles. Some students learn best through verbal instruction, others by watching a demonstration and then trying a skill themselves, and others by reflecting on an experience. By using a combination of visual aids (e.g., writing on a white trash bag with dry erase markers), lectures, demonstrations,

and discussions, you increase the likelihood of accommodating different learning styles. The lesson plans on the CD-ROM accompanying this book will also help you prepare.

- **Coaching and feedback.** You can learn a great deal about how to teach different topics by watching other instructors. Ask others to give you feedback on your presentation style. Do you establish good eye contact? Do you stick to the basics? Do your demonstrations emphasize major points? Do you model your school's values and expectations? Do you provide ample opportunity for practice and exploration? Give students time to demonstrate to you that they are learning the material. Also, consider how your students are positioned. Are they gathered in a horseshoe for lectures and circles for discussions? The more scattered the students are, the more scattered the class will feel.

- **Teachable moments.** Good instructors learn to exploit teachable moments, which surface constantly in the outdoors. Stopping to identify mystery tracks in the snow is a perfect time to discuss how students can learn about animals not by watching the animals themselves but by following their tracks and observing the evidence they have left behind such as scratches, gnaw marks, rubbings, droppings, and dams. While a teachable moment should not be contrived, you still need to be flexible to take advantage of opportunities as they arise during an outing. If only part of the group is exposed to a teachable moment, share what was learned with the rest of the group at a later time.

- **Reflecting.** An intense learning experience can lose its effects unless you ask students to sort out their thoughts and emotions. Focused discussions can help to identify and reinforce important lessons gained from an event or activity. Personal and group journals also provide an excellent way to help students reflect on what they have learned or accomplished. Journals might include descriptions, stories, poems, illustrations, observations, and class notes. Don't force a discussion or a journal entry if there is nothing to deliberate or capture. By the same token, allow adequate time for reflection to enhance the learning process and honor the learning.

Following these tips, as well as using many other tools such as games, storytelling, and guest speakers, can help you sharpen your lessons. But most important is that you be yourself, know your limits, and share with your students your own heartfelt commitment to the subject and to their ability to learn.

CONCLUSION

Physical education teachers can introduce students to the many benefits of outdoor pursuits. For example, in the outdoors there are endless prospects for exploration and discovery through which students can exercise both their bodies and their brains. A student may discover how long it takes to hike or bike a certain distance while also learning how to orient a map or follow a bearing. Students also can learn to master new and challenging skills (e.g., tying knots, packing a day pack, traversing steep terrain) while experiencing the satisfaction of overcoming previously difficult tasks. Social development and interaction are also important aspects of outdoor activities; communicating, negotiating, and sharing can lead to greater awareness and acceptance of one another's strengths and limitations. Moreover, in an environment that is different naturally from the indoors, students must learn risk management and the hazards of certain actions. Finally, outdoor pursuits offer opportunities for developing an interest and understanding of the natural world and our place in it.

REFERENCES

Association for Challenge Course Technology. (2008). www.acctinfo.org.

Baumgartner, S. (2004). Questionable practices in physical education. *Journal of Physical Education, Recreation, and Dance, 75*(5), 4, 9.

Bender, T. (1997). *Don't squat with yer spurs on! II.* Layton, UT: Gibbs Smith Publisher.

Ford, P., Blanchard, J., & Blanchard, A. (1993). *Leadership and administration of outdoor pursuits.* State College, PA: Venture.

Hammerman, D., Hammerman, W., & Hammerman, E. (2001). *Teaching in the outdoors.* (5th ed.). Upper Saddle River, NJ: Prentice Hall.

Louv, R. (2006). *Last child in the woods.* Chapel Hill, NC: Algonquin Books.

Miles, J., & Priest, S. (Eds.). (1999). *Adventure programming.* State College, PA: Venture.

National Association for Sport and Physical Education. (1991). *The physically educated person: Outcomes and benchmarks for quality education programs.* Reston, VA: Author.

National Association for Sport and Physical Education. (2004). *Moving into the future: National physical education standards.* (2nd ed.). Reston, VA: Author.

Neill, J. (2004). Experiential learning cycles (Kolb). www.wilderdom.com/theory/ExperientialLearningCycles.html.

Outward Bound. (2006). The history of outward bound. www.outward-bound.org/lic_sub3_history.htm.

Roberts, J. (2007, April 10). Teaching in the outdoors: A primer. *OutdoorEd.com Internet News.* www.outdoored.com/anm/templates/default.aspx?a=2958&template=print-article.htm.

Rohnke, K., & Butler, S. (1995). *Quicksilver.* Dubuque, IA: Kendall/Hunt.

Rohnke, K., & Grout, J. (1998). *Back pocket adventure.* Needham Heights, MA: Simon & Schuster.

Siedentop, D. (1980). *Physical education: Introductory analysis.* New York: McGraw-Hill.

Siedentop, D. (1990). *Introduction to physical education, fitness, and sport.* New York: McGraw-Hill.

Sigman, E. (2009). Well connected?: The biological implications of 'social networking.' *Biologist, 56*(1), 14-20.

Stiehl, J. (2000). Outdoor and adventure programs. In D. Hellison, N. Cutforth, J. Kallusky, T. Martinek, M. Parker, & J. Stiehl (Eds.), *Youth development and physical activity: Linking universities and communities* (pp. 67-85). Champaign, IL: Human Kinetics.

Stodden, D., & Langendorfer, S. (2008, February 11). BGSU study asks: Do good motor skills promote fitness? *BGSU Monitor.* www.bgsu.edu/offices/mc/monitor/02-11-08/page45537.html.

Tilton, B. (1998). *The wilderness first responder.* Old Saybrook, CT: Globe Pequot Press.

Wurdinger, S., & Steffen, J. (Eds.). (2003). *Developing challenge course programs for schools.* Dubuque, IA: Kendall/Hunt.

SAMPLE LESSON PLAN

This is a sample lesson plan from chapter 8 on learning pacing in orienteering.
Each lesson plan on the CD-ROM includes these same sections.

> The CD-ROM is organized by chapter and by **day** within that chapter. You'll find CD-ROM icons in chapters 2-12 referring you to specific lessons on the CD-ROM that will help you teach the skills and techniques described in the chapter.

DAY 2
PACING

> Each lesson plan provides **objectives** and identifies the NASPE standards the activity addresses.

Objectives

At the end of this lesson, the student will be able to do the following:

- Demonstrate effective pacing (standards 1, 6)
- Explain the function of pacing (standard 6)
- Describe the drawbacks associated with poor pacing (standard 6)
- Describe the benefits of proper pacing (standard 6)

> Each lesson lists the **equipment** needed.

Equipment

Measuring tape, rope or some other way to mark off 100 ft (30 m), bungee cord with ends tied together, hula hoops, rope tied in a circle

> The **introduction** lists the focus of the lesson and briefly describes what the students will do.

Introduction

The focus of this lesson is for students to learn how to count paces in order to calculate distance traveled.

> Each lesson includes a **warm-up** section. The warm-up gets students energized and prepared for the activity to come.

Warm-Up

Circle the circle: This activity helps elevate students' heart rates and provide a quick stretch. Have the students stand in a circle and hold hands with the person to the left and the right. Instruct the students that once the activity begins, there is no talking. Once students understand that they cannot talk, place the hula hoop around the forearm of one of the students (two students must let go of their hands to allow you to add the hula hoop to the circle). Have the student shake the arm until the hula hoop slides down to the hand. Now that the hula hoop is encircling the hands of two students, the group must pass this hula hoop around the entire circle without letting go of one another's hands. Students will be required to step through the hoop to pass it along. To increase the challenge, try passing around a bungee cord tied in a circle or passing another hula hoop in the other direction. Another variation is to have every third person sit on the ground with the legs straight out in front. The sitting students cannot physically lift their legs to pass the hoop (other students will have to assist them).

> **Central activities** make up the main part of the lesson. Here you'll find a detailed description of the activities for the lesson.

Central Activities

Part A: Introduction to Pacing

Overview

Students should learn that pacing is necessary in order to approximate distances covered. Each person has a slightly different leg stride, and this stride affects pace. A student's pace is the measurement of the distance traveled while navigating a course. Usually the pace is a measurement of a person's double step. A student who starts walking by stepping with the left leg first should count a step each time the right foot hits the ground. Measuring leg stride is the first step in learning how to pace a distance. Stride multiplied by two equals pace. The following activity helps students to determine their stride and pace. Pace can also be defined as the amount of distance a student can travel in

Orienteering, Day 2, from J. Steffen and J. Stiehl, eds. 2010, *Teaching Lifetime Outdoor Pursuits* (Champaign, IL: Human Kinetics).   1

an allotted duration. For example, students might know that they can comfortably walk 1 mi (1.6 km) in 15 min and know what that pace feels like.

Part B: Activity

Pacing Walk

Mark off a distance of 100 ft (30 m) and then add marks showing 1 or 2 ft (0.3 or 0.6 m) intervals. Having a 100 ft (30 m) tape measure is handy in this activity but is not required. You and your students can mark off the gymnasium floor using a ruler and masking tape. Have each student walk the 100 ft (30 m) distance while using a normal stride and counting out the pace (every second step). When students reach their 10th pace, they should stop and measure the distance traveled by noting the measurement of the forward foot. This measurement can be divided by 10 (number of paces) to determine the distance of the stride in feet. Dividing this number by 2 provides a stride length.

Closure

Summarize the lesson, reviewing the goals of the lesson. Get feedback from the students on how successful they were at maintaining a similar pace. Remind students that knowing their pace will be useful in future lessons. For example, in order to travel 200 ft (61 m) to get to a control, a student must know how many paces to count in order to figure this out.

The **closure** section provides discussion topics and suggestions on how to end the lesson.

Assessment

Teacher observation: Complete the Teacher Observation Pacing Checklist.

Written assessment: Have students describe how to determine stride.

Journal response: Describe how you can determine your pace and then explain why pace is important in orienteering.

The **assessment** section provides you with the tools to assess students' learning.

Orienteering, Day 2, from J. Steffen and J. Stie

TEACHER OBSERVATION PACING CHECKLIST

- Student counts every second step out loud.
- Student keeps leg strides constant.
- Student maintains measured pace.

Use the following marks to record your observations:

+ Student meets *all* objectives.

√ Student does not meet all objectives.

– Student does not meet any objectives.

Student	Observation

Each lesson includes an **observation checklist** with a rubric.

chapter 2

Overnight Hiking

Daniel L. Chase

L ook deep into nature, and then you will understand everything better.

Albert Einstein

H iking is an exhilarating outdoor activity enjoyed by thousands of people every day. Defined simply as an extended walk, hiking has provided people of all ages and abilities the opportunity to discover countless wonders of the world. Hiking is relatively inexpensive and can occur in a variety of locales such as school campuses, city parks, established trails in forests, and remote jungle settings. Basically, hiking can occur just about anywhere. While many early settlers relied on hiking as a mode of transportation for exploration and hunting, individuals of today include hiking in their lives for exercise and pleasure. Although some people still use hiking as a mode of transportation (e.g., the only way to access a climbing area or hunting location), most hikers participate in the activity for its physiological, psychological, and social benefits.

The benefits associated with hiking are as diverse as the hikers themselves. While many people hike for exercise, others hike for relaxation or for the benefit of being with friends. In addition to offering countless benefits, hiking also poses minimal dangers. However, as with all outdoor pursuits, there are a few inherent dangers associated with hiking. These dangers can be minimized and managed with proper education and training. As hikers gain more experience and lengthen their outings to include an overnight stay, they will require a bit more training. There are a number of fundamental rules hikers should learn and adhere to in order to make their experience and others' experiences safe and enjoyable.

While this chapter focuses on overnight hiking, providing specific information for planning a safe and enjoyable overnight hiking adventure, the basic skills and techniques presented here apply to all day hikes as well. Many physical education teachers, including yourself, may be reluctant to extend their day trip into an overnight trip because of the unknown. The intent of this chapter is to help quell anxieties by providing the fundamental information needed to be able to take a small group on an overnight hike. This chapter also helps newcomers become more acquainted with the planning process for an overnight hike. Specifically, this chapter highlights overnight hiking equipment, hazard evaluation (for staying safe), hiking techniques and etiquette, outdoor ethics, basic first aid, and helpful resources.

This chapter was written with the assumption that you will be taking students on an overnight hike in close proximity to the school and keeps the following question in mind: "What information would teachers and students need if they were dropped off at a trailhead for an overnight hike?" While many schools and teachers face limited funding or administrative resistance for excursions such as an overnight hike, the lessons included for this chapter (see accompanying CD-ROM) can be taught and built upon in the classroom regardless of whether the class ever embarks on an overnight trip. If you are unable to bring students off campus for an overnight hike, you might try conducting the overnight excursion on your campus field. Many younger or inexperienced students might even appreciate this. A great aspect of teaching overnight hiking is that all of the fundamental components can be taught in the gymnasium, classroom, or backcountry.

This chapter in no way presents all of the information you need for bringing students to a remote locale for extended durations or under situations of impending foul weather. While there can be great benefits associated with these types of adventures, this chapter presents only the fundamental information needed for overnight hiking. A goal of this chapter (and this book) is to expose students to outdoor adventures and create excitement for outdoor pursuits as a means to encourage lifelong participation in such pursuits. The following sections provide a solid base for teachers and students to build upon.

The beauty of teaching overnight hiking is that the lesson components do not have to be taught in a particular order. For instance, it is completely acceptable to teach students first aid before teaching them how to pack a pack. Similarly, it is acceptable to teach students how to set up a tarp or tent before teaching them how to plan a trip. Although the first topic presented in this chapter is equipment (a reasonable starting point), this topic can also be taught as a culminating lesson of trip planning. The lesson sequence outlined in this chapter is only one recommendation on how to present the fundamental principles of overnight hiking.

EQUIPMENT

Figure 2.1 provides a sample equipment list developed by students embarking on an April overnight hike in Colorado. Use this list as a starting point to help students generate their own equipment lists. A checklist helps ensure that needed or intended items are not left behind. A closer examination of the sample equipment list reveals that the 10 essentials mentioned in chapter 1 are included. These 10 essentials need to be brought along on every outing, including day hikes. There are a number of stories from hikers who were overjoyed to have these 10 items with them when a short summer day hike turned into an overnight excursion due to injury, getting lost, or being pinned down in foul weather. For each of these stories there are also stories in which hikers wished they had the items with them. In fact, there are tales of people freezing to death after getting lost on summer day hikes. This information is not intended to scare you—it is meant only to highlight the importance of packing the 10 essentials.

Aside from the essentials, the sample list includes many other items, some of which many hikers deem unnecessary (e.g., board games, stoves) but happened to be preferred by the students compiling this particular list. Have fun when creating your equipment lists with your students. Many people compete to see who can create the lightest pack without sacrificing essentials. Some go as far as cutting the handle off their toothbrush

SAMPLE EQUIPMENT LIST

Personal Equipment

Clothing

- ❑ Heavy wool or synthetic socks
- ❑ Light wool or synthetic socks
- ❑ Hiking boots
- ❑ Underwear
- ❑ Wool or synthetic thermal underwear (tops and bottoms)
- ❑ Heavy pants (fleece or wool)
- ❑ Heavy sweater (fleece or wool)
- ❑ Hooded parka (synthetic or down)
- ❑ Wind pants (synthetic)
- ❑ Rain gear (tops, bottoms, and head covering)
- ❑ Gloves with liners (polyester) or mittens (fleece or wool)
- ❑ Stocking hat (wool or fleece)
- ❑ Scarf
- ❑ Bandana
- ❑ Camp footwear (e.g., old sneakers, no open-toed shoes)

Other Personal Items

- ❑ Backpack
- ❑ Map and compass
- ❑ Sleeping bag and stuff sack
- ❑ Insulating ground pad
- ❑ Large garbage bags
- ❑ 50 ft (15 m) of 0.125 in. (0.32 cm) rope (parachute cord)
- ❑ Water bottles
- ❑ Bowl
- ❑ Mug
- ❑ Knife
- ❑ Utensils

- ❑ Waterproof matches
- ❑ Flashlight (with extra batteries and bulb)
- ❑ Whistle
- ❑ Toothbrush and toothpaste
- ❑ Biodegradable soap
- ❑ Tampons or sanitary napkins
- ❑ Legal medications
- ❑ Lip balm and sunscreen
- ❑ Sunglasses

Group Equipment

Cooking Gear

- ❑ Stove, fuel, and fuel bottle
- ❑ Pots and frying pans
- ❑ Pot lifter
- ❑ Pot scrubber or scraper
- ❑ Can opener
- ❑ Cooking utensils

Food-Related Gear

- ❑ Containers (no glass)
- ❑ Plastic storage bags
- ❑ Condiment containers
- ❑ Foodstuff sacks

Camping Gear

- ❑ Shelter (tarp, tent, footprint)
- ❑ Trekking poles (ski poles or hiking stick)
- ❑ Repair kit
- ❑ Games (e.g., board games, cards)
- ❑ Toilet paper
- ❑ Trowel
- ❑ First aid kit
- ❑ Water filter or water treatment pills

Figure 2.1 This equipment list can be used a starting point to create your own lists specific to your trip.

From J. Steffen and J. Stiehl, eds. 2010, *Teaching Lifetime Outdoor Pursuits* (Champaign, IL: Human Kinetics).

and snipping unnecessary pieces of fabric off their packs to lose ounces of weight. This minimalist approach to packing has benefits to some hikers but is outside the scope of teaching overnight packing to newcomers. In most cases students realize that they packed too much after the first mile and thus through experiential learning realize they could do with less.

Using the sample list as a guide, the following sections describe major hiking equipment items (e.g., clothing, shelter, packs). Technology has provided hikers with increasingly sophisticated equipment, much of which is fashionable and quite expensive. The aim of this chapter is to provide you with the fundamental information needed to embark on an overnight hike. Overnight hikers can and do use less-fashionable, inexpensive, functional equipment. Thus the following sections describe basic, necessary, and functional equipment.

Sleeping Bags and Pads

Sleeping bags and ground pads provide much comfort on a cool evening, although they do not provide as much comfort as sleeping in bed at home provides (in terms of support, firmness or softness, and so on). Sleeping bag comfort refers simply to being able to wiggle your way into the bag in order to remain warm as the temperature drops. With so many different sleeping bags available to consumers, beginning overnight hikers can become overwhelmed with the many options and features offered. Try to remember that the basic function of the sleeping bag is to hold in your body heat to help keep you warm.

Focus on the fit (ask yourself, "Do I fit in the bag?") and the temperature rating of the sleeping bag. Most sleeping bags have a temperature rating printed on their tag. Choosing a temperature rating close to the temperatures your group expects to encounter is important. In the summer, carrying and sleeping in a bag rated for –20 °F (–6.7 °C) is quite uncomfortable (too hot). Conversely, bringing a 40 °F (4.4 °C) bag on a winter trip is equally uncomfortable (too cold). Ratings are approximations, and students should be able to regulate their temperature inside the bag by adding or removing layers of clothing or zipping or unzipping the bag.

Helping to keep an overnight hiker warm is the ground pad. Although ground pads vary in type (from an inflatable air mattress to open cell foam), they should not be likened to your mattress at home. The function of a ground pad is to provide a layer of insulation against

the cold ground rather than provide support like a bedroom mattress provides. Used in combination, a sleeping bag and ground pad can provide you and your students with a warm place to rest.

Tents and Tarps

Tents and tarps provide shelter and protection from the elements (rain, snow, wind, sun). Weather cannot be predicted exactly; therefore, some type of shelter is necessary for overnight hikes. Many experienced hikers prefer sleeping under the stars and will not sleep under or in a shelter if the conditions appear amenable. However, these experienced hikers usually carry a simple shelter with them and can set it up quickly if the conditions change unexpectedly. Here again, preparation is key. It is better to have a shelter and not need it than to need a shelter and not have it. When working with students, have everyone build their shelter even if the weather appears perfect with a zero chance of turning foul. Doing so not only provides practice for setting up a tent or tarp but also ensures that each student has shelter if needed. Plan to arrive at the camping location early enough so that students can set up during daylight.

You should take into account a number of considerations when choosing the type of shelter (tarp versus tent) to use with students. Many instructors prefer to use tarps over tents for a number of reasons and especially for their inexpensive cost. Table 2.1 lists the pros and cons of tarp use compared with tent use. You may find it helpful in determining your equipment needs.

Many overnight hikers refuse to use a tarp as a shelter. Most often their reason for doing so is that creepy and crawly critters can enter the tarp as easily as they can. Others have noted that tents are a lot easier and quicker to set up. While this may be true and is a benefit of using a tent, the additional skills necessary to create a shelter from a tarp should be embraced as an experiential learning opportunity for students. Tarps also allow for creativity, since there is not one specific way to set up a tarp (whereas tents come with clear instructions). Tarp shelters can be set up in a variety of styles (classic A-frame, teepee, and so on) (see figure 2.2). When setting up a tarp (and often when setting up a tent), you need to consider the wind direction, number of people sleeping under the shelter, impending foul weather (driving rain requires tarp sides to be staked closer to the ground), terrain, and amount of ventilation needed.

Tarp shelters can be set up in a variety of ways. Setting up a tarp shelter begins by finding a suitable loca-

Day 5

Table 2.1 Pros and Cons for Tents and Tarps

	Pros	Cons
Tent	• Easy to set up • Keeps out creepy crawlers	• Expensive • Heavy to carry • Not easy to set up on uneven terrain • Setup does not allow for creativity • User must fiddle with zippers to get out
Tarp	• Inexpensive • Lightweight • Can set up on uneven terrain • Setup allows for creativity • Easy to get in and out	• Difficult to set up • Does not keep out creepy crawlers

tion. A good location is found, not built. The location should be somewhat smooth, devoid of low spots where water may collect, and away from fragile overhanging tree branches. A functional tarp shelter (one that does not blow down in the wind or sag in the rain or snow) requires a tight ridgeline, a taught roof that is steep enough to shed water, corner tie-down lines pulled 45° from the corners, stakes placed on an angle of 30° to 45° angled back from the tarp and buried almost completely, and lines tied with a knot easily untied (e.g., trucker's hitch). Whether using a tarp or a tent, students should also carry a footprint to place under their shelter. *Footprint* is a fancy term for a sheet of plastic. This sheet of plastic should not be ripped or have any holes in it because its primary purpose is to keep out the dew or any water that might run along the ground.

Stoves and Fire Pits

In some locations and especially during dry seasons, open fires are prohibited. Depending on the fire restrictions, stoves might also be banned. While stoves and fires offer a variety of benefits to overnight hikers, your group should discuss and evaluate these benefits to determine whether they are a necessity or a luxury. The obvious benefit of using stoves or fires is that they

provide the means to prepare hot meals. While stoves are much more convenient and efficient than campfires are for cooking hot meals, students typically prefer campfires. When asked whether they want a fire or a stove, students usually respond that they *need* a fire. Campfires are typically preferred to stoves because of the American tradition of socializing around the fire while making s'mores. The value of s'mores and campfire bonding is just one of the many considerations you must take into account during planning. Thousands of miles have been hiked (including overnight trips) without the use of a stove or fire (and without s'mores). Choosing not to use a stove or fire may limit menu options; however, creativity can present opportunities to experience foods in new ways.

If stoves and fires are an option (there are no restrictions), you need to decide which one is the better option. Aside from considering the popularity of campfires, you must consider the following to make an informed decision about campfire use: the inefficiency of campfires as a heat source, the availability of wood, the damage done to the earth, and the hazards and safety concerns. There are also a number of factors to consider when deciding whether to use a stove. First and foremost, stove operation is the most hazardous activity on an overnight hike second to traveling to and from your hiking destination. Other considerations include the availability of stoves, the extra weight of stoves and fuel, and the trip menu. Groups who choose to use a campfire should adhere to the regulations of the agency responsible for managing the land being visited. Most often fire rings are available. Fire rings should be used and kept clean for future visitors (food waste and trash should be packed out rather than burnt in the campfire). If your group

Figure 2.2 Proper tarp setup using the A-frame style.

decides to use a backcountry stove you should be very comfortable with operating it. Please read and follow all of the manufacturer's instructions.

Packs

Backpack design and construction continue to evolve. Packs are getting lighter, more durable, and more expensive. While there are hundreds of options available, many of the older packs are quite suitable for an overnight hike. In addition, hikers generally can buy an older, slightly worn pack for a fraction of the cost of a new pack. Whether choosing a brand-new fancy pack or a slightly worn pack, you must take into consideration the size of the pack (and whether all of the necessary equipment will fit inside the pack) and how the pack will fit once all of the equipment is packed inside of it. Note that equipment should be packed inside of the pack! Packs should not resemble the Beverly Hillbillies' car—that is, there should not be a bunch of junk hanging from all sides. There are a couple of reasons for this. First, packing all items inside the pack (lined with a garbage bag) can provide a level of waterproofing. Second, items hanging from a pack can fall off and get lost or can disrupt the hiker's balance or snag on trees and shrubs, contributing to falls and injuries.

Pack Packing

As with most skills, packing a pack improves with practice. Pack packing should be viewed as an art. No two packs are ever packed the same, even if the same person packs the same gear twice! Inevitably, there will be subtle differences. Differences are OK, as there are no standardized methods for packing a pack, only recommendations. In addition to the recommendation that all necessary equipment be packed inside a pack that is lined with a garbage bag, there are two other recommendations for pack packing that can provide you with a more enjoyable experience.

These two recommendations for pack packing are *A* for *accessibility* and *B* for *balance*. Accessibility refers to the location of the equipment in the pack. Items of necessity or items that are used often, such as rain gear, extra clothes, snacks, water, first aid items, and so on, should be packed in an easily accessible location. Items that are likely to be used only when camp is reached, such as the sleeping bag, tarp or tent, stove, cooking equipment, and so on, can be packed in less-accessible areas. A balanced pack is a pack in which the weight is distributed equally from top to bottom, left to right, and front to back. It is easy to see how a pack with gear

strewn all over the outside could unbalance a hiker. A balanced weight makes a pack more comfortable. You should also be aware of the shape of the end product (the packed pack). Sharp, pointy, or lumpy items should not be packed so that they place continuous strain on a small area of the pack (leading to tears) or your body.

Pack Fitting and Adjustments

Depending on the style of pack used, there are a number of different techniques for making pack adjustments. Regardless of the pack used, the following points can make wearing a pack more comfortable. The waist belt of the pack should rest above your hips. This allows the weight of the pack to be carried by the trunk rather than the shoulders. The pack should not hang from your shoulders, as occurs when the waist belt is not high enough or not tightened appropriately. Packs hanging from shoulders can become uncomfortable very quickly. The primary function of the shoulder straps is to keep the pack against the back and prevent it from swaying side to side. You may want to have students try on a loaded pack without buckling the waist belt so they can see how it compares with wearing a well-adjusted pack.

Appropriate Clothing

Overnight hikers have no control over unexpected weather changes. Appropriate clothing is a hiker's defense against changing conditions. Clothing is the gear that you use to regulate body temperature, stay dry, and keep comfortable. In the outdoors, temperature and humidity can change abruptly for a number of reasons, the most obvious of which is an oncoming rain- or snowstorm. Perspiration can also soak a hiker's clothes. You should seek to regulate your body temperature and avoid excess perspiration while hiking. You can do this by increasing or decreasing your activity level, using a layering system, and opening or closing layers (changing the ventilation).

A common approach to layering is the three-layer system (wicking layer, insulating layer, and outer shell; see figure 2.3). This system is critical to regulating body temperature. The layer closest to the skin should be a wicking material such as polypropylene. This layer allows perspiration to be wicked away from the skin, through the material, so it can evaporate. The next layer is the insulating layer. The insulating layer should be made of a material such as fleece or wool and comes in many different thicknesses. Depending on the expected weather temperature (very cold, for instance) a second insulating layer may be necessary. The third layer is a

Figure 2.3 Layering is one of the best ways for hikers to regulate their body temperature. The three-layer system includes the *(a)* outer shell, *(b)* insulating layer, and *(c)* wicking layer.

shell that goes over the insulating layer to protect you from the elements (wind and rain). Cotton should be avoided whenever possible because it holds moisture rather than wicks it away. When cotton gets wet, it usually stays wet.

> **TEACHING TIP**
>
> Let students know that there is no such thing as bad weather, just bad attitudes. Many students and adults quickly associate bad feelings with rain, cold, heat, or snow, mainly because they have been caught off guard by it. This unfortunately gives a rainy, cold, hot, or snowy day a bad name. Remind students that with proper equipment, changing weather can be fun.

Depending on personal differences (some people tend to always be cold whereas others seem to always be hot) and changing weather conditions, hikers can adjust their body temperature by adding or removing layers. You should try to regulate your perspiration and temperature so that you do not soak through your layers. If a layer of clothing gets too wet (due to perspiration, rain, snow, and so on), remove that layer and put on a dry one. As the outside temperature falls, wet clothing drastically reduces core body temperature. Do not rely on one heavy, warm, waterproof layer. Also, since most heat is lost from the head, putting on a hat is a great way to warm up without putting on another insulating layer.

Appropriate Footwear

Appropriate footwear provides warmth, dryness, support, and comfort. A basic rule of thumb is to choose footwear that provides ample support and protection against the distance and type of terrain to be traveled and the possible weather conditions that may be encountered (rain, snow, sleet, and so on). This footwear could range from walking sneakers to mountaineering boots. For the sake of safety, do not allow students to wear any open-toed shoes, even when sitting around camp. Hikers' feet are much too important to take the chance of stubbing a toe, kicking a cactus, or suffering any other seemingly small injury to an exposed foot. Socks are also a part of footwear, and many hikers recommend layering socks. A thin wicking layer on the foot covered by an insulating sock helps feet stay dry. Layering socks also reduces friction on the feet, which decreases the chance of developing blisters. Another recommendation is to leave the cotton socks at home. They have poor insulating properties and are generally a coarser fabric, which can lead to heel blisters.

OVERNIGHT HIKE PLANNING

The planning phase for hiking and other outdoor pursuits is critical for developing a safe, enjoyable outing. As noted in chapter 1, you can use the seven principles of

Leave No Trace (www.lnt.org) as guideposts throughout your planning process. For instance, the first principle, plan ahead and prepare, is exactly what students need to do to begin their planning. While there is no standard method for you to use when developing a trip plan for an overnight hike, one recommendation is to begin by asking, "What do students need to know in order to plan a safe and enjoyable overnight hike?" When students are asked this question, many respond immediately by listing the types of equipment they *think* they will need. This is certainly an important aspect of trip planning, but it may be putting the cart before the horse. Knowing the answers to the questions of why (trip goals), where (location), when (season), and what if (possible unknowns) will help determine what equipment will actually be needed. A closer look at why, where, when, and what if is useful for developing a comprehensive trip plan. As you work your way through these questions with your students, the answers you arrive at should incorporate the remaining Leave No Trace principles (the six principles after plan ahead and prepare). The end result will be a written itinerary for an overnight hiking trip.

Why?

A great start to trip planning is to answer the following question: Why am I going hiking (what are my goals)? This is an important question to ask not only of yourself but also of any group members who are planning to go with you. If your goal is to travel as fast and far as possible, with minimal breaks, it is important to know if the goals of the other group members are similar. Suppose you invite a friend to go on a hike with you without exploring the different reasons why people enjoy hiking and just assuming everyone hikes for exercise. Imagine the dismay of the friend who agrees to go with you because he believes everyone hikes to enjoy leisurely walks with multiple stops for enjoying the scenery. Imagine the comments you and your friend make about one another after the hike. For instance, you might say, "I can't believe I brought him hiking; the only thing he wanted to do was stop and smell the flowers. We made so many stops I never got my heart rate up and I knew we would never make it to the summit." Conversely, your friend might comment, "What a horrible hike! All she wanted to do was drag me to the top of the mountain. She kept pushing me to go faster and faster. I never did get to stop and look at anything." It is often a mismatch of goals that negatively affects the hiking experience. Letting others know your intentions for the hike allows them to make an informed decision about whether to join you. In the case of an entire class embarking on an overnight hike, the teacher can determine the goals to accommodate the class.

Where?

There are a number of ways to determine a location for an overnight hike (books, Web sites of land management agencies, outdoor retail stores, friends, and so on). Regardless of the method you use to determine the location, conduct basic research of the site in advance of the trip. Considerations about where to take a hike go beyond simply choosing a location. Once a location has been determined, you need to gather additional information such as land use regulations (group size limitations or fire and stove restrictions), permit requirements (camping fees, entrance fees, fishing licenses), closures (specific trails, entire areas), typical weather patterns, ways to get there, available emergency response systems, and best times to visit. This list of considerations is not exhaustive; it merely provides a starting point for thinking about proper trip planning.

Allowing students to generate questions about choosing a location is recommended. Students generally think of things that many adults overlook. For instance, one student wanted to know how bad the mosquitoes would be for a trip planned in Maine. Until this student asked this question, everyone in the group, including the instructor, had overlooked this finer detail. Most, if not all, people who have been unfortunate enough to spend a night with mosquitoes unprepared (without repellant) do not make that mistake twice. This example highlights the importance of researching the finer details about locations and also shows how previous experience can help in future planning.

When?

Making plans on when to go on an overnight hike can be an extension of planning *where* to go. Most often the timing of the trip will be determined by preexisting school schedules. Considerations for when to conduct an overnight hike should include, at the very least, typical weather patterns, visitation rates (and possible overcrowding), water availability (unless packing all water), and location availability.

What If?

The answer to this question is helpful because it prepares hikers for emergencies. You should think about the many different scenarios that, while not likely to occur, could occur. Developing answers to the following what-ifs before embarking on a hike is a great place to begin this type of planning. The following is only a partial list of questions to consider. Having students create other questions is useful in developing an appreciation and understanding of the necessity of preparedness.

Sample What-Ifs

1. What if I get separated from the group?
2. What if someone gets injured?
3. What if I fall in a fast-moving river?
4. What if I cannot get along with others in the group?
5. What if my feet get wet?
6. What if I encounter large wildlife (e.g., bears, mountain lions, moose)?
7. What if we break down on the way to the trail-head?
8. What if I get a blister or experience sunburn?
9. What if the teacher gets injured?
10. What if I get bitten by a venomous snake?

Knowing the answers to questions like these helps reduce the anxiety and knee-jerk reaction that can occur in response to one of these unlikely events. The point of asking these questions is to prepare hikers in advance for worst-case scenarios so that they can respond more effectively. For example, before going on a hike, you should know how to treat a blister so that it does not turn into an open wound (which sometimes might require an evacuation). Having answers to questions like this also assists in developing an equipment list. For example, treating a blister requires a basic first aid kit (assuming you know how to use its contents), and thus a first aid kit is an item to include on your equipment list. Hikers generally do not go out on hikes with the intention of getting injured, but knowing the different injuries that are possible assists in providing care.

Most of the answers to the why, where, when, and what if of planning can be determined by group brainstorming and simple research. Simple research can include contacting different land management agencies, using Internet resources, reading guidebooks, speaking with others who have previously gone on this or similar outings, and so on.

Creating an Itinerary

During the trip planning, encourage your students to think about their overnight hike in sequential order from start to finish. This is useful in helping students think about the process of events and not simply the overall event (the overnight hike). Once all of the questions are researched and answered, you should develop a trip itinerary. The itinerary should be left with at least one person not going on the hike. This person assumes the responsibility of sending help in the event that the group does not return at a predetermined time. With that said, it is paramount that you follow the itinerary closely. This includes following the directions of travel to and from the location and also the daily plans for the overnight hike. Table 2.2 provides a sample itinerary with instructions on how to fill it out.

BASIC SKILLS AND TECHNIQUES

Overnight hiking can be a satisfying, rewarding, and comfortable adventure, or it can be a less than desirable night in the woods. Chances for satisfaction, reward, and comfort can be increased by understanding and learning some basic skills and techniques. These skills and techniques include food menu planning, sanitation and hygiene, and travel techniques and trail etiquette.

TEACHING TIP

To avoid scaring students away from the lifetime activity of overnight hiking, discuss a less than desirable night as uncomfortable rather than dangerous.

Food Menu Planning

As noted previously, menu planning depends on whether you need to use a stove or fire to cook your food. Other considerations for food planning include the preferences and allergies of the individuals in your group, packaging waste, caloric values, spoilage, amount of time you want to spend preparing meals, and amount of weight you are willing to carry. You can have the entire class plan the same menu or can split the class into small groups of 3 or 4 students and have each group plan a menu. While planning meals as an entire class allows you to economize and take advantage of bulk food purchases (that you then repackage into group portions), it is usually more difficult to come up with a menu that everyone can agree on.

Generally people burn more calories when hiking versus walking on city streets due to the increased

Table 2.2   Sample Overnight Hiking Trip Itinerary

Leader	Give the teacher's name.
Students	Attach a list of all participants.
Dates	Include both start date and end date with times.
Location	Describe location as exactly as possible.
Activities	List intended activities (e.g., overnight hiking, fishing, swimming).
Maps	Provide a detailed map of the area with your hiking trails and camping area highlighted.
Travel time	Note the amount of time planned to get to the destination.
Starting point	Provide the starting point of the hike.
Ending point	Provide the ending point of the hike (often the same as the starting point).
Narrative	Begin with the travel directions to and from the overnight hiking location. Next, describe in detail the hiking trail and camping area planned. Include enough detail for someone to follow you in the event of an accident or the need for search and rescue.
Total hike time	Include the time it will take to hike to the camping area with intended breaks and also the amount of time scheduled to hike back to the trailhead the next day.
Hazards and obstacles	List the potential hazards or obstacles that could be encountered throughout the entire trip. For example, automobile travel to and from the location is perhaps the greatest hazard. Other hazards could include rockfalls, stream crossings, bug bites, scratches, or cold temperatures.
Emergency contacts	Include emergency numbers for the local land management agency (e.g., U.S. Forest Service), local police and fire department, nearest hospital (with directions), and administrative personnel from school. Noting whether 911 is operational in the area is also helpful.

level of exertion required to carry a pack, climb steeper grades, and traverse uneven and changing terrain. Thus hiking is a good excuse for students to choose foods high in calories. However, students should still plan meals balanced in carbohydrate, fat, and protein. The U.S. Department of Agriculture food guide pyramid is a useful resource for meal planning. Beginners should keep meal plans simple. As they gain more experience with overnight hikes they can then experiment with different backcountry cuisines.

Sanitation and Hygiene

Proper sanitation and hygiene are critical for reducing the incidence of illness and the spread of disease. Many camping areas have facilities with toilets that flush and sinks that have running water and soap. When camping in one of these areas, you should use these facilities. However, there will be many times when facilities such as these will not be available. Knowing that bathrooms are unavailable can incite panic in many. Students and teachers alike should rest assured that relieving the

body of waste is a natural process for *everyone!* Where you should dispose of human waste is another issue. Teach students to dispose of human waste as early on as possible (nature calls each of us at different times). The third principle of Leave No Trace (www.lnt.org) covers waste disposal extensively. Most importantly, always dispose of human waste in cat holes at least 200 ft (61 m) from water sources, trails, or camp areas, and use hand sanitizer when finished.

> **TEACHING TIP**
>
> To reduce the chances of contaminating shared food, remind students to pour food from a container into their hands instead of diving into the container with their hands. We cannot assume everyone has been keeping their hands clean.

Aside from using hand sanitizer, hikers can also clean their hands with water. Soap is not necessary; friction is the key. Instead of plunging your dirty hands into a small stream (which might serve as a source of drinking water), have a partner slowly pour water from a bottle over your hands as you rub them together with much friction. During snack and food preparation times it is critical that all hikers have sanitized their hands. Bacteria such as *E. coli* can spread quickly among hikers when proper hygiene is not followed. Use common sense. For example, when sharing food from a common bag, do not stick your hands inside the bag to dig around and scoop a handful of food; rather, have someone pour the food into your opened hands.

Travel Techniques and Trail Etiquette

Using different travel techniques during a hike can help students to conserve energy. Hikers are generally much happier when they arrive at their camping destination with enough energy to set up their tarps and tend to other matters. Using trail etiquette not only benefits other visitors you may encounter on the trail but also benefits your group and the environment.

Energy Conservation

Hiking on a trail with a pack strapped to your back requires greater exertion than walking around town or school requires. Students need to be taught methods for conserving energy so that they do not burn out early during the hike. Often students get summit fever, in which they are so excited at the start that they want to go as fast as they can to reach their destination. Starting off at a quick pace can drain energy needed later in the trip. Learning how to develop an appropriate pace helps students conserve energy.

Encourage students to hike at a pace that they could continue all day long. Individual paces differ because each person has a different level of physical fitness and comfort. Individuals should hike in a rhythmic, controlled pace that matches the rhythm of their breathing. Furthermore, students should be able to carry on a conversation with others while they hike. This is a good way to assess whether a hiker is going too fast or too hard. The rhythmic pace should be kept when hiking on a flat surface, uphill, or downhill. Racing ahead for a few minutes only to have to rest for a few minutes is not a good idea, unless you are involved in another type of fitness training. When moving at an appropriate pace, most students are able to hike for about an hour. After each hour of hiking, stop and rest for 5 min.

Aside from taking necessary rests, you and your students can conserve energy by stepping over or around small rocks or downed tree limbs rather than stepping up onto each rock or downed limb. Each step-up is cumulative, and near the end of a hike these step-ups can add up. Use hiking poles or a walking stick to take some of the weight off of your knees and other joints. Shorten your stride length when going up or down a hill. By using these simple techniques, you can be better assured of having enough energy to complete the upcoming tasks associated with setting up camp.

Etiquette

Knowing when to rest is one thing, but understanding where to rest is another. Hikers need to be aware of the surrounding environment when choosing a place to rest. Choose rest areas that are off of the trail so that others can pass by and that do not place any hikers at risk of injury (e.g., do not rest near a cliff edge). Choosing a shady or sunny rest stop can also be helpful. If students are hiking in the scorching sun, it might be advantageous to lengthen the distance traveled so that they can rest under a shade tree. Conversely if students are hiking on a cooler day, you might seek a sunny area. Rest stops are a great opportunity to rehydrate and eat a quick snack. However, students must remain hydrated throughout the outing. Waiting until they are thirsty is too late to begin rehydrating. Have students encourage one another to take sips of water throughout the day. Or have students propose toasts periodically. For instance, one student can say, "I would like to make a toast to the beautiful surroundings." In response, the rest of the students and teachers in your group can hold up their water bottles to toast one another and take a drink.

As with other outdoor pursuits, you should exercise general etiquette while hiking. Proper etiquette not only helps prevent possible user conflicts but also adds to the hiking experience. General etiquette includes yielding to bikes, pack animals, and hikers moving uphill. Slower hikers should allow faster hikers to pass by, and faster hikers should be polite and ask if they can pass by. Other considerations for general etiquette include preserving the land as you found it. For instance, stay on the trails, follow rather than cut any switchbacks (cutting switchbacks increases trail erosion), and, if the trail is muddy, go through the mud rather than around the mud. Hiking around muddy sections on a trail widens both the trail and the muddy area. As you can see, the principles of Leave No Trace are integral to all aspects of hiking.

Choose rest areas that are off of the trail so that others can pass by and that do not place any hikers at risk of injury.

SAFETY CONSIDERATIONS

Overnight hiking is an inherently dangerous activity involving the risk of injury and even death. Hikers are susceptible to hazards such as weather, falling rocks, uneven terrain, poisonous plants, stinging insects, small and large critters, and snakes. This short list in no way includes all the risks involved in overnight hiking; it merely provides a starting point to help students develop an awareness of what they could encounter.

Hazards

During the trip planning process, have students research potential hazards associated with their chosen location. The next step is to figure out what to do in the event that a group member encounters one of these hazards. For example, if the students determine that they will be spending the night in bear country, they should know what to do if they encounter a bear and also what they can do to decrease their chances of encountering a bear. Although overnight hiking can never be guaranteed

as safe, common sense and appropriate planning can minimize the inherent dangers. There are two types of hazards that you and your students need to consider: human factors, also referred to as *subjective hazards,* and environmental factors, also referred to as *objective hazards.* Human factors are errors in judgment and environmental factors involve environmental risks.

Proper planning coupled with vigilant hazard evaluation minimizes many risks. During trip planning, have students research and determine how to navigate both subjective and objective hazards.

Subjective Hazards

- Getting lost
- Carelessness, complacency, poor judgment
- Fatigue
- Panic, fear

Objective Hazards

- Talus, scree, and boulder fields
- Plants
- Animal encounters (with bear, elk, moose, coyote, or mountain lion)

- Stinging insects
- Rockfall
- Dry crossings
- River crossings
- Weather
- Flash floods

Being prepared before embarking on your overnight hike—that is, knowing what your group could encounter and how to deal with those encounters—greatly minimizes the risk of injury. Encourage students to point out potentially unsafe conditions and hazards throughout the hike. As students note potential hazards, use teachable moments to reinforce learning. For example, if a student encounters a rattlesnake on the trail, use this opportunity to reinforce how to react to this situation. Remind students not to approach the snake, throw things at it, or try to pet it. Instruct the students to go around the snake, giving it a wide berth. Try sharing other useful facts about rattlesnakes. For instance, rattlesnakes are not found in Hawaii and they do not eat people.

In addition to knowing how to minimize risks, students should understand how to treat minor scrapes, cuts, abrasions, and blisters. While the following paragraphs on first aid do not replace the need for professional training, they do highlight some of the common injuries hikers may encounter.

Common Injuries and First Aid

Even with the best-laid plans, hikers on an overnight hike cannot be guaranteed 100% safety. Although most people begin their hikes with safety in mind, they cannot be certain that an accident will not occur. Having the knowledge and skill to respond to the minor injuries that may occur can provide much relief in an overnight setting. Students should carry a small first aid kit with them to treat minor wounds, and you as the leader should carry a more substantial first aid kit and be trained in first aid and CPR.

The most common injuries hikers experience are cuts, scrapes, and blisters. These injuries are usually only bothersome and do not pose a threat to life. However, if left untreated these injuries could become exacerbated and require an evacuation. A small first aid kit should handle most minor injuries. These minor injuries can be likened to those that children experience while playing on the playground. Minor first aid, such as cleaning and covering an injury, is the key. Blisters, on the other hand, can become troublesome rather quickly for the entire group. Untreated foot blisters can lead to an unwanted and unexpected evacuation. Since your feet are your mode of transportation, they must be watched over vigilantly.

Be on the lookout for the warning signs associated with blisters (hot spots, friction, discomfort), and address them immediately. Hikers who feel a hot spot should stop and treat it. Cleaning the area with an antiseptic wipe and covering it with a bandage usually suffice. If a blister does occur, do not rip the skin off. Ripping the skin off creates an open wound, which is a much more serious injury. Popping the blister can provide some relief. To do this, poke the base of the blister with a sterile needle (found in the first aid kit). After the blister is drained, clean it and cover it. Often you will have to build up the area around the blister to prevent further friction. A small piece of foam from a first aid kit can be used. Simply cut a small hole out of the center and place the foam over the blister. The hole can be filled with antibiotic ointment and covered. The best advice is to avoid a blister in the first place. Remember, hot spots and feelings of friction should be addressed immediately to prevent blisters!

ENVIRONMENTAL CONSIDERATIONS

As when teaching all outdoor pursuits, you should encourage your student hikers to develop a personal outdoor ethic. As mentioned in chapter 1 and developed as a theme throughout this book, practicing the seven principles of Leave No Trace (www.lnt.org) is a great way to help students to become stewards of the land. Explore the seven principles listed in chapter 1 with your class to help your students develop and practice methods that will minimize their effects on their environment.

During the exploration and development of an outdoor ethic, encourage students to think about their time spent in the outdoors as well as their time spent near their homes and schools. Doing this can help students develop an outdoor ethic that includes responsible care for all "public lands." Students and instructors should walk away from this exercise understanding that caring for the outdoors is not reserved only for the times they visit the mountains, parks, beaches, deserts, or wooded areas. Caring for the outdoors needs to include the areas around homes, businesses, and schools.

CONCLUSION

The benefits of overnight hiking are vast. Whether you plan your trip for exercise, relaxation, or socializing with friends, there are a number of basic skills you need to manage the inherent dangers of overnight hiking. Developing a detailed trip plan is perhaps the most critical step in planning a safe and enjoyable outing. The seven principles of Leave No Trace should be used as guideposts throughout your entire journey. Adhering to these principles not only protects you and others but also protects precious public lands.

RECOMMENDED WEB SITES

Land Management Agencies

Bureau of Land Management: www.blm.gov
National Park Service: www.nps.gov
U.S. Fish and Wildlife Service: www.fws.gov
U.S. Forest Service: www.fs.fed.us

Retail Stores

REI: www.rei.com
Eastern Mountain Sports: www.EMS.com

OVERNIGHT HIKING UNIT PLAN

General Lesson Information

Each lesson contains the following seven elements:

1. Objectives—primary learning outcomes
2. Equipment—specific materials and gear
3. Introduction—opening concepts, ideas, and questions that identify the focus of the day
4. Warm-ups—not necessarily appropriate for this topic
5. Central activities—activity progressions that increase in difficulty and lead to more advanced skills
6. Closure—suggested discussion and reflection items
7. Assessment—examples of evaluation strategies

Day 1

Focus: Introduction to overnight hike planning

- Fundamentals of planning
- Developing an overnight hike trip plan and itinerary

Day 2

Focus: Introduction to overnight hiking equipment

- Considerations for choosing equipment

Day 3

Focus: Introduction to pack packing

- Fundamentals of pack packing
- Pack packing activity completed in groups of four

Day 4

Focus: Introduction to the potentially adverse effects humans have on natural areas and on ways to reduce these effects

- Adverse human effects on natural resources
- Leave No Trace charades

Day 5

Focus: Introduction to tarp setup

- Benefits of tarps versus tents
- Fundamentals of tarp setup
- Setup game (set up tarp cord and stakes using groups of four)

Day 6

Focus: Introduction to travel techniques and etiquette

- Fundamentals of energy conservation
- General trail etiquette

Day 7

Focus: Introduction to hazard evaluation

- Subjective hazards
- Objective hazards

Day 8

Focus: Introduction to food planning

- Fundamental considerations for menu planning
- Introduction to MyPyramid

Day 9

Focus: Introduction to backcountry stove operation

- Fundamental safety considerations for operating backcountry stoves
- Considerations for using stoves

Day 10

Focus: Introduction to appropriate clothing

- Fundamental considerations for regulating body temperature
- Layering

chapter 3

Bouldering

Kristen Csiacsek

For me, climbing is a form of exploration that inspires me to confront my own inner nature within nature. It's a means of experiencing a state of consciousness where there are no distractions or expectations. This intuitive state of being is what allows me to experience moments of true freedom and harmony.

Lynn Hill

Bouldering is the art of climbing horizontally, rather than vertically, on an artificial or authentic rock surface. It may occur in a remote backcountry locale or on a decorative wall in a local gymnasium. Bouldering was first introduced as a way for climbers to practice certain moves and techniques without venturing onto high peaks, especially during inclement weather. As more and more climbers exercised and practiced on large rocks—or boulders—even in fair weather, bouldering matured into a challenging outdoor pursuit in its own right. No longer is bouldering considered merely as training for the mountains. It is now thought of as a legitimate and artistic climbing activity with its own intrinsic value. Today, elite climbers compete for speed and for degree of difficulty on real rock and climbing walls in bouldering events all over the world.

Unlike traditional climbing, which demands endurance over long stretches of rock, bouldering focuses on short sequences of moves, or problems. Although the individual moves in bouldering are often more difficult than they are in traditional climbing, the opportunity for repeated attempts and frequent planning when bouldering can help climbers acquire essential skills more quickly. Bouldering continues to increase in popularity, and today there are climbing gyms dedicated to bouldering. Although there is no official standard for height limit in bouldering, instructors should use discretion and be conservative.

Although some enthusiasts distinguish between boulderers (people who climb outdoors on real rock) and gym climbers, much of the information presented in this chapter applies to both. In fact, an indoor climbing wall can be a great site for learning the basics of outdoor bouldering.

In bouldering, rather than being protected by the roped belay system used in traditional climbing, the climber is protected by other students who serve as spotters. A spotter is someone who is trained to stand behind a climber and who physically helps to protect a falling climber against landing badly on the ground.

Bouldering has numerous benefits, not the least of which is its relative safety when compared with vertical climbing; that is, falls in bouldering are limited to short distances (although with improper spotting and no rope to arrest a fall, a bouldering accident can be serious). Without the need and cost of specialized equipment (such as ropes, harnesses, carabiners, and artificial protection), bouldering is affordable, exhilarating, and fun. Furthermore, bouldering can be challenging for both novice and experienced climbers, some of whom may be afraid of heights! Whether performed indoors or outdoors, a short climb of less than 10 ft (3 m) off the ground can present a variety of problems that afford genuine climbing challenges.

In addition to being a low-risk, low-cost, highly challenging activity, bouldering comes with numerous other benefits. For example, as climbers "stretch and grab their way across appropriately demanding traverse routes, they enhance their physical proficiency (balance, strength, and coordination) while confronting cognitive challenges and building interpersonal skills" (Stiehl and Chase, 2008, p. vii). All of these attributes are directly related to the standards recommended by the NASPE (2004).

EQUIPMENT

One of the greatest parts of bouldering is that there is no need for expensive equipment. The most basic equipment needed for a boulder includes a climbing surface and crash pad. Climbing enthusiasts might also bring climbing shoes, a brush, towel, chalk, and athletic tape.

- **Artificial walls.** There are many varieties, both indoor and outdoor, of artificial walls. These include simple flat traversing walls; portable traversing walls; walls with corners, edges, overhangs, and convoluted surfaces; self-standing bouldering islands; and bouldering caves. Each must meet industry standards, including providing a safe landing surface. These walls are good for practicing basic and advanced climbing movements that easily transfer to outdoor settings. In fact, many artificial walls now offer features and heights that are analogous to those of real rock, thereby helping to maintain a climber's interest while also increasing the wall's value as a training aid. Bouldering can be done on any type of wall as long as the climber doesn't go too high.

- **Authentic boulders.** When practiced outdoors, bouldering usually occurs at the base of a rock face or on large boulders and outcrops. Rock types vary across geographic areas. Hard rock, such as granite, provides good footholds but can be painful on the hands, whereas softer rock, such as sandstone, is kinder to the hands but allows the feet to slip more. Nonetheless, bouldering routes can be found on almost all rock types.

> **TEACHING TIP**
>
> Introduce these personal items to students at the beginning of the unit. As the instructor, it would be appropriate to have climbing shoes available for those students that don't have their own personal gear.

- **Crash pad.** When bouldering on real rock, climbers sometimes use a foam landing pad or mat, which when placed at the bottom of a boulder problem can reduce the likelihood of injury. Similarly to people who climb on artificial surfaces, outdoor climbers usually employ the assistance of spotters, who work to direct the climber's body toward the crash pad during a fall.

- **Climbing shoes.** Although not an absolute necessity, climbing shoes can be worn to increase climbing performance. These shoes enhance the climber's ability to use the feet on small edgy holds, provide better friction on holds, and provide a better feel (sensitivity) for footwork. They are lightweight and fit snugly. When climbing the typically short, low routes of bouldering, many climbers prefer the convenience of slip-on shoes. If students are using shoes not specifically designed for climbing, they can make their shoes perform better by lacing them tightly, especially toward the toe of the shoe. A shoe that has little rubber sole protruding past the toe of the shoe itself also aids in climbing.

- **Chalk.** Some climbers prefer to use loose, powdered chalk as a hand-drying agent. The chalk is often carried in a small bag designed specifically for climbing. The bag straps around the climber's waist and, for easy access, hangs in the middle of the back at about the end of the tailbone.

- **Brush.** It is not uncommon to see people bouldering with a small brush. This brush can be used to clean holds, including chalk residue left over from an earlier climb.

- **Towel.** Some climbers bring along a towel that they use to wipe their feet before ascending the rock.

- **Clothing.** Most outdoor clothing outlets carry outdoor apparel promoting design, performance, and comfort. However, clothing for bouldering usually includes a shirt and shorts or anything that is comfortable and flexible.

- **Athletic tape.** Athletic tape can be useful for covering cuts or blisters and can provide support for strained joints.

ROCK FEATURES

Before teaching climbing skills and techniques, it may be helpful to describe to students the common features on real rock and artificial walls. Although not an exhaustive list of protuberances and hollows, the following terms are used throughout this chapter and are linked frequently to specific climbing techniques:

jug (also called a *bucket*)—a hold large enough to allow the climber to reach an entire hand inside or around it, making it easy to grasp.

crimper (also called a *pinch* or *edge*)—a small knob with a thin edge that can fit only a climber's fingertips.

horn—a rounded, knoblike hold that is considerably larger than a crimper.

pocket—a hold that is similar to a jug but has a more pronounced recess; a hold into which a climber can place the fingers and sometimes the entire hand.

sloper—a large, severely rounded hold that resembles the bottom of a bowl and sometimes is very difficult to grasp.

TEACHING TIP
Provide visual examples of these rock features through demonstration, pictures or video.

BASIC SKILLS AND TECHNIQUES

While good climbers must have strength and agility, they also must have well-practiced techniques in order to negotiate the climbing surface with speed and skill. A successful climber moves effectively from one balance position to another, all while conserving energy. Climbing relies heavily on the arms and legs, so it is important that beginners learn to use their limbs in ways that conserve strength and energy for difficult moves. Since muscles tire, techniques for resting during a climb can further help to conserve strength. Finally, regular breathing keeps muscles oxygenated and ready to function. The following suggestions are the most essential techniques for improving bouldering performance.

Climb With Your Eyes First

This old saying means to look at and study the boulder problem before starting to climb. Bouldering provides the advantage of having the whole problem visible and often within reach. Since you can touch and feel most of the holds, route finding becomes relatively simple. By visualizing the best sequence, you can anticipate weight shifts, reaches, and sections that may present the most difficulty (a crux, or the hardest part of a climb). Though climbing with the eyes first takes practice and is not used as much as it should be, previewing a route guarantees better climbing.

Keep Your Weight Over Your Feet

Climbing requires balance, which means keeping your center of gravity squarely over one foot or both feet (i.e., keeping your nose over your toes). Taking small steps aids balance by permitting a smoother transfer of weight from foot to foot. A good sense of balance is the key to moving smoothly. A simple exercise for improving balance is to practice traversing a slab at a 60° (or greater) angle using only your feet. Traverse back and forth, using your hands for balance only occasionally or not at all.

As a rule, keep your body close to, but not pressed against, the climbing surface. Leaning out from the rock will increase the friction between your shoe sole and the rock. However, your general body position should be upright with your weight squarely over your feet. A common beginner's mistake is to lean in with the head and shoulders while sticking out the behind. This position displaces the center of gravity as well as places undue strain on the hands. Experiment with different stances and distances so you can adjust to various conditions.

Maximize Your Steadiness

The steeper the climbing surface, the more it becomes necessary to use the arms and hands. When using a combination of the hands and feet, the climber's maxim is to maintain three points of contact with the rock at all times. If, for instance, you are moving your left hand, don't also move your right hand or either foot. In general, this maxim is sound advice, and yet there may be times when a lunge works better than a controlled reach. Nonetheless, when transferring weight from hold to hold, maintaining three points of contact is a valuable principle for the beginner. Using fewer than three points of contact compromises balance and forces you to make difficult adjustments to regain stability.

There are two ways in which a climber can move from one location or position to another. One way is static climbing, in which the body position is controlled by muscle movement rather than momentum. Maintaining the three points of contact is useful for this way of moving. When practicing static climbing, first move the hand or foot and then shift the body weight.

More difficult routes may require the more advanced dynamic climbing, which involves using momentum to reach a hold that is farther than can be reached by using the limbs alone. To practice this technique, identify holds that are not quite out of reach but might require extending your body position and briefly losing your three points of contact. Quickly move your weight toward the hold, using your momentum to reach the hold just before you begin to drop. The moment when you can grip the hold is called the *dead point* (the climber is at the point of maximum height and is weightless). When you reach the dead point, let go with one hand while reaching for the more distant hold with the other hand. For a brief moment neither hand will be in contact with the rock. Obviously this requires precise timing. By practicing both static and dynamic techniques, your movement across the rock will become more fluid.

Use Good Footwork

Developing good foot placement is essential for improving climbing technique and balance. The following tips are indispensable for helping students to improve their climbing.

- **Deliberate foot placement.** Teach students to be deliberate in choosing their footholds. The security of a foothold largely depends on how much weight you can put on it. Again, keeping your body positioned over your feet is critical to remaining on a hold. After making a precise foot placement, keep it still. When moving a foot from one hold to the next, the supporting foot must be firmly placed.

Figure 3.1   Edging.

- **Edging.** This technique involves using the inside edge or outside edge of the foot to stand on sharp holds (see figure 3.1). When the edge of the shoe is placed directly on the best part of the hold and then weighted, the shoe bites into the hold and provides firmer footing (also known as *purchase)*. The inside edge, which is generally the most effective technique, is mostly used when the knee and hip are turned out from the wall so that the inside of the knee is facing the wall. Outside edging involves using the outside of the foot with the small toe against the surface and is mostly used when the hips are perpendicular to the wall and the outside of the leg is against the wall.

Figure 3.2   Smearing.

- **Smearing.** For less-defined holds that do not permit edging, smearing might be a more appropriate technique (see figure 3.2). Smearing involves placing as much of your shoe sole as possible against a surface to obtain enough friction for support. When smearing, hold your body as upright as possible, thus increasing your foot pressure on the rock. Avoid leaning in, as doing so reduces the friction and can cause you to lose your footing.

On some occasions it might be better to push than to pull. The following are some of the different ways in which you can grab a simple handhold:

Figure 3.4 Open grip.

- **Open grip.** This grip involves using your whole hand (including the palm, fingers, and thumb) to grasp a big or rounded feature (see figure 3.4). Typically this grip is used on jugs and larger pockets, horns, and slopers. Since the open grip spares the finger tendons severe stress, it is the hold least likely to produce an injury.

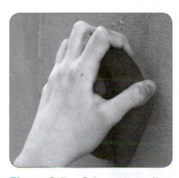

Figure 3.5 Crimper, or cling grip.

- **Crimper** (sometimes called the **cling grip**). This grip is used on edges with flat tops, and only the fingertips contact the rock (see figure 3.5). Although this grip is very strong, it leaves the fingers vulnerable to tendon injury.

Figure 3.6 Pinch grip.

- **Pinch grip.** For this grip you use your thumb and fingers like a lobster claw to squeeze two surfaces toward each other (see figure 3.6). This grip is not very powerful, but it will help you grasp a tiny knob.

Figure 3.7 Side pull.

- **Side pull.** This grip involves pulling sideways on a vertically or diagonally oriented hold that is off to the side (see figure 3.7). Lean away from the side pull to make the grip work. A variation of the side pull is the **undercling** (see figure

Figure 3.3 Heel hook.

- **Other foot techniques.** Additional techniques include the heel hook (see figure 3.3), in which the inside part of your heel is placed on a protruding hold. Some people refer to this technique as *using a third arm* since the intent is to use the foot as a hand. One use of a heel hook is for taking weight off one arm and redistributing it to a leg. This allows you to release one arm in order to reach a different hold and can save you energy. Another technique, the toe-in, is a head-on approach in which your knees and hips are parallel to the climbing surface, the front of your foot is on the hold, and you are standing on your toes. This technique requires strong toes but can be handy in small pockets. Although these and other specialized techniques can be useful, much success can be found by refining the basic edging and smearing skills.

Check Your Grip

Unlike footwork, grip is not often considered a feature of good bouldering. Since hands and arms are not as strong as legs are, climbers are encouraged, to the greatest extent possible, to use arms for balance and legs to hold body weight. But the weight on the hands and arms increases as the rock gets steeper and the footholds get smaller. As a result, the hands and arms are the first muscle groups to tire.

New climbers have a tendency to use too tight a grip, which quickly drains strength, technique, and confidence. The key to the right grip is simple: Relax. While a vicelike grip may seem essential, you should use the lightest possible grip to make moves. Overgripping wastes strength!

Day
2

Handholds, both on real rock and on indoor walls, come in every shape imaginable. You have to adjust your grip to the demands of each hold. There are many ways in which you can use your hands to take full advantage of a hold. You can pull down, pull sideways, or pull up.

Figure 3.8   Undercling.

3.8), which involves grabbing hold with your palm up and pulling upward. This can be useful as a balancing tactic until a free hand can reach for a better hold. Yet another variation is the **Gaston,** in which you pull on a vertically oriented edge that is directly in front of you. The movement looks the same as the one you would use to open an elevator door.

- **Palm.** This grip is for when no hold exists. You can palm the rock with an open hand, pushing on the rock surface rather than pulling on an available hold. Palming is like smearing with a hand instead of a foot.
- **Mantle.** This grip involves gaining a vertical boost by stepping up with one foot (often onto a thin ledge) and pressing down on a handhold with your palm (see figure 3.9).

Figure 3.9   Mantle.

Use Bone, Not Muscle

Climbing can be exhausting. Since muscles tire, resting on your skeleton is an important means of conserving energy. Climbers who look for and take rests do better than those who do not simply because they are better at resisting fatigue. Tips for conserving energy while climbing include the following:

- Stand tall on straight legs and hang down on straight arms.
- Lower your heels to relax the calves and straighten your elbows to relax the biceps.
- Take short rests and rest your smaller muscles frequently.
- If you must rely on your muscles, choose a full contraction or extension over intermediate positions involving a partially bent arm or leg.
- To relax and get the blood flowing, dangle and shake your limbs one at a time.
- Search for resting spots, especially while still on the ground. Good climbers are good resters. When resting, relax and take a few regulated deep breaths.

TEACHING TIP

If your students are complaining about sore forearms, it might be because they are not applying the "use good footwork" and "use muscle not bone" techniques.

Watch and Learn

Observation and imitation can be great teachers for your students and you. Observe the techniques used by good climbers, and try to develop new techniques yourself. Though a new climbing technique might seem awkward at first, practicing new moves while rehearsing the fundamentals of good bouldering will help you progress to a new level.

SAFETY CONSIDERATIONS

Whether performed indoors or outdoors, bouldering is an inherently dangerous activity involving the risk of injury and even death. Indoor climbers are susceptible to hazards such as loose or damaged holds, falling to the ground or on other participants, abrasions from the wall and holds, and climbing out of control and above acceptable heights. Outdoor climbers face additional hazards such as the weather, falling rocks, poison ivy, wasps, and rattlesnakes. Although bouldering can never be guaranteed as safe, maintaining a reasonable margin of safety can minimize the inherent dangers.

Falling

No matter how good you are, you will fall. Many climbers fall when attempting moves that push their limits. But even climbers who find full satisfaction in doing moves that are close to the ground and well within their current skill level occasionally fall. Falling is a part of bouldering and is a skill to learn just like any other good climbing technique. While fear of falling is part of the underlying thrill of climbing, it also can inhibit learning and progress. But the more experience and skill you can gain in falling, even if it means taking deliberate falls, the more comfortable you will become when bouldering.

Learning to fall in control involves landing in a balanced position and bending your knees to help absorb the energy of the fall. Also, most falls come as a surprise, so you should always be aware of what is below you (rocks, shrubs, uneven surfaces). If you are using a crash pad, avoid landing on an edge, which can lead to a twisted ankle. Finally, rather than leaping to the ground, try to jump lightly away from the rock at the moment you slip.

A common question is, "What is a safe height for bouldering?" The answer depends on how far you are willing to fall, how controlled you will be when you fall, and what kind of landing surface you might encounter. Some instructors prefer to establish height limits; for example, you might tell your students that a climber's feet should be no higher than 3 ft (about 1 m) off the ground.

Spotting

An important safeguard against injury from a fall is spotting. A spotter is someone who is trained to stand behind a climber and who physically helps to protect a falling climber from a harmful landing. Good spotting takes practice. Therefore, you should teach and assess proper spotting *before* presenting bouldering activities.

Spotters are not catchers! The purpose of good spotting is to absorb part of a climber's fall rather than catch the climber by taking the whole of a climber's weight during a fall (see figure 3.10). Good spotting requires the following:

Figure 3.10 It is important to teach and assess proper spotting before students begin bouldering.

- A balanced and stable stance: The spotter should stand with the feet about shoulder-width apart and one foot slightly in front of the other and with the knees slightly flexed to absorb impact.

- A proper upper-body position: The spotter should extend the arms and hands at the level of the climber's waist, with the palms facing the climber and the fingers together (spoons, not forks).

- Moving along with the climber and being ready for a fall at any time: This includes anticipating the path of the climber and being ready to be in a good position should the climber fall. A useful principle is to follow the climber's center of gravity and not the climber's moves.

- An adequate number of spotters: If a boulderer keeps changing positions on the rock, thereby changing the possible path of a fall, then two or more spotters may be necessary.

At times, all a spotter can do is protect a climber's most vulnerable areas—the back, head, and neck. Occasionally a spotter might even end up on the ground with the fallen climber. As long as spotters remain with their climbers in an attempt to protect them, the spotters have done their job.

Students also should learn a communication sequence that tells everyone what the climber intends to do. The following is an example of a good sequence:

> Climber: "Ready?" This cues the spotter that the climber is ready to begin.
>
> Spotter: "Ready." This reassures the climber that the spotter is ready.
>
> Climber: "Climbing." This notifies the spotter of the intent to begin; the climber awaits permission from the spotter before beginning.
>
> Spotter: "Climb on." This gives the climber permission to begin climbing.

Some people prefer to end the communication once the climb is completed:

> Climber: "Off spot?"
>
> Spotter: "Spot is off."

Objective Hazards

Unlike subjective hazards, which are errors in judgment, objective hazards are potentially unsafe conditions and primarily involve environmental risks. Bouldering

presents many of the same objective hazards that are encountered in other outdoor pursuits (e.g., weather and wet or slippery terrain). In addition to the issues already mentioned, such as an uneven landing surface, a few hazard considerations include the following:

- **Loose rock.** When bouldering at the base of a rock crag, you should watch for potential rockfall. Rocks can spontaneously fall from above or can be dislodged by a hiker, another climber, or an animal.

- **Rock quality.** Holds can break unexpectedly, even on the most solid rock. Examine holds carefully. If a hold sounds hollow when you tap it, don't use it. Even when holds are secure, sharp rock can abrade and tear flesh. When bouldering on abrasive rock, consider wearing long pants made of durable material. In addition, taping your fingers before some climbs can help you to avoid Band-Aids and antibiotic ointment afterward. To tape your fingers, use athletic tape and wrap individual fingertips. See chapter 4 for more information.

- **Plants and animals.** Bouldering sites can be home to unfriendly plants, insects, and other creatures. Teach students to recognize and avoid poison ivy and poison oak. Also be on the lookout for hornets and wasps, snakes, and the occasional bird which, when frightened, might startle the unaware climber and lead to an unexpected fall.

ENVIRONMENTAL CONSIDERATIONS

Today there are more climbers out in bouldering areas than there ever were before. Climbing enthusiasts affect the outdoors in very visible ways, and bouldering can be more destructive than the other forms of climbing. Heavy traffic in popular areas, trash at bouldering sites, crash pads laid over plants, and disrespect for nesting birds all take their toll on a fragile environment. To address some of these issues, teach students to do the following:

- **Pick up trash, whether or not they brought it to the site.** Seeing litter is offensive but unfortunately not at all uncommon. In addition to having students take care of litter, ask them to use chalk sparingly. Keeping the trails, climbing areas, and rock itself clean reduces signs of human use.

- **Practice good sanitation.** When outhouses are available, students may use them. When they are unavailable, students should know how to deal with getting rid of their own waste. Otherwise they risk damaging the environment (e.g., contaminating water sources) and spoiling the experience of other outdoor visitors.

- **Use established trails and paths.** Traveling outside the main trail tramples vegetation and contributes to the formation of wider and more numerous paths, both of which can lead to rampant erosion.

- **Respect wildlife.** Remember, you and your students are a guest of the outdoors and its inhabitants. When you disturb and feed wildlife, they may experience greater competition for food and cover, suffer nutritionally, and become more vulnerable to predation.

- **Be considerate of others.** Etiquette at a bouldering site is important. For more popular sites, those who arrive first should have preference. However, while it may be polite to offer a site to other climbers, it is rude to rush another group to hurry up and leave. If a climb is taken, have students move on to something else. You can also avoid popular sites, or visit them during times when crowds are small.

- **Request access permission from landowners and respect** *No Trespassing* **signs.** Landowners and government agencies are concerned about liability, environmental effects, overcrowding, and other issues. Therefore, you and your students must earn their respect and their willingness to allow you to use their property.

As bouldering becomes more and more popular, access to bouldering areas could become a significant problem. It is our shared responsibility to preserve bouldering areas by minimizing environmental effects, practicing safe bouldering, and respecting public and private property. We can also help to ensure that areas remain open to bouldering by volunteering for trail-building and maintenance projects, participating actively with forest rangers and rescue teams, and looking for other ways of demonstrating that we are responsible users of outdoor resources.

CONCLUSION

Bouldering is one of the simplest outdoor pursuits in terms of required technical equipment and skills, and yet it can provide the ultimate challenge for the outdoor athlete in grades K through 12. The task for the physical education teacher is to locate a bouldering site that presents adequate challenge, easy supervision, and level landing surfaces. In the evolution of climbing, many students may choose bouldering as a method to practice the climbing techniques used in rock climbing. A variety of challenges allows you as the instructor to meet the ability levels of all students.

REFERENCES

National Association for Sport and Physical Education. (2004). *Moving into the future: National standards for physical education* (2nd ed.). Reston, VA: Author.

Stiehl, J., & Chase, D. (2008). *Traversing walls: 68 activities on and off the wall*. Champaign, IL: Human Kinetics.

RECOMMENDED READINGS

Everlast Climbing Industries. (2001). *Vertical expressions: Teacher manual.* Mendota, MN: Everlast Climbing Industries.

Stiehl, J., & Chase, D. (2008). *Traversing walls: 68 activities on and off the wall.* Champaign, IL: Human Kinetics.

Stiehl, J., & Ramsey, T. (2005). *Climbing walls: A complete guide.* Champaign, IL: Human Kinetics.

Wilderness Education Association, Kidd, T., & Hazelrigs, J. (2009). *Rock climbing.* Champaign, IL: Human Kinetics.

BOULDERING UNIT PLAN

General Lesson Information

Each lesson contains the following seven elements:

1. Objectives—primary learning outcomes
2. Equipment—explicit materials and gear
3. Introduction—opening concepts, ideas, and questions that identify the focus of the day
4. Warm-ups—routines to stretch or strengthen muscles and tendons specific to climbing
5. Central activities—activity progressions that increase in difficulty and lead to more advanced skills
6. Closure—suggested discussion and reflection items
7. Assessment—examples of evaluation strategies

Day 1

Focus: Spotting

- Spotter stance
- Spotter communication
- Paired spotting
- Trust circle
- Wobbly walk
- Trust walk
- Assessment with spotting checklist

Day 2

Focus: Explore bouldering, climbing with the eyes first, maximizing your steadiness

- Stay low
- Stay high
- Zigzag climb
- Pattern traverse
- Hula hoop pass
- Caving
- The tunnel
- The hole

Day 3

Focus: Footwork and handholds, placing your feet carefully, checking your grip

- Jigsaw handholds and footholds
- Freeze frame
- Handholds and footholds check-off
- Intermediate technical climb
- Backward traverse
- Follow the leader
- 360° turn
- Advanced technical climb
- Multiple 360° turn
- Blindfolded climb
- Intelligent traverse

Day 4

Focus: Starting with your legs

- Beanbag traverse
- Every other foothold
- Missing arm
- Three-arm climb
- Three-leg climb
- Hoop connection

Day 5

Focus: Keeping weight over the feet

- Bulging brain
- Bag pickup
- Cone head
- Ring grabber
- Point to point
- Dwindling resources
- Maximize traverse

Day 6

Focus: Using bone, not muscle

- Cone-to-cone tennis
- Collection bags
- Toss and catch
- Elbow-lock traverse

Day 7

Focus: Building strength and endurance while bouldering

- Endurance climb
- Speed climb
- Scrunch

- Weighted pack
- Backward scrunch
- The wild traverse

Day 8

Focus: Team climbing challenges

- Capture the flag
- Shuttle relay
- Copycat
- Four-leg or four-arm climb

Day 9

Focus: Creative climbing

- Making up bouldering challenges
- Student-marked routes

Day 10

Focus: Individual climbing competition

- Bouldering contest
- Share challenges

chapter 4

Rock Climbing

Ryan Hammes
Ryan Olson

What we get from this adventure [climbing Mt. Everest] is just sheer joy. And joy is, after all, the end of life. We do not live to eat and make money. We eat and make money to be able to enjoy life. That is what life means and what life is for.

George Leigh Mallory

Rock climbing is the sport in which people climb vertically on a natural rock surface or a manmade artificial rock wall with the goal of climbing to the top or other end point. Historically, climbing on rock features was simply a means for indigenous peoples such as the Anasazi of what is now New Mexico to trade with others within their cliff dwellings. Explorers used rock climbing techniques to cross over mountain passes. Sometime in the 1800s, outdoor rock climbing transcended from a means of transportation to a popular recreational sport, and today specialized equipment and climbing techniques allow people to climb for the sheer enjoyment of reaching mountain summits. With the technological advances and design of safe, lightweight equipment in the late 1900s, North American guide services and schools began to understand the value of such a sport. Outdoor rock climbing is done all over the world and offers an incredible diversity of opportunities. Today climbers are pushing the envelope of technique, speed, safety, difficulty, and style. Depending on the location, outdoor rock climbing can happen year round. Climbers of all abilities and ages can find enjoyment, whether participating in competitions for speed and difficulty or climbing for personal satisfaction. Even people with disabilities can participate, as climbing is adaptable with available equipment and training. The reflection and transformative opportunities are endless, as this sport challenges the climber both mentally and physically.

As the sport of rock climbing grows, it is important to understand that even the words *rock climbing* offer a variety of meanings due to the creativity that is employed within the sport. Although this chapter focuses on top-rope and free climbing on outdoor rock faces, many of the techniques described here also apply to using an artificial wall. Free climbing is a method in which a participant climbs up a rock feature without the aid of artificial equipment to move upward. In the top-rope system, a climber ties into one end of a rope. The rope attached to the climber goes to the top of the climb, passes through an anchor master point, and then drops back down to connect to the belayer. The belayer is someone who is trained to manually operate the rope to protect the climber. This person plays a key role, as the belayer is responsible for the climber's life if the climber falls. It is recommended that a trained professional or accredited guide service set up each climbing route to ensure that the anchors are secure.

Climbing participants must learn a wide array of skills to move efficiently from hold to hold, as rock climbing requires endurance over large stretches of rock (30-70 ft, or 9-21 m), as opposed to bouldering,

which focuses on short, powerful sequences (8-18 ft, or 2-5 m). Other forms of climbing include ice climbing, traditional lead climbing, sport lead climbing, aid climbing, mixed climbing, and alpine climbing or mountaineering. All of these variations share the fundamental movements and safety techniques learned in top-rope climbing.

Rock climbing offers numerous benefits for both climber and belay team. While on a rock face, climbers learn new movement and motor skill patterns. They must strategize and be creative to find their own path to the top, as various climbers may differ in their technique. Belayers must learn to be responsible, attentive, and respectful to one another when performing their duties. The physical and mental benefits resulting from rock climbing include building strength, learning balance and agility, increasing flexibility, improving communication, developing coordination, overcoming fears, practicing problem solving, developing trust, and so on. These benefits meet most, if not all, of the standards recommended by the NASPE (2004). Although rock climbing offers many benefits, it also requires specialized training and equipment (e.g., rope, carabiners, harnesses, helmets, belay devices, and artificial protection). Given the right location and oversight, rock climbing is a safe sport. In fact, experience has proven that more accidents happen going to and from the rock site than during the actual climb.

Whether 25 ft (7.6 m) or 100 ft (30.5 m), an individual route is subjectively rated by the first person who climbed it. There are many types of rating systems throughout the world, but the one most commonly used in North America is the Yosemite Decimal System. This system uses a 5.0 scale (see table 4.1). Individuals scrambling talus (broken rock fragments) and boulder fields find themselves on class 3 and 4 terrain. Although this level can be dangerous and technically is a form of

Students listen to their instructors as they prepare for a top-rope climb.

Table 4.1 Yosemite Decimal System

Rating	Description
5.3-5.6	Beginner
5.7-5.8	Beginner to intermediate
5.9-5.10	Intermediate
5.11-5.12	Advanced
5.13-5.15	Very advanced, extremely difficult, professional

outdoor rock climbing, an area is designated as class 5 terrain only when the rock becomes vertical and thus requires the use of technical equipment. Easier routes begin around 5.3 (pronounced "five three") and reach as high as 5.15. When choosing a climbing site it is a good idea to find a site with a variety of difficulty levels that can meet the needs of all physical abilities in your class. A climbing guidebook for the area or a local guiding company should be able to detail the climbing levels of each route. Take classes to climbing sites in the 5.3 to 5.7 range, as the sport can be intimidating for some students, especially if they are unable to climb to the top. As your students become more comfortable with rock climbing, a more challenging environment may be appropriate.

Once your students understand some of the history and theory of rock climbing, they should learn what equipment is used and how to properly take care of this lifeline. It is easy to be overwhelmed by all the various pieces of equipment needed in outdoor rock climbing, but an overview of the function of the equipment will help students respect the property and the sport. Students who learn about the differing rock features, the uses of technical equipment, and the proper movement techniques will be sure to succeed in this adventurous outdoor pursuit.

EQUIPMENT

Rock climbing requires specialized equipment for safe participation. Purchasing the equipment is a large investment initially, but fortunately the investment lasts many years. Climbing equipment should be used and stored with care, as some of this gear is a lifeline for the students.

- **Shoes.** Like bouldering shoes, climbing shoes help to increase climbing efficiency. Many brands and styles cater to different shapes and sizes of feet as well as different styles of climbing (see figure 4.1). For example, a traditional lace-up shoe offers comfort while a sporty technical shoe is more pointed and creates a bend in the foot bed. A sporty technical shoe is worn by advanced climbers who desire to climb on routes that have smaller footholds and thus require a shoe that offers support for smaller surface areas. A traditional shoe can be worn for hours at a time, while more technical shoes are worn just for the climb. For beginning climbers a traditional lace-up shoe works great. Some companies such as Five Ten and La Sportiva carry a line of shoes that have the size printed on the outside of the shoe

Figure 4.1 The two lace-up shoes on the left offer a traditional shape and are preferred for novice climbers. The shoe on the right is a sportier technical shoe that has a smaller toe box for greater precision on smaller holds.

to make it easier for fitting large groups. A climber's preference for brand or style depends on comfort and fit. At all times a climbing shoe should be snug but not painful. The sticky rubber of a climbing shoe helps the foot to maneuver on small surface areas. Weather, primarily precipitation, can hinder rock climbing, as the rock must be dry in order for the sticky rubber of the climbing shoes to stick. Climbing shoes help climbing efficiency tremendously, but if the cost of outfitting an entire class is too cumbersome, students may climb in normal tennis shoes.

- **Harness.** Once upon a time it was common practice to simply tie into the end of the ropes with a few loops around the waist. This is no longer the case, as the force of a fall could lead to injury. A seat harness is always necessary when rock climbing outdoors. A harness should fit properly to ensure safety. Adjustable leg loops and an adjustable waist strap allow a climber to maintain a snug fit. The waist strap should ride just above the hip bones. This allows the force of a fall to be distributed over the entire pelvic area in the event that the falling climber flips upside down. Harnesses traditionally have a buckle for the leg loops and waist strap to be threaded through and doubled back. Some newer harnesses now come with an adjustable buckle system that is already doubled back and only requires the climber to tighten the straps by pulling in a singular direction. Whichever style you use, become familiar with the manufacturer's instructions for proper use.

Although not necessary, a belay loop helps to orient the belay device in a more anatomical position during belaying or rappelling (see figure 4.2).

Figure 4.2 Proper orientation of belay device attached to belay loop with brake strand on the bottom.

Most harnesses come with gear loops attached to the waist strap. Gear loops help climbers carry additional climbing equipment when progressing to more advanced styles of climbing such as lead climbing. Whatever brand or style you decide to purchase, be sure that the harness fits comfortably and has a Union Internationale des Associations d'Alpinisme (UIAA) certification guaranteeing that it is designed specifically for rock climbing. The UIAA is the international federation that sets safety standards for both mountaineering and rock climbing equipment. It is recommended that all technical equipment used in rock climbing be certified by the UIAA. Most equipment sold in the United States has been approved by the UIAA.

• **Rope.** Rope comes in all lengths, thicknesses, colors, and prices. A kernmantle climbing rope is made up of a protective sheath and an inner core that is made of synthetic fibers. The right rope to purchase depends on where you are climbing and at what height you intend to set your top-rope routes. A rope that is 197 ft (60 m) long with a diameter of 0.4 in. (10.2 mm) is a good choice for most popular rock sites. This length allows for setting climbing routes that are up to 90 ft (27 m) in height. Of course, it is imperative that you purchase a rope that is certified by the UIAA and designed specifically for rock climbing.

A rope can also have different stretch characteristics. A dynamic rope stretches up to 10% to absorb a fall, while a static rope stretches by only about 2%. Static rope sometimes is used to set anchors, but a dynamic rope

should always be used for the main belay line. Ropes also have special features such as dry treatment (water repellent sheath), markings for the middle of the rope, and a change in sheath design in the middle of the rope. Since the climbing rope is one of the main lifelines in the top-rope system, it should be protected from dirt, abrasion, and long exposure to ultraviolet rays from the sun. One way to protect the rope is to store it in a dry, cool place inside a rope bag. Most rope bags can be flattened out and used as a ground tarp at the rock site. The belay team can then stack the slack of the rope on the tarp to keep it free of dirt and debris that can harm the rope (see figure 4.3).

Figure 4.3 Rope bags and tarps help to protect the climbing rope from the ground.

• **Carabiners.** Carabiners are used in rock climbing for joining different items together (figure 4.4). They come in many different sizes, shapes, materials, and locking abilities. For top-rope climbing, locking carabiners are best, as they have a twist lock on the gate that helps to keep it from inadvertently opening. A recommended carabiner for a physical education class is a pear-shaped locking carabiner. Pear-shaped locking carabiners are versatile and work well for clipping the belay device and rope to the climbing harness since they have a larger gate opening. Whichever carabiner you decide to purchase, be sure that it is intended for rock climbing and the spine displays the strength of the carabiner in kilonewtons. A kilonewton (kN) is a measurement of force used in physics. Since most modern carabiners are made from aluminum, a cautionary practice is to retire a carabiner that has been dropped from a great distance, as dropping a carabiner can sometimes lead to microscopic fractures. It is always better to be safe than sorry, so if you ever question a carabiner, retire it immediately!

Figure 4.4 Different styles of carabiners. From left to right, wire gate D, oval, locking oval, locking D, locking pear-shaped, and autolocking pear-shaped carabiner.

- **Belay device.** Belay devices are used to safely control the rate of descent for the climber. Operated by a member of the belay team, this device is the braking mechanism in the rope handling system. Each brand has a slightly different look, but most brands operate with the rope entering and leaving the belay device while being wrapped around a locking carabiner. The three most commonly used types are the tube-style, figure-eight, and self-locking (Petzl Grigri) belay devices. Figure-eight devices are becoming less popular, as they kink the rope and create a rat's nest to deal with later on. Self-locking (Petzl Grigri) belay devices are great because they automatically pinch the rope even if the belayer lets go with the brake hand. However, they are more expensive than other devices and are limited to only one strand of rope. Also, this type of device is not useful for rappelling. It is recommended that climbers learn how to belay with a basic tube-style device such as the Black Diamond ATC or Mammut Fuse (see figure 4.5).

Figure 4.5 Different styles of belay devices. From left to right, Black Diamond ATC-XP tube-style device, Mammut Fuse tube-style device, and Petzl Grigri self-locking device.

- **Chalk bag and chalk.** Although chalk is not necessary, some climbers prefer to use loose chalk to dry their hands while climbing. Chalk is usually carried in a small bag attached to the waist with a small belt (see figure 4.6).

Figure 4.6 Chalk bags are traditionally worn around the waist.

- **Clothing.** For the most part, clothing for climbing is a personal preference. Clothes should be stretchable, have good breathability, and not inhibit movement. Chapter 2 provides suggestions for proper layering.
- **Tape.** Athletic tape can be used to protect the hands from abrasion or to add support to finger tendons. Some climbers use tape as a preventative measure against scrapes by making tape gloves. Such protection is optional and depends on the type of rock being climbed. Climbers use tape to support their tendons by wrapping strips of athletic tape around their fingers between the knuckles.
- **Helmet.** You should wear a helmet at all times while at a rock site whether you are climbing, part of the belay team, or simply watching your peers. As with other climbing equipment, make sure the helmet is designed for rock climbing and holds a UIAA rating.
- **Rock protection.** Rock protection is used to set up a top-rope anchor system. Protection can be natural or artificial. This chapter does not cover the use of rock protection, but it is important to teach students new to rock climbing that there are various ways to construct a safe top-rope system that utilize specialized pieces of equipment such as passive wedging chocks or nuts, hexes, and spring-loaded camming devices (see figure 4.7). Placement of these variously sized artificial protection items requires training and experience and should not be attempted without proper instruction.

Trees and boulders are known as *natural protection* and may be used when the rock site allows for it. Large trees and boulders are often wrapped with webbing, static rope, or cordelette to create a master point where two locking carabiners join multiple separate anchors into one. The rope passes through the master point and becomes the top of the climb—thus the label *top-rope climbing* (figure 4.8). Only a trained professional or accredited guide service should set up anchors for a top-rope site.

Figure 4.7   Artificial rock protection. This rack of equipment contains many different sizes of passive wedging chocks and spring-loaded camming devices. This equipment is used by professionally trained climbers to set anchors at the top of climbing routes.

Figure 4.8   This master point has been extended from the anchor protection pieces with static (nonstretching) rope to make sure the climbing rope does not rub over any edges.

- **Artificial walls.** Outdoor rock climbing offers advantages over artificial walls, such as scenery, connection to nature, diversity of technique, amplified problem solving, natural rock surfaces, weather, differing heights, and diversity of rock types. It also requires additional training, safety parameters, transportation, land access, and equipment. For these reasons schools have begun to build artificial walls to better control some of the hazards encountered in and logistical support needed for group climbing. Modern walls use materials that create the texture and look of a real rock site. Anchors can be placed into a welded infrastructure that can literally withstand the force of an earthquake. Differently sized and shaped holds can accommodate different levels of climbing ability and can be changed to keep climbing routes fresh. Walls should meet industry standards and be inspected regularly by professionals.

ROCK FEATURES

Just as climbing style, equipment, climate, and terrain differ across the world, so do the types of rocks. Outdoor rock climbing can be experienced on sedimentary, igneous, or metamorphic rock. Rock quality is not determined by aesthetic appearance but by the integrity of the rock's breaking strength. Rock quality helps determine the safety of the climb. A rock site is good quality if it holds the protective pieces of artificial protection and will not break apart when the climber pulls on the holds. Certain cliffs are good quality and safe for rock climbing, while others crumble apart. Climbing sites across the United States mostly feature sandstone, limestone, and granite, but depending on where you live, you may find yourself climbing on a variety of other types of rock faces. The rock type usually, but not always, determines the style of climbing. Some of the techniques used to climb the various rock features are covered later in this chapter.

When climbing granitic formations such as those of California's Yosemite National Park or Joshua Tree National Park, you can expect to do a fair amount of crack climbing. Crack climbing is a technique in which you use your hands and feet in a jamming formation to hold your weight without pulling on any actual hold. This style of climbing is difficult for beginning climbers.

Sedimentary formations offer face climbing, in which you use the alterations in the rock face to find irregularities, or holds, you can use to pull your way up to the top. Areas such as Zion National Park and Indian Creek in Utah are composed of sandstone and offer sustained crack climbing routes. Sandstone sometimes offers cup-shaped or pocket-shaped holds called *huecos*. Most rock sites will have a little of both crack climbing and face climbing. Regardless of what type of rock you climb, you will always encounter different features that provide additional challenges to problem solve. A positively angled rock face involves slab, or friction, climbing, in which you lean into the rock face and use both balance and footwork to overcome this awkward technique of climbing. A negatively angled rock face is referred to as an *overhang* or *roof* and not only is intimidating but also requires endurance and upper-body strength. Two parallel walls between which a climber must stem, or use oppositional forces to climb, are called a *chimney*. Cracks in the rock have different names depending on their size. For example, a small crack in which only the fingertips can fit is called a *splitter,* while a gaping crack that swallows the entire arm and shoulder is called an *offwidth*. Climbers use these words to communicate and provide information, or beta, to help each other. Using these commonly used terms can help students improve their skills and technique while being up off the ground.

SKILLS AND TECHNIQUES

The joyous sport of rock climbing allows participants to challenge themselves both physically and mentally. With that said, it is important that climbers learn to be efficient with their movements so that they can conserve their energy for the entire climb. Although experiential learning is best for climbing, studying a few pointers ahead of time can help ensure safety and enjoyment of the sport. Chapter 3 on bouldering also outlines good techniques that can be applied to top-rope climbing.

Getting Started

Before allowing your group to begin climbing on a rock face, take the time to make sure your students understand the fundamental safety measures of climbing. Then you can begin getting ready to climb.

Stretching

Since climbing requires flexibility and agility, it is important to stretch properly before beginning the activity. Some of the muscle areas to target are the forearms, biceps, triceps, quadriceps, calves, and gluteal muscles. Yoga poses can help with warming up for climbing.

Putting on a Harness

Putting on a harness for the first time can be a little tricky. First, be sure there are no tangles in any of the straps, as this causes discomfort later on. Position the waist strap over the hips and tuck your clothing inside the strap. Tighten the waist strap snugly and then double back the buckle (some harnesses may differ). Repeat this process for the leg loops. Figure 4.9 shows step by step how to put on a harness.

> **TEACHING TIP**
>
> Demonstrate putting on a harness on yourself before letting students attempt to put on their harnesses.

Tying Into the Harness

There are many different knots used to tie into a harness. The knot most commonly used in North America is a figure-eight follow-through:

1. Tie a figure-eight knot, leaving 4 to 5 ft (1.2-1.5 m) of tail at the end of the rope. This tail is used to tie into the harness (see figure 4.10, *a-d*).

2. Thread the working end of the rope through both the leg loop and the waist strap junctures. Do not tie directly into the belay loop (figure 4.10*e*).

3. With the working end of the rope, rethread the figure eight to make a uniform knot with at least 6 in. (15 cm) of tail exiting from the finished figure-eight follow-through knot. The knot should be 2 to 4 in. (5-10 cm) from the harness and should not interfere with the climber's movements (figure 4.10, *f-h*).

Taping Fingers and Hands

Using athletic tape is an optional method that can help prevent the straining of a tendon. Tearing a strip of athletic tape that is 1 in. (2.5 cm) wide lengthwise down the middle offers the proper width to apply short (2-3 in., or 5-7.6 cm) strips of tape between the knuckles. When

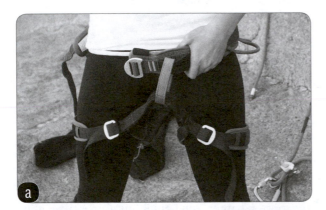
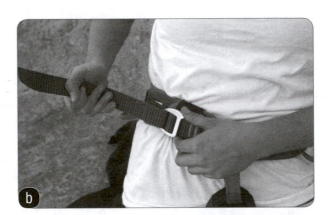
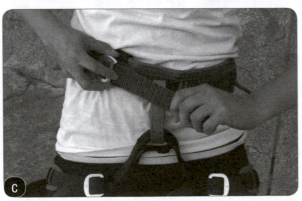
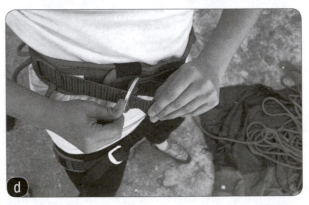

Figure 4.9 Putting on a harness. *(a)* Step into the leg loops and pull up the harness so that the waist strap rests above the hip bones. *(b)* Next, tighten the waist strap by inserting the strap into the buckle and pulling backward. *(c)* Next, thread the strap through the other side of the buckle, making sure the waist belt is snug. *(d)* Finally, double back the buckle by rethreading the strap as shown. Repeat this process for the leg straps.

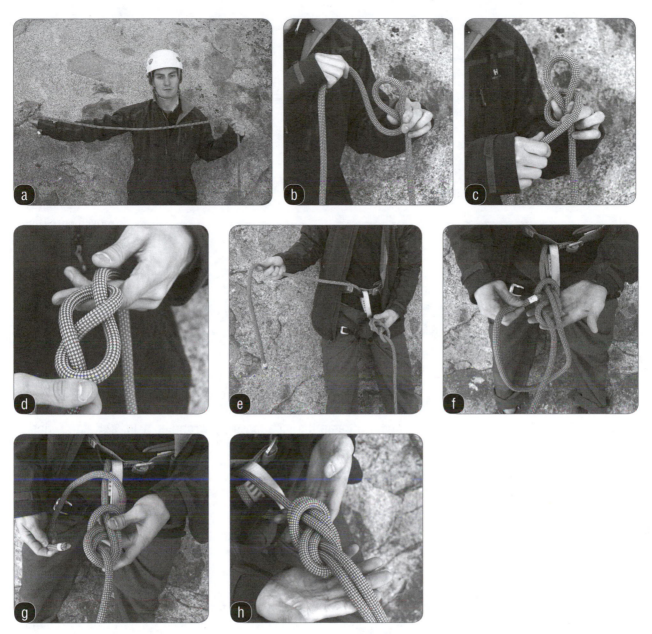

Figure 4.10   Tying into a harness is a multistep process. *(a)* Begin tying a figure-eight knot by measuring about 5 ft (1.5 m) of rope from the end. *(b)* At this point create a pinch, or bight, of rope. *(c)* With the working end of the rope, wrap the bight one complete rotation as shown. *(d)* Thread the remaining tail of rope through the open loop. Notice the symmetrical shape of the figure-eight knot. *(e)* Thread the working end of the rope through both the leg and waist connections, pulling the figure eight close to the harness as shown. *(f)* With the working end of the rope, retrace the figure-eight knot, beginning with the strand that is closest to the harness. *(g)* Continue to retrace the figure-eight knot. *(h)* The finished figure-eight follow-through knot should look symmetrical and be no more than 6 in. (15 cm) from the harness.

climbing on sharp granite or crack climbing, it is a good idea to tape the back of the hand for protection. To do this, apply strips that are 1 in. (2.5 cm) wide around the wrist and palm and knuckle areas of the hand (see figure 4.11*a*). This helps hold the rest of the tape in place. Next, tear the tape down the middle and make eight 10 in. (25 cm) strips that are 0.5 in. (1 cm) wide (figure 4.11*b*). Starting from the wrist, apply the strips to the 1 in. (2.5 cm) wrist wrap that is already in place. Follow around the inside of the finger and then back

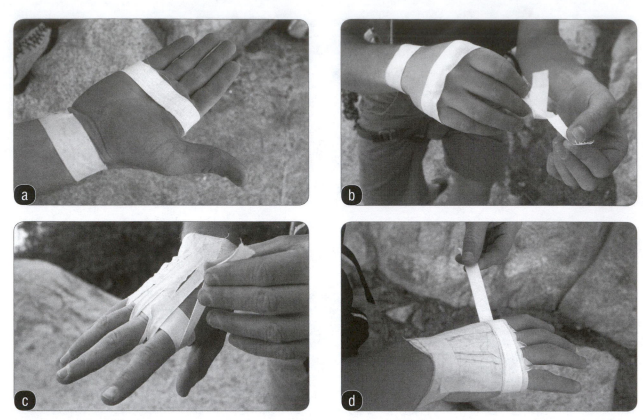

Figure 4.11 Taping the fingers and hands. *(a)* Begin the tape glove by wrapping 1 in. (2.5 cm) strips of athletic tape around the wrist and upper palm. *(b)* Tear eight 10 in. (25 cm) long pieces of tape lengthwise down the middle. *(c)* Starting at the wrist strap, place pieces of tape on the back of the hand and wrap around the finger before returning back to the wrist strap. Overlap strips of tape when possible. *(d)* Fill gaps with extra tape and then secure the glove with another layer of wrist and palm straps.

to the wrist (figure 4.11*c*). Follow the same procedure for all of the fingers (but not the thumb) and fill in any gaps with pieces of tape (figure 4.11*d*).

Putting on a Helmet

Proper use of the helmet helps protect the head against falling objects such as rock or equipment from a climber. A climbing helmet should fit snugly on the head and not wiggle freely when the head moves. It should cover the skull and protect the forehead in the event of a direct fall into the rock face. A common mistake is wearing the helmet loosely and tilted back. Secure the chinstrap to a comfortable, tight position. Figure 4.12 shows the correct and incorrect ways to wear a helmet.

Belaying

Proper belay technique is essential for the safety of the climber. A pinch of rope, or bight, is pushed through the belay device and is attached to the belay loop of the

belayer's harness with a locking (preferably pear-shaped) carabiner (figure 4.13).

There are many styles of belaying that can be used in rock climbing. A preferred beginning style is the overhand belay method. This is a four-part process. The dominant hand is the brake hand and the other hand is the guiding hand. Make sure that the brake hand *never* lets go of the rope.

1. As the climber ascends, slack is created in the rope system. The first step is to pull the slack through the belay device. The guiding hand pulls rope toward the belay device at the same time the brake hand pulls the rope away from the device (figure 4.14*a*).

2. The brake hand is used to lock off the rope into the brake position (figure 4.14*b*).

3. The guiding hand reaches below the brake hand (figure 4.14*c*).

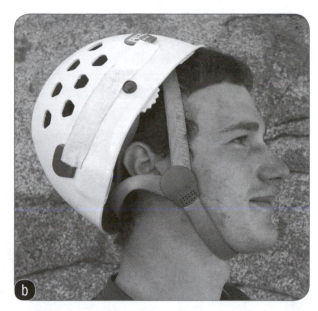

Figure 4.12   *(a)* Correct helmet position: Helmet covers the front of the head with the chinstrap connected. *(b)* Wrong helmet position: Helmet is worn too far back on the head.

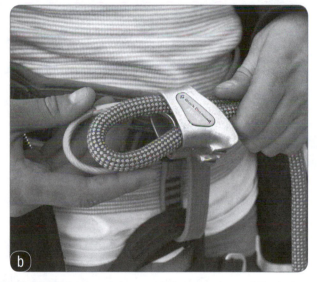

Figure 4.13   *(a)* Create a bight by pinching the rope. *(b)* Push the bight through one of the two slots of the belay device so that it matches up with the belay wire.

4. The brake hand slides toward the belay device while the guiding hand secures the rope in the brake position (figure 4.14*d*).

The belaying process is repeated as many times as needed until the climber reaches the top or end point of the climb. Should the climber fall at any point, the belayer always has a hand on the brake side and can simply lock off and hold the climber in a static position. In the event a climber needs to rest, the belayer can use the guiding hand to help hold the climber's weight by simply positioning it beneath the brake hand. The overhand belay method works best in quick, short increments. It is important for a new belayer to show competency in belaying before being allowed to practice on a real person.

Lowering

When a climber reaches the top of the climb, she will communicate to the belayer that she is ready to be lowered. The belayer then takes in all of the slack and positions the guiding hand below the brake hand, easing both grips to allow the rope to slide through in a slow, controlled manner. The climber positions herself in an L formation with her legs straight and perpendicular to the rock face and with her hands up in front of her so she is ready in case she swings unexpectedly (figure 4.15).

Day
2

Figure 4.14   Belaying using the overhand belay method. *(a)* Pull rope slack through the belay device as high as the chin (pull no more than 12 to 18 in. [30.5-45.7 cm] of rope out of the belay device). *(b)* Move the brake hand from the chin downward to brake the belay strand. *(c)* Position the guiding hand below the brake hand. *(d)* Slide the brake hand toward the belay device. Repeat the process.

Figure 4.15   The student being lowered in the foreground is showing proper lowering positioning. The hands are on the rope and the legs are perpendicular to the rock face.

Backup Belaying

Having a backup belayer is a good idea both for safety and for including more of your students in the climbing process. The role of the backup belayer is to hold the rope in the brake position should the climber fall at the same time that the main belayer lets go of the rope (figure 4.16). This is a cautionary measure that also helps students who are not at a level to do the main belaying still feel involved. The backup belayer stands on the brake-hand side of the main belayer. There should be approximately 4 ft (1.2 m) of slack in the rope between the main belayer and the backup belayer. The backup belayer positions the rope along his lower back and uses the hip belay method. A hip belay is similar to the slip, slap, slide method that is covered in day 2 of the accompanying lessons (see the CD-ROM) except that it doesn't involve a belay device. With this method, you *slip* or pull the working end of the rope until your arm is almost stretched fully out in front of you. Then you *slap* the rope into your helping hand (the helping hand goes farther away from you than your brake hand does).

Finally, you *slide* your brake hand back to your hip and start the process over again. As slack is pulled around the waist to the brake hand, the guiding hand pinches both strands of rope in front of the waist while the brake hand slides back toward the hip bone. This process is done repeatedly. The hip belay method creates friction by pulling on the brake hand to hold the rope and keep it from sliding through the belay device attached to the harness of the main belayer. In this method friction is created around the back of the backup belayer and creates redundancy in safety should the main belayer accidentally let go of the rope.

Communication

Proper communication between the climber and the belayer makes both feel supported along their journey to the top. There is nothing more unnerving than when you are 40 ft (12 m) off the ground and your belayer is having a side conversation with a friend. Since the climber and belayer grow farther apart as the climber advances up the wall, common commands are used between the climber and the belayer to make communication concise and consistent (see table 4.2). When climbing at a popular rock site or when multiple routes are set up close together, it is a good idea to follow the command with the person's name (e.g., "On belay, Jenny"). Whatever words you decide to use for the commands, be consistent in using them.

Figure 4.16   This belay team (belayer and backup belayer) is demonstrating good form, keeping their attention on the climber. Notice the hip belay method the backup belayer is using.

Table 4.2 Communication in Climbing

Commands	Description
Climber: "On belay?"	Climber is tied into the rope and has double-checked to make sure the belayer is properly set up to do his job.
Belayer: "Your belay is on."	Belayer is making a verbal contract with the climber, letting her know that he is ready to belay her knowing that all safety measures have been double-checked.
Climber: "Climbing."	Climber puts her hand on the rock but does not leave the ground until the belayer responds.
Belayer: "Climb on!"	The belayer gives the climber the green light to proceed up the wall.
Climber: "Tension." or "Take."	Climber uses these commands interchangeably to communicate to the belayer to take in any slack in the system and to make the rope tighter. These commands are often given at the top of a climb or when the climber needs to rest in the middle of the route.
Climber: "Slack."	Beginning climbers rarely use this command as they usually like the reassurance of a tight rope. Occasionally the rope pulls on the climber and she may wish for the belayer to loosen the rope a bit and thus will call out "Slack."
Climber: "Falling!"	The climber prepares the belayer to lock off on the brake hand quickly.
Climber: "Rock!"	If anything falls or is knocked loose, the climber yells "Rock!" and the belayer remains in his stance and does not look up.
Belayer: "Stop." or "Wait."	If the belayer needs to catch up from a climber ascending too quickly, he uses these commands to have the climber wait for him to catch up and take in the remaining slack through the belay device.
Climber: "Ready to lower."	The climber lets the belayer know that she is in the proper lowering position. It is common courtesy for the belayer to respond with "Lowering." This lets the climber know that slack is about to be given.
Climber or belayer: "Thank you."	This command lets either the climber or the belayer confirm a command was heard. It can also be used after a command. For example, Climber: "Slack." Belayer: "Thank you."

Movement

Successful climbers are efficient in many different techniques so they can be prepared when the rock's surface texture and shape change as they work their way to the top. Most moves are made in a static manner, meaning that the climber maintains control of his movement from one hold to another. Static movement is fluid and focused as opposed to dynamic movement, which requires a burst of energy and sometimes forces many limbs to leave the rock to latch onto new holds (figure 4.17).

Dynamic movements, sometimes referred to as *dynos,* require experience and can be dangerous if not practiced properly. Proper stretching, breathing, and resting are all required for the endurance needed for long climbs. Breathing and resting between difficult moves allow the muscles to reoxygenate and may reduce cramping. The use of good handwork and footwork will get students on their way to being better climbers.

Figure 4.17 This climber is demonstrating a dyno, in which he essentially leaves contact with the rock wall to jump for a hold that is normally out of his reach.

Handwork

Teaching students the names of the different grips and the proper technique in which to use a handhold will help you communicate with them when giving climbing advice. Some of the climbing handwork does not feel natural at first, but with practice the students will become more confident and able to apply less force and thus become more energy efficient. Some grips are more common than others, but usually the type of grip used depends on what type of rock you are climbing.

Day 6

Cling grip. The cling grip is probably the most commonly used grip, especially on artificial handholds. This grip feels most natural—it feels like hanging from a pull-up bar.

Crimper. The crimper is similar to the cling grip but is applied to either a thin edge or a small knob. Only the fingertips touch rock.

Pocket grip. In the pocket grip, one or two fingers are applied on a divot on the rock face or cupped in an actual pocket.

Undercling. The undercling is the same as the cling grip but is used upside down. The motion is similar to opening a drawer.

Pinch grip. The pinch grip is pinching small seams or squeezing larger portions of rock to hold yourself upright.

Mantle. The mantle is pushing in a downward motion with the palm of the hand.

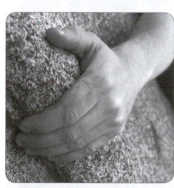

Side pull. In a side pull, you pull in a horizontal direction to stabilize yourself.

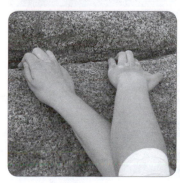

Crossing over. Crossing over occurs when the route traverses or goes at a diagonal and the hands must overlap each other.

Counter pressure. Counter pressure is created in a number of ways: *(a)* one hand can pull while the other pushes, *(b)* both hands can pull away from each other, or *(c)* both hands can pull or squeeze toward one another.

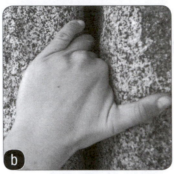

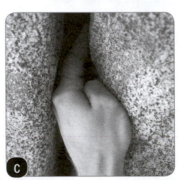

Jamming. Jamming is the technique used when climbing cracks. There are many variations, but the main idea is sticking the hand into the crack and torquing it so it becomes wedged in the crack just long enough to pull up to the next jam. Variations shown here are *(a)* positioning the hand with the thumb down and applying counterclockwise torque, *(b)* stacking the fingers and applying torque, or camming, to fill any void in the crack, and *(c)* using a cupping motion while tucking the thumb on the inside of the palm for added stability (used for wider cracks).

Matching. Matching occurs any time both hands or feet need to share a hold before moving to the next hold.

Footwork

Proper footwork leads to a higher-performing, more-efficient climber. Since leg muscles are stronger than arm muscles, practicing proper footwork technique helps you to conserve energy. For beginning climbers, the forearms are typically the muscles that are easiest to fatigue. For this reason, provide students with reminders and helpful tips early on, before they can develop bad habits. A simple tip is to keep your nose over your toes. This reminder makes a climber realize where her body is located in relation to the rock and where her center of gravity is being weighted. By looking down at the feet a climber can determine which maneuver is best for that particular foothold.

Edging. Edging is the proper way to stand on small rock features. Most of the time the inside edge of the shoe by the large toe will give you purchase on the rock. At other times you may use the outside edge, such as when conducting side pulls or lie backs or any time when the feet are pointed in the same direction. Avoid standing on the arch of the foot when rock climbing.

Smearing. When climbing on slabs or when there are not any features on the rock face, you may have to press the balls of the feet on the rock and use the friction created to climb upward.

Foot change. Climbers often have to change their footing on a small hold. It is good to practice switching feet by stacking one foot on top of the other and then moving the bottom foot quickly while the top foot replaces it on the hold.

Heel hook. Some features such as a horn will allow you to hook your heel around them and act as a third arm to hold you in place while you are reaching for the next handhold.

Flagging. Stretching to your fullest reach may tip you off balance. Flagging, by simply applying pressure to the rock when needed, can help stabilize your footing. Flagging can be done by either *(a)* extending a leg outward (photo shows the right foot stabilizing outward to prevent the body from swinging to the right) or *(b)* applying pressure from behind (photo shows the right foot stabilizing from behind to prevent the body from swinging to the left).

High stepping. High stepping is a technique that makes climbing more efficient, as using less movements will speed up your climb. High stepping does require greater flexibility.

Stemming. Stemming by spreading your legs out can be a good way to rest since the pressure is evenly distributed through your feet and your legs are straightened out for stabilization. This technique is especially useful in chimneys.

- **Lie back.** A lie back uses both handwork and footwork. The arms are extended to apply the weight on the skeletal system in a side-pull fashion, while the feet push off the wall or crack in opposition. This technique requires endurance and experience.

Coiling a Rope

Teaching students how to coil a rope can give them opportunity to help set up and take down the rock site. Although there are many variations on how to coil a rope, the backpacker's butterfly coil works well if students want to help carry some of the gear.

1. Start by flaking (putting the rope in a pile or stack on the ground after running it through your hands and checking for irregularities or damage) the rope from one end to the other, checking for any irregularities (figure 4.18*a*).

2. Take both ends of the rope and begin to stack about 12 ft (4 m) from both ends (figure 4.18*b*).

3. Take full arm lengths of the doubled strand and coil it back and forth around the shoulders (figure 4.18*c*).

4. Wrap the 12 ft (4 m) of slack left at the rope ends around the middle of the coil 5 to 7 times (figure 4.18*d*).

5. Push a bight through the hole (figure 4.18*e*) and pull the rest of the tail on through (figure 4.18*f*).

6. Make the coil into a backpack by wrapping the tails over the shoulders and around the waist (figure 4.18, *g-i*).

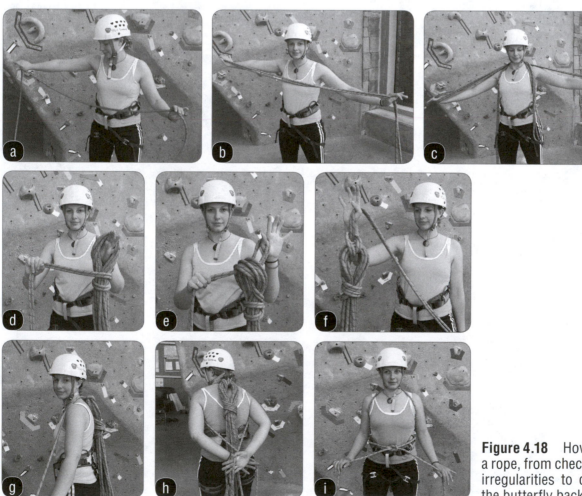

Figure 4.18 How to coil a rope, from checking for irregularities to creating the butterfly backpack.

SAFETY CONSIDERATIONS

Whether performed on an overhanging roof of granite or an artificial slab wall, rock climbing is an inherently dangerous sport involving many risks that cannot always be avoided. Some of these risks can lead to injury or even death. It is the responsibility of the group leader to set the tone and seriousness of the activity before the climbing begins. When taking a group outside to climb, keep in mind how you plan to manage the rock site, handle liability, and adhere to principles of Leave No Trace. Since safety is your number one concern, know as much about the area as possible before leading the climb.

Site Management

As a group leader, you must do your homework before taking a group out to a new rock site. Going out for a reconnaissance trip will help answer questions during the planning stage, such as the following:

- What are the permit or access requirements for the area?
- Is there parking close by?
- What is the approach like? How long is the approach? What is the terrain like?
- What is the base of the site like? Is the terrain even or a boulder field?

- How many ropes can be set close to one another?
- Are the ratings (difficulty) of the routes appropriate for the group? Is there enough variety?
- Is the site in the sun or shade?
- Where are the closest bathrooms?
- What is the rock quality like?
- How high are the routes?
- What type of equipment will be needed to construct the anchor?
- Is there another suitable site that can be used in case a group is already using this location?

When you arrive at the rock site, establish a safe zone in which participants can sit, observe, and cheer their peers on. This is an area where students can pull items out of their pack, drink water, and, if safety allows, take off their helmet. A safe zone should be on a durable surface, such as an area that has been trampled previously or an area of flat rocks. It is important for the future of the sport to keep climbing sites natural and free of trash.

As much fun as it is to cheer for a friend who reaches the top, being too loud can also take away from others' climbing experiences. Be aware of your surroundings at all times. A good rule of thumb is to climb earlier in the day before other climbing parties reach the site. Be respectful of others since the area is for everyone—not just climbers—to enjoy.

A well-organized rock site includes a safe zone, a number of routes of various difficulties (3-6 routes), and

A good example of site management: instructors watching closely as novice belayers practice their new skills.

a level base from which the group leader can easily hear and see what is going on at all times. A common question is, "How many students can I take out climbing and how many chaperones are required?" The answer depends on many conditions. A good rock site might be a group of 15 students with four ropes set up and 2 to 3 instructors managing the site. The students can be middle school to high school aged as long as their maturity can handle the belaying and knot tying and they can communicate as instructed. In an indoor artificial wall setting, the environment is much more controlled and can accommodate larger groups. Regardless of setting, if you feel hesitant at all, belay for the students and include them in the process by assigning them jobs such as backup belayer, rope stacker, knot checker, and so on.

Leave No Trace

Taking a large group out rock climbing can be very invasive to the land as well as disrupt hikers out for a quiet stroll in the woods. It is for these reasons that we must all do our best to educate others on how to tread lightly on the earth and at all times follow the Leave No Trace ethics. Chapter 1 includes a full list of the Leave No Trace principles. Some ways in which we as rock climbers can help teach Leave No Trace ethics as they relate to outdoor climbing include the following:

- Plan ahead and prepare by researching the area and reading the rock site guidebooks.
- Create a safe zone that is located on a durable surface.
- Travel single file on the trails approaching the rock site.
- Keep group size small to minimize affecting the experience of others in the area.

To lessen their effects on the natural setting, students travel in single file on a class 3 trail on their way to the rock site.

Day 8

- Minimize the use of chalk so the rock does not become painted with white spots.
- Pack out your trash, including fruit cores.

Hazards

Whether climbing indoors or outdoors, there are many hazards associated with climbing you need to take into account. Indoor hazards include long hair caught in the belay device, jewelry constricting digits or getting caught on holds, items falling out of climbers' pockets, one climber swinging into another climber, and abrasion from the artificial wall. Outdoor rock climbing presents even more hazards, including rockfall, insects, poisonous plants, weather, and hazards associated with transportation to and from the site. Climbing equipment, although made incredibly strong, does not last forever. All equipment is susceptible to abrasion from the rock, microfractures, and ultraviolet degradation, and thus it must be retired before the possibility of failure. Follow the manufacturer's recommendations for proper use and know the lifespan of the product.

Liability

Nobody would imagine a parent suing a school district for their son coming home with a twisted ankle from a game of flag football played in physical education class. However, if an injury occurs while rock climbing, regardless of the severity, there is more cause for alarm, as climbing is an activity that is sometimes misunderstood and often viewed as an extreme sport. It is for this reason that as an outdoor pursuits leader you must be professionally trained or must hire a guide who holds an accredited guide certification. There are many advantages to hiring a guide service, such as knowledge of the area, expertise in anchor setups, knowledge of permitting procedures, available equipment for participants, and additional insurance. The two most widely respected certification organizations in the United States are the American Mountain Guides Association and the Professional Climbing Instructors Association. Be sure to check that your hired guide holds a current certification for the type of climbing your group is doing. Although controversial, waivers are a must. They are at a minimum a good way of informing parents of the inherent risks associated with rock climbing. Since some rock sites are isolated from immediate medical help, it is a good idea to carry a well-stocked first aid kit and have one of your leaders hold a current wilderness first aid or wilderness first responder certification. A cellular phone or satellite phone provides communication to emergency medical help.

CONCLUSION

Rock climbing isn't just about safety and physical fitness. It also challenges participants in the affective domain. Working toward the top of a climb can provide endless opportunities for reflection, transference, and real-life metaphors. Creating a chance for students to be 25 ft (7.6 m) off the ground or to hold their classmate's life in their hands allows for a wonderful opportunity of facilitating a group discussion.

As the sport of outdoor rock climbing increases in popularity, it is important for educators to make sure the experience is a safe and enjoyable one for students. Practicing safe and proper etiquette while at the rock site ensures that others can enjoy the same experience. It is the responsibility of each group to practice Leave No Trace ethics, respect the rules of the land, safely manage the rock site, and have fun!

REFERENCE

National Association for Sport and Physical Education. (2004). *Moving into the future: National physical education standards.* (2nd ed.). Reston, VA: Author.

RECOMMENDED READINGS

Cox, S.M., & Fulsaas, K. (2003). *Mountaineering: The freedom of the hills.* (7th ed.). Seattle: The Mountaineers Books.

Hurni, M. (2003). *Coaching climbing: A complete program for coaching youth climbing for high performance and safety.* Guilford, CT: Globe Pequot Press.

Luebben, C. (2004). *Rock climbing: Mastering basic skills.* Seattle: The Mountaineers Books.

RECOMMENDED WEB SITES

American Mountain Guides Association

www.amga.com

Professional Climbing Instructors Association

http://pcia.us/pro/

Professional Climbing Guides Institute

http://climbingguidesinstitute.org/site/

ROCK CLIMBING UNIT PLAN

General Lesson Information

Each lesson contains the following seven elements:

1. Objectives—primary learning outcomes
2. Equipment—specific materials and gear
3. Introduction—opening concepts, ideas, and questions that identify the focus of the day
4. Warm-ups—routines to stretch or strengthen muscles and tendons specific to climbing
5. Central activities—activity progressions that increase in difficulty and lead to more advanced skills
6. Closure—suggested discussion and reflection items
7. Assessment—examples of evaluation strategies

Day 1

Focus: History and equipment

- Harnessing
- Rope care
- Carabiners
- Helmets
- Knots (see chapter 13)

Day 2

Focus: Body belay and backup belay

- Brake hand
- Slip, slap, slide
- Relay races

Day 3

Focus: Using a belay device

- Rope jousting
- Threading a belay device
- Using the slip, slap, slide or brake, under, slide (BUS) belay method
- Relay races
- Fishing in the dark

Day 4

Focus: Belaying on the wall

- Stretching
- Belay contract
- Half-wall climbing

- Lowering
- Repetition

Day 5

Focus: Belay check-off day

- Stretching
- Assessment (Belay Training Checklist)

Day 6

Focus: Handhold techniques

- Various grips
- Mantle
- Side pull
- Counter pressure
- Jamming
- Crossing over
- Matching

Day 7

Focus: Footwork techniques

- Edging
- Smearing
- Foot change
- Heel hook
- Flagging
- High stepping
- Stemming
- Lie back

Day 8

Focus: Leave No Trace ethics

- Group effects on climbing areas
- Climbing etiquette
- Leave No Trace principles

Day 9

Focus: Finding appropriate rock climbing sites

- Introduction to Yosemite Decimal System

Day 10

Focus: Outdoor climbing assessment

- Final exam

chapter 5

Caving

Steven J. Eggerichs

Only those who will risk going too far can possibly find out how far one can go.

T.S. Eliot

Unseen by most, the mysterious underground world of caves offers an extremely different environment for exploration. Darkness, a sense of the unknown, gigantic rooms, vertical ascents and descents, beautiful cave formations, underground creatures, winding tunnels with tight squeezes, and the anticipation of what lies on the other side all lead adventurous individuals to seek out these massive structures that lay beneath our feet. Caving provides an avenue for physical activity in the natural environment that challenges participants both physically and emotionally. Caving is the act of visiting or exploring a cave, and the responsible people

who visit or explore caves are called *cavers*. Cavers are often called *spelunkers* by noncavers. No one person can claim to have invented caving, as people have been using caves for shelter and exploration for thousands of years. However, one of the first persons to conduct studies inside of caves was a gentleman from France named Édouard-Alfred Martel. Martel began venturing into caves for scientific studies around the late 19th century, and since then caving has become a hobby for many individuals seeking recreation and adventure. In virtually every area of the United States there are local caving clubs or other organizations dedicated to caving and cave conservation. These groups are referred to as *grottos*. More than 200 grottos and 12,000 individual members make up the National Speleological Society (NSS; National Speleological Society, 2009). There are a variety of reasons why people visit caves. Some people visit for the physical challenge, others visit for pure enjoyment of the natural environment, others visit to help preserve the cave by cleaning it, and still others visit to scientifically study the cave's underground environment (Jones, 2003). *Speleology* is the term used to describe the scientific study of caves, and a person who scientifically studies caves is called a *speleologist* (Jones, 2003).

As a physical education teacher, one of your goals is to teach students to be active for a lifetime. Teaching young people basic physical skills and exposing them to a variety of avenues for being physically active may help them to find an activity that they enjoy enough to incorporate into their lifestyle. Teaching students the basics of caving, such as equipment needs, safety procedures, and preservation of the underground, taking students on a trip to a cave, and teaching students how to connect with others who enjoy caving may give them enough information to connect with a group that they can learn from and enjoy caving with for a lifetime. This caving unit provides the opportunity for students to challenge themselves both physically and mentally while working with others. Working in a group, students will crawl, squeeze, slide, climb, and work their way through the underground while using interpersonal skills, exercising physical skills, and choosing their own challenges. The experiences and knowledge acquired during this unit can meet the 2004 standards recommended by the NASPE.

HOW CAVES ARE FORMED

Teaching students about the environment they will be venturing into provides important benefits. Understanding the cave environment and how it is formed may help the students to respect, appreciate, and value the living organisms and formations that they will be viewing. Understanding the basic features and formations can also provide opportunities for activities inside of the cave, such as a scavenger hunt using a digital camera.

A cave is "a naturally formed void in the earth generally large enough for a man to enter. It is not necessary for a cave to have an opening to the surface" (Rea, 1992, p. 175). Every cave is different; caves come in all shapes

and sizes and may be made out of a variety of materials. The vast majority of caves are formed in limestone, and thus caves are most prevalent in areas that contain a great deal of limestone rock. Caves do not form overnight; rather, the unique cave formations are caused by thousands of years of surface water and rainwater seeping and flowing through cracks in the rock that lie below the ground surface (Wood, 1990). As rainwater travels through the ground, it picks up carbon dioxide that has developed from dead and decaying plants. When the water and carbon dioxide mix, a mild acid called *carbonic acid* is formed. The acid dissolves and deteriorates the limestone, forming what we know as caves. If the area of the cave being dissolved happens to be close to the ground surface, the surface can break open to expose the cave and provide an entrance (Kerbo, 1981, p. 11).

As the water flows, seeps, and drips in the cave, it carries with it the dissolved limestone. When the water drips or drops in the cave, it loses the carbon dioxide, and when the carbon dioxide leaves the water, traces of the limestone are left behind in the form of deposits. The mineral deposits of limestone form cave features or decorations known as a *speleothem* (Kerbo, 2002, p.13).

CAVE DECORATIONS AND FEATURES

Before taking a trip to a cave, it may be helpful to describe to students the common features, known as *cave decorations,* that the class may see in the cave (see figure 5.1).

The following is a list of a few, but not all, cave decorations that students may encounter on their trip (Rea, 1992; Jones, 2003). Some of these decorations are also illustrated in figure 5.1.

anthodite—A mineral deposit that looks like a clump of needles that are all growing from a common point.

boxwork—A decoration that looks like honeycomb and is formed by erosion within the cave. Very thin, finlike calcite formations join each other to create what looks like a box.

breakdown—Rock slabs, blocks, or chips on the floor of a cave that have fallen from the walls or ceiling (Rea, 1992, p. 175).

cave pearl—A small, round calcite concretion that has formed in a shallow cave pool or floor depression.

column—A cave formation created when a stalactite and stalagmite grow together.

dogtooth spar—Spearlike or pointed projections of calcite crystals found in small nooks and crannies of limestone. The formation looks like a bunch of teeth stuck to the rock.

flowstone—Mineral deposits that have accumulated as water slowly seeps over a wall or floor of a cave.

guano—This material is a feature found on the floor of bat caves and is made up of the excrement of the bats.

helictite—A smooth stalactitic form that grows in curved paths instead of hanging vertically.

lily pad—Sometimes called a *cave raft,* this unique decoration is formed when calcite is suspended in a pool of water. As the calcite accumulates it becomes heavy and eventually sinks. Calcite continues to deposit on the formation until it looks like a lily pad. Sometimes stalagmites form on top of the pad.

moon milk—A very fine, white-colored deposit that is formed when water drips in a cave. This pasty deposit has a moist and squishy texture when wet. A dry deposit of moon milk has a more chalklike texture.

popcorn—Also referred to as *cave coral,* these calcite deposits form round, knobby clumps that look very similar to popcorn.

rimstone pool—Mineral or calcite buildup in a cave formed when water flows down. The buildup causes a ridge or rim to form and water to pool on one side of the rim.

soda straw—A thin, hollow stalactite resembling a sipping straw. It grows from the tip by water flowing down the inside.

speleothem—A formation inside of a cave that is formed from secondary mineral deposits.

stalactite—A speleothem of cylindrical or conical shape hanging from a ceiling or ledge and resembling icicles.

stalagmite—A speleothem of cylindrical or conical shape rising from a floor or ledge.

Figure 5.1 Cave decorations: *(a)* soda straw stalactites, *(b)* draperies, *(c)* stalactites, *(d)* breakdown, *(e)* stalagmites, *(f)* column, *(g)* rimstone, and *(h)* flowstone.

Courtesy of Indiana Geological Survey.

EQUIPMENT

The equipment needed for caving can make up a relatively small and simple list of supplies or can create a vast list needed to cover extended or very technical trips. The equipment need for extended or technical trips, such as underwater caving or vertical caving, is out of the realm of this chapter and beyond what most physical education classes would cover. The equipment listed in this chapter is geared toward a relatively short day trip that is not very difficult and requires little to no technical equipment. Most of the basic equipment can be found in the home or can be purchased very inexpensively. There are a few simple ideas that help students find the equipment they need for the trip included in the day two and day three lesson plans for this chapter.

- **Helmet.** A helmet is a must on every caving trip. The helmet protects the head from bumps when navigating in low or tight spaces and also protects the head from falling rocks, gear, and other debris. There are many varieties of helmets on the market today, and when choosing a quality helmet for caving a few things should be taken into account. Look for a helmet that can be adjusted to fit multiple sizes of heads and that also has an adjustable chinstrap. Also choose a helmet that provides a clip that will hold a headlamp securely in place. Above all, use a helmet that meets or exceeds the standards set by the International Mountaineering and Climbing Federation (UIAA).

- **Headlamps and lighting.** Having light during a caving trip is obviously a necessity. Most cavers have a primary source of light and two backup sources of light. The primary source should attach either on the side or on the front of the helmet. Mounting the light on the helmet frees up the caver's hands for crawling and climbing and provides light wherever the caver looks. The backup sources of light do not need to be able to be mounted on the helmet, but they should always be carried. There are several types of lights to choose from, including light-emitting diodes (LEDs), xenon bulbs, krypton bulbs, and halogen bulbs. Each of these bulbs offers advantages and disadvantages, such as bulb life, brightness, and energy consumption. Whichever light sources you choose for the trip, be sure to carry extra batteries and bulbs for each source.

- **Gloves.** Gloves serve two purposes. The first is to protect the caver's hands from the elements inside the cave. These may include cold temperatures, sharp or abrasive rocks, dirt, and mud. The second purpose is to protect the cave from the caver. Human hands contain oils that can damage the formations and fragile ecosystem of the cave. Gloves used for caving vary in thickness, waterproofing, insulation, durability, and cost depending on personal preferences. Leather gloves, cotton chore gloves, and gloves with a rubber exterior are all popular choices.

- **Padding.** Since a great deal of time may be spent crawling and sliding on the hands and knees, it may be a good idea to invest in elbow and knee pads to protect the elbows and knees from scrapes, bumps, and bruises. Elbow and knee pads used for inline skating usually provide a hard plastic cover over a soft pad that can be secured in place with adjustable straps. Knee pads used for volleyball, wrestling, or construction are also viable options.

- **Caving boots.** Caves have uneven terrain and because of this it is important to choose correct footwear to maximize comfort and reduce the risk of injury. When choosing a boot make sure that it has adequate ankle support to decrease the chances of twisting an ankle. Also choose a boot that has plenty of traction to reduce the risk of slips and falls on wet and uneven terrain. Depending on cave temperatures and the amount of water in the cave, some other things to consider may be the amount of insulation in the boot and the waterproofing of the boot. There are several types of hiking and hunting boots that incorporate synthetic insulation and waterproof material that work very well for caving and keep the feet warm and dry. No matter what footwear you select, make sure that it is broken in and does not cause blisters when worn for extended durations.

- **Clothing.** Before selecting the clothing to wear on a caving trip, gather information on the underground environment to be visited. Two things to consider are the average temperature and the amount of water or wetness of the cave. As a general rule, caves are cool and can be wet. So dressing in layers is important. It is easy to take layers off in the cave but it is hard to add layers in the cave if the extra layers are still in the car. Choosing clothing made from synthetic materials over cotton is also important, since synthetic materials can wick moisture away from the body, dry quickly, and hold a limited amount of moisture. These features help to insulate the body better than cotton does, as cotton does not perform well when wet or sweaty. Most clothing stores carry high-performance athletic gear that is made from synthetic materials. The outer layer of clothing will take the most abuse on a caving trip and can become muddy, torn, and wet. Because of this the outer layers should be somewhat abrasion resistant and should provide enough room for additional layers to be worn underneath. Coveralls, army fatigues, or jeans would work well for this purpose.

Also pack a second set of comfortable clothing, including shoes and socks, to put on after the trip. Upon exiting the cave, cavers may be muddy, wet, and cold, and cleaning up and changing into clean, dry clothes can feel pretty good after a hard day of caving. Washing off dried mud can be a challenge, and a towel and baby wipes can make cleaning up a little easier if water is not available. Muddy clothes and boots should be placed in a plastic garbage bag for the ride home. These clothes should be cleaned soon after returning from the trip. Spraying the clothes clean with a garden hose before placing them in a washing machine seems to help get the clothes cleaner and reduce the mess left in the machine.

- **Caving pack.** Packing in necessary gear is a given on any caving trip. The type of pack used depends on the personal preference of the caver; however, there are a few helpful hints for selecting a cave pack. The packs are going to take extensive abuse while in the cave, so finding a pack that is fairly rugged and tear resistant is an important factor. Also, since some of the navigated areas are fairly small, a compact pack may be more practical than a large, bulky pack. Packs should also be comfortable, as carrying around an uncomfortable pack for a day could provide for a negative experience. Lastly, the gear in the bag must be easily accessible, so having a pack that is easy to open and close should be taken into consideration. A local military surplus store is a good place to start when looking for a pack that fits the needs of most cavers. Many of the packs found at these stores are carried as a satchel over the shoulder and can be removed easily.

- **Pack contents.** What to carry inside of the pack may differ for every trip. You must consider the length of the trip, the technical difficulty of the trip, and what you know of the cave. It is better to be overprepared than underprepared, so pack more than you anticipate needing. There are a few things that should be packed every time you go into a cave. A quick day trip can turn into an extended trip if an emergency occurs, and it is important to be as prepared as possible. When caving with a group, some of the following pieces of equipment should be carried by everyone in the group, while other pieces of equipment, such as the first aid kit and risk management plan, can be carried by just the group leaders.

- **Extra light source.** Carry two reliable backup light sources in case of failure or damage to the primary light source.

- **Extra batteries.** Carry extra batteries for each of the light sources.

- **Multipurpose tools.** These tools often fold into a small case and incorporate several tools in one; a pair of pliers, a knife, a bottle opener, scissors, and a file are just a few of the available options. These tools can be useful for repairing equipment.

- **Duct tape.** This is a multitool in and of itself. It can be used to cover blisters or to repair clothing and equipment.

- **Food and water.** The amount of food and water you need to take with you will depend on the length of the trip, but pack more than what you anticipate needing. High-energy foods such as energy bars and trail mix packed in durable containers such as a widemouthed water bottle work well.

- **Rain poncho.** A disposable rain poncho can help keep you dry.

- **Handkerchief or bandana.** In an emergency first aid situation, this can be used to apply pressure or to create a sling.

- **Basic first aid kit.** This kit could include the following: a first aid manual, bandages, dressing strips, butterfly closures, battle dressings, moleskin, safety pins, a razor blade, tweezers, scissors, sterile gauze pads, a gauze roll, cloth tape, triangular bandages, elastic bandages, an oral thermometer, a flexible splint, a space blanket, antibacterial cream, calamine lotion, instant chemical ice packs, alcohol swabs, a personal barrier for CPR, pain-relieving drugs, personal prescription drugs, athletic tape, and shoelaces.

- **Risk management plan.** This plan should include medical history information for participants and staff members, emergency phone numbers, evacuation plans, missing person report forms, accident report forms, evacuation report forms, extra pens, and paper to record important information.

- **Whistle with a lanyard.** This can be used to signal group members in an emergency or to signal rescuers.

- **Watch.** Carry a watch to keep track of time, and give yourself plenty of time to exit to avoid rushing through the cave.

- **Laminated map and compass.** These two items can come in handy when trying to maneuver throughout the cave. In larger caves with multiple rooms, twists, and turns, it is very easy to become disoriented, turned around, or even lost. Learning how to use a map and compass will be necessary if visiting such a cave. Since most caves are at least a little wet and muddy, laminating the map is a great idea so that the map is preserved for the entire trip.

- **Camera.** Students may want to take pictures of their experience, be sure to keep the camera dry by carrying it in a waterproof protective case.

- **Spare bottle.** Bring in a spare plastic bottle that can be used to carry out human waste.

BASIC CAVING TECHNIQUES

When preparing students for a caving trip, there are several things you should discuss during the pretrip lessons. Taking the time to prepare your class for the upcoming trip can increase the success of the group, protect the underground environment, and reduce the risk of injury and accidents as well as physically and emotionally prepare the students for what they will encounter once underground and what they should do in case of an emergency during the trip. Teaching students basic caving techniques and other safety considerations is a good way to prepare for an upcoming trip.

Moving Inside of the Cave

As a trip leader, you should make sure the students stay together and that the group moves at a pace that allows everyone to stay within their physical limits. Place one group leader at the front of the group and one group leader at the back of the group and tell the students that they are at no time to pass the group leader at the front or to fall behind the group leader at the back. In addition, consider placing several adult leaders or chaperones throughout the group to help keep the group focused and on task. If at any time someone in the group needs to rest, eat, or take a break, the group leader at the front needs to be notified to stop the group until everyone is ready to continue. Remind students to never leave the group for any reason. While moving through the cave it is important to stay within voice and visual contact of the group and to always wait for teammates before continuing (Waldron, 2007). An individual who does become separated from the group should remain calm, find a dry place to stay put, and blow the whistle until help arrives.

Cave terrain may vary greatly from cave to cave but in general demands a wide variety of movements from cavers. Some of the common ways to move include crawling, sliding on the belly, sliding on the back, duck walking, bending and walking, walking on hands and feet, army crawling, and sliding (Rea, 1992, p. 56). Whatever movement you use, remember that the footing inside caves may be unstable, wet, muddy, slippery, and uneven and may cause hazardous falls and slips. One easy way to practice cave movements during the learning process is to set up relay races and obstacle courses to get the students active. Share the following simple tips with students to help reduce the risk of injuries during the trip:

- Avoid drugs and alcohol while caving, as they impair your ability to make good decisions and move in a safe manner.

- Understand your own physical limits and be sure to stay within them. If you become fatigued, take a break.

- Stay focused on what you are doing, and watch where you place your feet and hands.

- Stay with the group, which should move only as fast as the slowest caver.

- While moving on unstable surfaces, try to keep at least three points of contact with the cave to help maintain balance, which will minimize the need for radical movements to regain balance (Waldron, 2007, p.25).

- On extremely unstable surfaces use "four-wheel drive" by maintaining four points of contact or crawling while moving.

- On unstable surfaces, use static movements, making sure movements are slow and controlled.

- Make a conscious effort to watch where you are going and where you place your feet.

- Avoid fast movements such as running, jumping, leaping, and horseplay, which can turn an enjoyable day of exploring into a potentially serious emergency in a matter of seconds.

Environmental Considerations

With more and more people venturing outdoors and heading underground for hobby, exploration, or science, the fragile environment of the cave system is at a greater risk of becoming compromised. It is up to those of us who use our natural environment for our enjoyment to maintain, enhance, and preserve it for future generations. Heavy traffic inside of popular caves, trash left behind in caves, and paths formed to and from caves take their toll on the natural resources and environment. As teachers, it is our responsibility to teach our students about proper etiquette and low impact practices that will help preserve the natural environment. The day 5 lesson for this chapter focuses on appropriate cave etiquette and low impact practices. The following are guidelines you can share with students to help them respect, preserve, and reduce their effect on the environment:

- Clean up anything that is not natural to the cave environment. Anything that is brought into the cave by the caver needs to be carried out. If you find trash or old equipment in the cave, pack it out as well. A good rule is to leave the cave and the trail leading to the cave as clean or cleaner than how you found them.

- Do not touch or climb on any cave formations. The oils that you leave on cave formations and speleothems after touching them can prevent the further formation of the delicate cave decorations. Climbing on speleothems can break and damage them and prevent further growth.

- Do not smoke or light fires inside of the cave. Smoke can alter and pollute the air, which may disturb local inhabitants of the cave as well as people who visit the cave.

- Avoid painting or marking the cave, which can permanently damage the fragile underground formations. For the same reason do not carve or dig out areas or remove things from the cave.

- Practice human waste removal. Try to use a restroom before venturing into the cave. If you need to relieve yourself inside of the cave, do so in a hard plastic widemouthed bottle used exclusively for waste. You are responsible for packing out your own waste and discarding of it appropriately.

- Stay on established trails and paths to preserve the natural environment and avoid disrupting fragile speleothems and organisms. If trails are not established, stay in the same line of travel as the rest of the group.

- Respect the local wildlife. Bats and other organisms use caves as their homes and it is important to remember that you are there to observe but not disturb their environment. By disturbing wildlife in the cave, you may compromise their ability to survive.

- Be considerate to other cavers. One way to do this is to not share the location of caves with people you do not feel would be responsible and treat the cave and other cavers with respect.

- Maintain good landowner relations. Introduce yourself and the group when asking for permission and always be polite and courteous while speaking with landowners. Ask them if there are particular areas that they would like you to park and if there are any particular areas to use or to stay away from while traveling to the cave. After the trip let them know that you appreciate being able to enjoy their property and that you are very thankful.

Safety Considerations

In addition to environmental considerations, there are various safety issues students need to be aware of before they begin caving. This section discusses these safety considerations.

Always Get Permission

Caves are often located on private lands and getting permission to access the cave is a must, especially when taking a school group. A good way to inquire about cave access is to contact a local grotto group. The grotto group may be able to provide information on who owns or manages the land, whether the cave is on private or public land, and if the cave is open to the public. If the

> **TEACHING TIP**
>
> If the cave is located on private property, always maintain good relations with the owner. Have the students make a thank you card or send pictures to the owner along with a gift certificate to a local restaurant.

cave is open to the public, the local grotto group may also be able to give assistance on where the group should park vehicles and where the group should change. The grotto group may also know the preferred route to access the cave entrance. Links for local grottos may be found on the NSS Web site (www.caves.org).

Never Cave Alone

Students need to understand that caving alone is extremely dangerous and should always be avoided. Kurt Waldron, the chairman of the NSS Safety and Techniques Committee, suggests that a group of three is the smallest sized group that should ever enter a cave (Waldron, 2007, p. 25). The reason for this is very logical: If one member of the group has a medical emergency, another person in the group can tend to the emergency and the third can go for help.

When deciding on what size school group to take underground there are some things to consider. One is the number of adult chaperones available for the trip and the desired adult-to-student ratio. This ratio may vary depending on the ability level of the group, the objectives of the class, and the physical demands of the cave that the group will be visiting. Assessing the physical and emotional capabilities of the group members before the trip may give insight as to how much assistance each participant will need and whether the trip poses a safety issue for the group or the participant. Limiting the number of participants or increasing the number of volunteers may be necessary to provide a more enjoyable trip for everyone involved.

Protect One Another

Remind students that caving is about the success of the team rather than the accomplishments of the individual, and competition should be avoided. The physical, emotional, environmental, and personal safety of the group should be protected and evaluated at all times. For example, on unstable areas group members should ask for help from other cavers when needed. If an individual in the group seems to be struggling, other group members should offer to help that person work through the physical problem or challenge. The physical performance of the group also needs to be monitored by the trip leader. Group members need to have enough energy and stamina to make their way out of the cave safely. Caving leaders must have previous knowledge of how long it should take the group to enter and exit the cave. They must also determine

when it is time for the group to start making its way out of the cave by assessing the group's physical and mental performance. Group members and adult leaders should also offer emotional support for cavers who become nervous or frightened.

Some groups use the code word *PEEP* as a signal that something is wrong within the group. *PEEP* is an acronym for the physical, emotional, environmental, and personal safety of the group. If at any time one or more areas of PEEP are being violated, a group member may say "PEEP!" and the group will work through the issue. The day 4 lesson of the caving unit provides additional information on PEEP. To increase the effectiveness of PEEP, many teachers lead their groups in team-building activities such acquaintance, problem-solving, communication, and trust activities. Doing this helps build cohesion and trust within the group, both of which increase the success of the group once in the cave.

Minimize Hazards

Before leaving for the cave, brainstorm and research potential environmental and human hazards that might occur during the trip and associated risks. Environmental hazards could include weather, open pits, slippery terrain, unstable surfaces, flooding, falling rocks, loose rocks, pools of water, and dark, twisty tunnels. Some of the risks associated with these hazards are cuts, bruises, broken bones, sprained ligaments, getting stuck, and hypothermia. Human hazards could include using poor judgment, running out of food or water, getting lost, and running out of light. There is also the risk of

---

TEACHING TIP

As a teacher, planning a simulated caving activity prior to the actual caving trip may help to physically and mentally prepare students for the trip. Try to set up a mock cave in a dark area of the school with hazards, pictures of decorations, and obstacles. Use equipment that the school already has to create the cave. For example, a rolled up wrestling mat works well as something to crawl in or on. Once the cave is set up, put the students into teams and have them navigate the cave making sure to use content from previous lessons such as moving safely in the cave, basic caving techniques, protecting one another, and minimizing potential hazards. See the day 7 lesson for a more detailed description of the simulated cave activity.

emotional dangers such as fear of tight spaces, fear of bats, fear of the dark, and other unforeseen fears participants may encounter. It is the responsibility of the entire group to recognize hazards and to make other group members aware of hazards.

Teach students to stay on previously established trails if possible and to avoid unstable or loose rocks, steep slopes, or unknown areas. Potentially dangerous areas such as an unstable rock should be pointed out to other group members to help them to avoid a dangerous situation. Cavers should also be aware of the potential for falling rocks. If a group member happens to notice a falling rock, he should yell "Rock!" so other group members can take cover and avoid looking up. Students should also avoid getting wet if possible since wet clothing does not keep the body as warm as dry clothing does.

PLANNING A TRIP

Culminating the caving unit with a trip can be an extremely rewarding and memorable experience for all involved. However, the planning of the trip can also be the most time-consuming and important part of your preparations. Things that need to be incorporated into the planning include developing a risk management plan, gathering health information, planning transportation and meal preparation, considering special student needs, communicating with parents and administrators, and finding a qualified and experienced trip leader. The following are some things to think about while planning the trip.

TEACHING TIP

Trip planning can seem overwhelming and a little stressful. Contacting a local grotto group or an experienced caver for guidance and information can help to make the process a little easier.

Find a Competent and Experienced Trip Leader

Finding an appropriate trip leader is as important as any other part of planning the trip. Taking a group underground should be attempted only by an experienced caver who has firsthand knowledge of the cave that the group will be visiting. An overconfident and underqualified or undertrained trip leader can be a

recipe for disaster. For this reason, you should research possible individuals who would be able to lead the caving trip and who could also aid in selecting a cave within the ability level of the group. Local universities that have an adventure or outdoor recreation program are a good place to start. Often theses universities provide basic equipment for the students and contract out to lead trips for school groups. Another way to find a competent leader is to contact a local grotto group. A benefit to having a university or a guide service leading the trip is that generally they take on the responsibility and the liability of leading the trip.

Develop a Risk Management Plan

A risk management plan should be developed before every off-campus trip. Give copies of the plan to an administrator, the school nurse, and the school secretary. Leave one copy in the vehicle on the trip and carry another in a pack inside of the cave. Giving a copy to an administrator can increase your credibility by showing that you have thought about several areas while planning.

Within the risk management plan, define who is teaching the course, which class is taking the trip, and where and when the trip takes place. The plan may also include a statement of the educational rationale for taking the trip that gives clear objectives for the trip and a description of how the trip enhances the learning experience of the students. Make it clear that the trip is a crucial part of the learning experience and that it is not just a fun day off from school.

An essential step to developing the risk management plan is gathering student information; this should start early when planning the trip. The school nurse is often a great resource for health and medical information. Compile a list for each student and include the participant's full name, emergency contact and phone number, medical diagnoses, current medication, and, if in existence, health plan that must be followed. Other pertinent information needed is the hospital of choice, family doctor, and any special qualifications or concerns. Make any adjustments to the trip you think is necessary after evaluating the gathered information.

In addition to being included in the itinerary, the phone numbers for the group leaders, police, hospitals, and rescue services must be included in the risk management plan. A few other things you might include in the risk management plan are meal provisions, an itemized budget for the trip, and a list of what equipment the school or guide service is providing and what equipment the students need to provide. Forms such as a missing person report, an evacuation plan, an evacuation report, an accident report, and waiver or permission forms could also be included in the risk management plan.

A travel plan and an itinerary are an important part of trip preparation. Determine the total number of students participating and plan accordingly. Decide if the group requires a school bus, a van, or both. Parking may be an issue, so research the cave area and figure out if there is a place for a bus to park. Within the risk management plan, describe the vehicles being used by the group. List what time the vehicles will depart to and from the cave and what time they are anticipated to return to the school. Including a map showing the travel route and the location of the cave may also be helpful. Try to plan out an itinerary between departing from and arriving back at the school. The following are examples of what to include in the itinerary: how long it will take to hike to the cave (once the vehicles park), what time the students will enter the cave, how long the students will explore the cave, what time the students will start exiting the cave, what time they will begin hiking back to the vehicles, how long it will take the group to change, when the students will eat, and when there might be any scheduled bathroom breaks during the ride to and from the cave.

Leave an Itinerary

As a responsible group leader and caver, you must give a detailed itinerary of the trip to an individual, or a group of individuals, who will not be attending the trip. In a school setting, these individuals should include the principal, a secretary, the school nurse, and another teacher. The itinerary should list the names of the individuals going on the trip; the time the group is leaving the school; the time the group is arriving at the cave, entering the cave, exiting the cave, and departing from the cave; and the anticipated time of return to the school. The itinerary should also provide the cell phone numbers of the group leaders; the phone numbers for the local police department, the local sheriff, the state patrol, and the nearest hospitals; and the phone numbers for the Air Force Rescue Coordination Center and the National Cave Rescue Commission. Arrange to contact a designated person when your group exits the cave; if the individual has not been contacted by a predetermined time she should begin contacting

the emergency groups for help. Some caves also have a sign-in and sign-out book for caving groups to use upon entering and exiting the cave.

Communicate With Parents

The thought of their child going underground may make some parents extremely nervous about allowing their student to participate in the caving outing. Sending home a letter to the parents well in advance of the trip so you can explain the objectives of the trip, the things that students will be learning about before the trip, and the potential risks of the trip can sometimes calm these fears. Along with the letter, send home a checklist of the equipment that the students will need to give parents and students enough time to gather the necessary items. Other forms that need to be sent home may vary among school districts. Check with an administrator to see what the school policy is for permission slips, informed consent forms, and release or waiver forms. District forms should be sent home and returned signed by the parents at least a few days in advance of the trip. In addition, if you are contracting out the trip to some type of guide service, make sure all of the necessary forms are sent home and returned.

CONCLUSION

Classroom activities are great for teaching students about the basic skills and knowledge needed to go caving. However, a culminating trip may be the ticket for hooking a young person on caving. Without a trip to a cave, the chances that a student will get excited about caving outside of the school setting are not very high. Since only experienced cavers should lead others underground, there are options for teachers who are not experienced to still take their class to a cave. One option is to contact a local grotto group, university adventure program, or guide service to lead the group underground in a wild, uncommercialized cave. The other is to take the students to a show cave or commercial cave where guides walk the students through the cave. Even though the second option may not be as exciting as going to a wild cave, it still exposes students to a basic caving experience. Whichever option you choose, the important thing is to culminate your unit with a visit to the mysterious underground.

REFERENCES

Jones, C. (2003). *A guide to responsible caving.* (3rd ed.). Huntsville, AL: National Speleological Society.

Kerbo, R. (1981). *Caves.* Chicago: Children's Press.

Kerbo, R. (2002). *The hidden world of caves: A children's guide to the underground wilderness.* Huntsville, AL: National Speleological Society.

National Speleological Society. (2009). www.caves.org.

Rea, G. (Ed.). (1992). *Caving basics: A comprehensive guide for beginning cavers.* (3rd ed.). Huntsville, AL: National Speleological Society.

Waldron, K. (2007, July). Safety and techniques. *NSS News, 65*(7): 25.

Wood, J. (1990). *Caves.* London: Two-Can Publishing.

RECOMMENDED WEB SITES

National Speleological Society

www.caves.org

National Park Service

www.nps.gov/wica/naturescience/cave.htm

CAVING UNIT PLAN

General Lesson Information

Each lesson contains the following seven elements:

1. Objectives—primary learning outcomes
2. Equipment—specific materials and gear
3. Introduction—opening concepts, ideas, and questions that identify the focus of the day
4. Warm-ups—routine to review or brainstorm cognitive information associated with caving or to stretch or strengthen muscles and tendons before physical activity
5. Central activities—activity progressions that increase in difficulty and lead to more advanced skills
6. Closure—suggested discussion and reflection items
7. Assessment—examples of evaluation strategies

Day 1
Focus: Introduction to caving
- History
- How caves are formed
- Play dough cave features
- Cave relay

Day 2
Focus: Clothing and equipment
- Preliminary slide show
- Scarecrow relay
- Packing a caving pack

Day 3
Focus: Virtual shopping
- Pricing clothing
- Pricing equipment
- Make an itemized budget

Day 4
Focus: Physical, emotional, environmental, and personal safety (PEEP)
- Explanation of PEEP
- Reverse the rug
- Test drive

Day 5
Focus: Caving etiquette
- Safety
- Behavior above and below ground
- Reducing your effects on the natural environment
- Caving etiquette poster

Day 6
Focus: Movements inside of the cave
- Relay race using movements
- Obstacle course

Day 7
Focus: Simulated caving activity

Day 8
Focus: Finding areas to cave
- NSS
- Grottos
- Finding experienced cavers
- Online search

Day 9
Focus: Review game

Day 10
Focus: Caving trip

chapter 6

Canoeing

Mark H. Zmudy

But love of the wilderness is more than a hunger for what is always beyond reach; it is also an expression of loyalty to the earth which bore us and sustains us, the only home we shall ever know, the only paradise we ever need—if only we had eyes to see.

Edward Abbey

One of the most magical ways to explore lakes and rivers, especially those in remote locations and not accessible by motor craft, is to travel by canoe. The beauty of canoeing is that it is possible to enjoy it with just a basic knowledge of a few paddle strokes. Enjoyment can then be enhanced with advanced stroke knowledge and ability to perform an increased number of strokes.

Skill development for canoeing may begin with an orientation to basics such as equipment, safety, getting in and out of a canoe, balance, and rescue techniques. These can be taught in a controlled and confined area such as a local indoor or outdoor swimming pool.

Instruction can then move to practicing and enhancing skills on flat water in an open area such as a pond, lake, or very slow-moving, flat river. People who wish to obtain more advanced skills can seek instruction in river environments where there are moving rapids and white water. In these environments, the difficulty of a river rapid is rated according to the river classification system, which rates rapids on a scale of class I through class VI and the amount of water, measured in cubic feet per second, traveling through a specified area.

Since the rebirth of the inclusion of outdoor and adventure activities in formal physical education curricula in the early 1990s, canoeing has become integrated into various K through 12 settings, including those in the United States (National Association for Sport and Physical Education, 1991) and the United Kingdom (Department of Education and Science & the Welsh Office, 1992; Qualifications and Curriculum Authority, 2007). Like other outdoor pursuits, canoeing provides a platform for learning identified technical skills linked to leading a healthy and active lifestyle (National Association for Sport and Physical Education, 2004), while also providing a less-competitive option for students who do not wish to pursue team sports as their main avenue for activity.

This chapter focuses on learning the basics of canoeing in a controlled and confined environment and on enhancing canoeing skills in open areas that are considered to be flat water (i.e., where there are no measurable rapids). Regardless of the paddling environment, knowing and staying within your abilities are crucial; paddling safety is always the top priority (American Canoe Association, 2009).

EQUIPMENT

To ensure a safe and successful canoeing unit, you must provide each student with a personal flotation device (PFD), also referred to as a *life jacket,* approved by the coast guard. You also need one paddle for each student and one canoe for every two students; if you have an odd number of students on a given day, you can always have a third passenger sit on the floor in the middle of a canoe.

Personal Flotation Devices

PFDs should be sized properly for each student and should be worn at all times when students are on any type of water (American Canoe Association, 2009). For times when communication may be hindered, such as when canoeing on open water in the wind, you can equip PFDs with a whistle so students can alert each other and instructors when assistance is needed in an emergency. Do not substitute other types of flotation devices for ones that are approved by the coast guard. Approved PFDs come in many styles. Base your decision about which type of PFD to purchase for your program on overall comfort interests and budgetary needs.

Paddles

Canoe paddles generally are made of wood, plastic, or aluminum. To maximize proper stroke performance, students should use a paddle that accurately fits their body height, at least to the extent that is possible. To determine proper paddle size, have students place one hand on the paddle grip and the other hand at the paddle throat and then hold the paddle above the head; both elbows should be at 90° angles. A simple solution for meeting the needs of your instructional setting is to stock a variety of paddle sizes. Prices may vary depending on paddle material and construction; it is best to research paddles before purchasing them so you will be able to choose the desired balance of quality and economy for your program.

For one of your instructional objectives, you should require students to be able to identify the parts of the paddle. The parts of the paddle are depicted in figure 6.1 and are defined as follows:

grip—the part of the paddle that is on the top. The paddler places the right hand on the grip if paddling on the left side or the left hand on the grip if paddling on the right side.

shaft—the long stick part of the paddle. The paddler places the hand that is not on the grip toward the lower end of the shaft near the paddle blade.

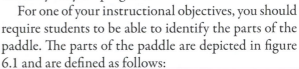

Figure 6.1   Parts of the canoe paddle.

throat—the curved part of the blade closest to the shaft.

blade—the part of the paddle that creates the force to propel the canoe forward during all forward strokes.

power face—the flat side of the blade that catches the water when moving forward.

back face—the flat side of the blade that does not catch the water when traveling forward.

tip—the sharp edge at the end of the blade.

Students should understand how to grip the paddle properly. Because the top of the paddle is shaped like a handle, it might seem logical that gripping it in any desired fashion should suffice. However, the paddle is used to its fullest potential mechanically when care is taken while placing the hand on the grip. One recommended method for gripping the paddle is the hitchhiker hand method. To help students grip the paddle using the hitchhiker hand method, try leading them through the following steps:

1. Open the grip hand so that all fingers are touching and the thumb is sticking out.

2. Lay the fingers over the top of the paddle grip and close the hand on the grip. The thumb is still sticking out.

3. Use the thumb as a visual guide for what direction the submerged blade is facing (i.e., the thumb is parallel to the paddle blade).

4. Take care not to simply grab the paddle grip as if it were a baseball, with the fingers clumped in a knot.

Canoes

Canoe type, construction, material, and size vary greatly and should match the interests and abilities of the canoeist. A good canoe for beginners is a flat-bottom canoe that has a rounded bow and stern, is constructed of either aluminum or plastic (e.g., Royalex, Polyethylene), and has a minimum rocker (rocker is the curvature in the shape of the boat from bow to stern). This shape of canoe is recommended because of its stability, both primary and secondary. Primary stability is the extent to which the canoe feels stable while sitting flat in the water, and secondary stability is how stable the boat is while on its edge, such as during a turn (McGuffin & McGuffin, 1999). Ample primary and secondary stability are essential for beginners, as stability is highly correlated with comfort level on the water, especially during unexpected wind and waves.

Before beginning skills instruction, make sure students have a basic working knowledge of the different parts of a canoe, as you will often make reference to the various parts when teaching students how to perform skills. For example, it is not helpful to instruct students to be careful with the deck plates on an aluminum canoe or to watch their fingers under overlapping gunwales (pronounced *gun-nel*) during a T-rescue if the students don't understand what a deck plate or a gunwale is. Figure 6.2 provides a labeled illustration of a canoe to assist in part identification. An unlabeled illustration of a canoe is included in the accompanying lesson plans. You can copy the unlabeled illustration and have students fill in the various parts of the canoe.

Day 1

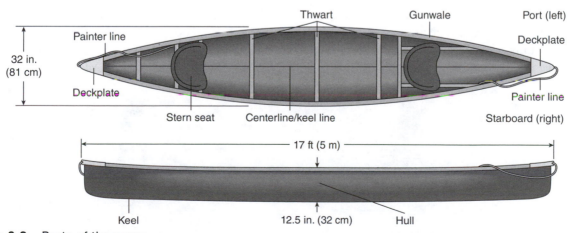

Figure 6.2 Parts of the canoe.

Reprinted from M. Wagstaff, 2009, *Technical skills for adventure programming: A curriculum guide* (Champaign, IL: Human Kinetics), 500.

Bail Buckets

There are times when water may unexpectedly get into the canoe and interfere with the canoe's ability to stay afloat. Tie a bail bucket to one of the thwarts with several feet of parachute cord (e.g., cotton clothesline) or rope so that it is available to bail water out of the canoe when necessary.

Buoys

Buoys are very useful when setting up paddling drills, as they provide students with identifiable markers to maneuver around. You will want to have enough buoys to create several teaching stations (e.g., a triangle with three buoys, a second triangle, a figure eight with two buoys, and so on). The following is an easy and economical way to make a buoy:

1. Start with a piece of P-cord approximately 25 ft (7.6 m) in length.

2. At one end of the P-cord attach an empty milk jug or laundry detergent bottle with the *lid on*.

3. At the other end of the P-cord attach a brick.

4. Adjust the length of the P-cord to match the water depth by wrapping the P-cord around the brick before submerging it.

Clothing

As when performing any outdoor activity, always dress for the weather. Take special consideration for rain gear, wind protection, sun protection, and thermoregulation with an appropriate layering system according to the season. Avoid wearing cotton clothes; once cotton becomes wet, it stays wet and contributes significantly to feeling cold and uncomfortable. An unexpected swim is always possible when canoeing, so have a change of clothes readily available. Instructors and students alike also need appropriate footwear for wet-foot entries and exits during outdoor canoe activities. Calf-high rubber boots that are 100% waterproof are recommended. Styles and exact materials of waterproof rubber boots and overshoes can vary greatly and range from a few dollars to well over $100 U.S. per pair. Again, it is suggested that you do a small amount of research before purchasing footwear. Typically, a program will purchase a small stock of inexpensive overshoes or boots in a variety of sizes to accommodate students who are unable to purchase their own.

CANOE BASICS AND RESCUES

Before students begin learning the full scope of canoe exercises on open water, there are many basic skills that they must know so that their initial canoe experience is safe and enjoyable. Do not take for granted that inexperienced students will figure out what seems to you the practical way of doing things, such as how to sit in a canoe for the most efficient paddle stroke mechanics or how to safely get in and out of a canoe. Taking the needed amount of time up front to cover basic skills allows for longer durations of engaged time later on, and that engaged time will be of higher quality for students and instructors. This section offers a set of canoe basics for students to practice and master.

Sitting in a Canoe

Generally, there are two ways to sit in a canoe. One way is to simply sit comfortably on the seat provided with the feet out in front. For this discussion, this position will be called *position one* (see figure 6.3). Position one is often used by beginners, as it appears to be the most logical way to sit in a canoe. However, there is another position, *position two,* that lends itself to better stroke mechanics. Position two involves sitting primarily on the knees with the feet tucked under the seat and the bottom placed on the forward part of the seat (see

Position 1   **Position 2**

Figure 6.3   Positions one and two for sitting in a canoe.

Reprinted from ACA, 2008, *Canoeing* (Champaign, IL: Human Kinetics), 141.

figure 6.3). Encourage students to use position two as their primary way of sitting in a canoe; position two is more classic in all types of canoeing and helps increase proficiency with proper form and stroke mechanics.

Stroke Mechanics

For proper stroke mechanics, paddlers should always paddle on opposite sides of the canoe. The side that a paddler chooses to paddle on is called her *onside*. The only way the onside changes is if both paddlers agree to call for a switch.

In addition to knowing the paddler's onside, it also is helpful to consider the paddler's box (see figure 6.4), which is

> an imaginary cube that contains the upper body. By paddling within the paddler's box, you are encouraged to use the muscles of your torso, which have much more strength and endurance than your arm muscles. By keeping within the box, you can avoid muscle strain and shoulder dislocations. (McGuffin & McGuffin, 1999, p. 24)

Dockside or Poolside Entering and Exiting

Taking the time to teach entering and exiting techniques in a swimming pool will save your students the trouble of potential hazards later on. Improper technique when getting in or out of a canoe at dockside or poolside can result in getting wet on one end of a continuum and serious personal injury on the other end. It is not necessary to have a full fleet of canoes available

Figure 6.4   The paddler's box.

Reprinted from M. Wagstaff, 2009, *Technical skills for adventure programming: A curriculum guide* (Champaign, IL: Human Kinetics), 513.

when practicing entering and exiting. In fact, it is neither practical nor safe to have too many canoes in the small confined area of a swimming pool. Nonetheless, a swimming pool is an ideal environment for teaching dockside entering and exiting techniques, for teaching self-rescue and assisted-rescue techniques in both shallow and deep water, and for allowing students to attempt various paddle strokes and maneuvers without the threat of wind and waves.

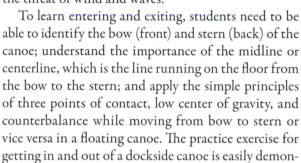

To learn entering and exiting, students need to be able to identify the bow (front) and stern (back) of the canoe; understand the importance of the midline or centerline, which is the line running on the floor from the bow to the stern; and apply the simple principles of three points of contact, low center of gravity, and counterbalance while moving from bow to stern or vice versa in a floating canoe. The practice exercise for getting in and out of a dockside canoe is easily demonstrated at poolside and should be practiced by students in partners.

Entering a Canoe Dockside or Poolside

As the students prepare to enter the canoe, position the canoe so that the length of the canoe is parallel to the dock or pool wall. Because the majority of steering maneuvers are initiated from the stern, the stern paddler should enter first while the bow paddler holds the canoe steady against the dock or poolside. This way if the canoe accidentally gets away from the dock or poolside before both passengers are aboard, the lone passenger will have an easier time maneuvering safely in the water. Likewise, the bow paddler should exit the canoe first while the stern paddler holds the canoe steady against the dock or poolside; the stern paddler then exits while the on-dock bow paddler returns the favor of steadying the canoe. The following is a sequence of steps that could be used for *entering* a canoe at dockside or poolside:

1. Bow paddler holds the canoe steady against the poolside or dock.

2. Stern paddler places one hand on the closest gunwale and places one foot on the canoe floor opposite the first hand placement—this creates an initial counterbalance so the canoe does not roll.

3. Stern paddler enters the canoe and moves both hands to opposite-side gunwales, places the feet on the midline of the canoe, and maintains a low center of gravity. From this position the stern paddler moves carefully to the back of the canoe.

4. Stern paddler, from inside the canoe, holds the canoe steady against the poolside or dock.

5. Bow paddler enters the canoe using the same techniques the stern paddler used.

Exiting a Canoe Dockside or Poolside

To *exit* the canoe, the two paddlers could do the following:

1. Reverse the process of entering, with the bow paddler exiting first while the stern paddler holds the canoe steady against the poolside or dock.

2. Take care to maintain balance and to carefully slide onto the poolside or dock in a seated position when exiting the canoe. This will help them avoid becoming off balanced and rolling the canoe.

Beachside Entering and Exiting

When you deem it appropriate, you may move the class to an outdoor setting on flat water. In this instance it may be necessary to implement the proper procedure for entering and exiting a canoe from a beach location.

Entering a Canoe Beachside

The following is an example of the steps paddlers could follow to *enter* a canoe at a beach location:

1. The paddlers place the canoe so that it is perpendicular (90°) to the beach, with the bow pointing into the water.

2. The paddlers slide the canoe into the water far enough that the bow is afloat. The stern may still be on the sand if the water is deep or may be in the water if the water is shallow; the goal is to place the canoe for an easy push-off (e.g., no getting stuck in the sand) from the beach after both paddlers enter the canoe.

3. The stern paddler straddles the canoe, holding it securely on the gunwales for stability. During this process, the stern paddler holding the canoe can cross the arms and place the hands on opposite gunwales (i.e., place the right hand on the left gunwale and the left hand on the right gunwale) to increase stability.

4. While the stern paddler holds the canoe in place, the bow paddler carefully enters in front of the

stern paddler. If the water is shallow, the bow paddler can enter the canoe in front of the stern paddler by walking one or two steps into the water before stepping into the canoe. If the water is deep, the bow paddler can move ahead of the stern paddler on dry land and then step into the canoe. Next, the bow paddler moves to the front of the canoe, using a low center of gravity, keeping the hands on the gunwales, and walking on the midline of the canoe.

5. The seated bow paddler uses balance to stabilize the canoe while the stern paddler enters.

6. When both paddlers are on board, they depart from the beach by carefully pushing off.

Exiting a Canoe Beachside

When returning to the beach, it is equally important to exit the canoe carefully to avoid an unwanted bath. The following is a sequence of steps paddlers could follow to *exit* a canoe at the beach:

1. The two paddlers paddle the canoe so that it lands bow first on the sand, perpendicular to the beach.

2. The bow paddler steps out of the canoe and straddles the canoe, holding onto the gunwales for stability the same way the stern paddler did upon entry.

3. The stern paddler moves to the bow using a low center of gravity, keeping both hands on the gunwales, and walking down the midline of the canoe.

4. Once at the bow, the stern paddler exits the canoe, and the two paddlers assist each other in pulling the canoe out of the water.

> ### TEACHING TIP
> In all entering and exiting activities, tell students to "stay low, equalize balance, and walk the midline"; this means that students should maintain a low center of gravity by bending at the knees, should maintain counter balance by placing the hands on the gunwales, and should be careful to stay on the center line of the canoe when entering so as not to tip over.

Rescues

Before canoeing on the open water, students must have a working knowledge of what to do in case of an unexpected capsize. Tipping over can happen in shallow water or in deep water and may be due to a variety of factors such as being improperly seated or being unbalanced in the canoe, leaning too far to one side during stroke execution, or encountering wind and waves. In any case, capsizing can be nerve wracking or even scary for students. Knowing what to do, both practically and methodically, can alleviate the tension surrounding a possible or actual capsize.

To help students understand the full scope of rescues, you should teach both self-rescues and assisted rescues. Self-rescue techniques are completed independently by the paddlers of the boat that capsized. Assisted-rescue techniques, usually associated with deep water far from shore, require the knowledge and assistance of other paddlers in a canoe that has remained upright.

Self-Rescue I: The Capistrano Flip

The Capistrano flip is good to teach first because it is a shallow-water rescue technique and gives students time to adjust to being out of their capsized canoe in easy-to-manage conditions. You or a student who knows the procedure should demonstrate the exact set of body maneuvers before trying it in the water. The Capistrano flip is done in partners, and there are two possible ways to complete the maneuver. One involves going under the capsized canoe with your partner and using the air space inside the hull for breathing and communication before lifting and righting the canoe by using the gunwales toward the middle of the canoe. The other involves staying outside of the canoe and using the gunwales at the ends of the canoe to perform the uprighting maneuver. The strategies are equal in value, and paddlers should learn both. In the case of an actual capsize, paddlers should perform the method they are most comfortable with. The following is an example of the steps paddlers could follow when practicing the *under-the-boat Capistrano flip:*

1. Both paddlers begin in the canoe.
2. After the paddlers determine that there are no obstacles or other paddlers in the water nearby, they tip the canoe in the desired direction (either left or right).
3. *Safety tip:* Make sure your partner is OK after capsizing.
4. The two paddlers feel under the canoe for the position of the thwarts, center yoke, and seats, locating the large space between the seats and thwarts.

5. When ready, the paddlers count to three and then go under the canoe together, emerging with their heads inside the open hull of the canoe. Each chooses a space between the seats and the thwarts.
6. Both paddlers face the same direction as if in single file.
7. Both paddlers place their hands on the gunwales of the canoe and lift it a few inches, breaking the seal of the canoe against the water.
8. The paddlers then decide which way they are going to flip the canoe. The command is "Up left!" for when the left arm goes up while the right arm stays down, so the canoe is flipped to the right, or "Up right!" for when the right arm goes up while the left arm stays down, so the canoe is flipped to the left.
9. The paddlers then stabilize and balance the canoe for each other so each can get back into the canoe.
10. *Safety tip:* Make sure there are no other paddlers or obstacles in the immediate area before flipping a canoe.

The following is a sequence of steps paddlers could follow when performing the *out-of-the-boat Capistrano flip:*

1. Once the canoe is capsized, each paddler goes to an end of the canoe, lifting it out of the water to break the seal of the canoe against the water.
2. The paddlers decide in which direction they will flip the canoe and then push it over to that side.
3. *Safety tip:* Make sure there are no other paddlers or obstacles in the immediate area before flipping a canoe.

Self-Rescue II: Deepwater Rock Wall

The deepwater rock wall self-rescue is important for those times when paddlers find themselves capsized in deep water next to a rocky shore or rock wall and are unable to retrieve their canoe due to it being filled with water. This technique works best with two people and simply involves getting an end of the canoe up on the rock wall (you can use the poolside for practice), breaking the water seal to allow the water to drain out, and flipping the canoe in the desired direction. The following is an example of the steps paddlers could follow to complete the deepwater rock wall self-rescue:

1. After capsizing, each paddler makes sure her partner is OK.

2. The paddlers carefully swim with the canoe, pushing it toward the rocky shore or rock wall.

3. The paddlers position the canoe so that it is perpendicular (90°) to the rock wall.

4. One paddler stays at the end farthest from the rock wall, while the other moves to the end next to the rock wall.

5. The paddler next to the rock wall positions his hands near the tip of the canoe and, using a scissors kick for upward momentum, pushes the end of the canoe onto the rock wall. At the same time, the paddler at the other end pushes the canoe slightly down and forward to assist.

6. The paddler next to the rock wall then joins the paddler at the other end. The two use scissors kicks for upward momentum to break the seal of the canoe and quickly flip it over in the desired direction before it falls into the water again.

7. *Safety tip:* You must decide on the direction of the flip before completing the maneuver so no one gets hit on the head with the canoe.

Self-Rescue III: Submerged Float

If it is not possible to self-rescue by using the Capistrano flip or the deepwater rock wall rescue, as a last resort you can bail out as much water as possible using your bail bucket and then sit in or on top of the submerged canoe and paddle to the nearest shore. Students should practice this rescue in the controlled setting of the swimming pool so they can feel what it is like to balance on a submerged canoe. The key to success is getting as much water out of the canoe as possible to avoid the canoe becoming a fully submerged surfboard. The following is an example of the steps paddlers could follow to complete the submerged float self-rescue:

1. The paddlers check to see that their partner is OK after capsizing.

2. The paddlers get control of their gear, paddles, and canoe and do a quick inventory.

3. The paddlers pull the submerged canoe up to the surface of the water to the best extent possible, trying to get the gunwales above the surface.

4. The two paddlers use the bail bucket to bail out as much water as possible; the canoe will likely still contain some water.

5. The paddlers gather their gear and paddles, carefully sit on top of the submerged canoe, and paddle to shore.

6. *Special note:* If you do not bring the gunwales at least a little above the surface of the water, the canoe will mostly likely sink even further when you try to sit on top of it.

Assisted Rescue I: The T-Rescue

The T-rescue is performed when a canoe is capsized in deep water and at least one other canoe is available to assist. The maneuver is somewhat complex, so students should practice it several times so that it becomes a sequence of rote movements; during the heightened excitement of a rescue, especially in hazardous conditions, is not the time to try and learn the steps for a safe T-rescue. The following is a sequence of steps paddlers could follow to perform a T-rescue:

1. The paddlers of the capsized canoe check to see that their partner is OK.

2. The assisting canoe approaches with caution, asking if the two submerged paddlers are OK.

3. One of the paddlers in the assisting canoe asks if either of the submerged paddlers can assist with the rescue; if both say no (due to fear, cold, or injury), they are quickly instructed to move to respective ends of the assisting canoe and hold on. The paddlers submerged in the water and holding onto the ends of the assisting canoe should try to get as much of their bodies out of the water as possible to avoid being injured by the cold.

4. *Safety tip:* The paddlers in the assisting canoe must stay in constant communication with the submerged paddlers, telling them what is going on with the rescue and offering reassurance.

5. The paddlers in the assisting canoe face each other and get on their knees. To do this, the bow paddler turns around and gets on her knees on the canoe floor. Often the stern paddler must move the thwart at the back toward the middle of the canoe so he has enough room to get on his knees.

6. One paddler then uses a wide and low center of gravity to stabilize the assisting canoe while the other carefully retrieves the submerged or flipped canoe, pulling one end up onto the gunwales of the assisting canoe.

7. The paddlers in the assisting canoe carefully pull the flipped canoe up onto the gunwales of their

boat in a perpendicular (or T) position to allow the water to drain out of the submerged canoe.

8. *Safety tip:* Be extremely careful not to allow your fingers to be caught between the gunwales of the two canoes.

9. The paddlers in the assisting canoe carefully flip over the newly drained canoe, slide it back into the water, and stabilize it so the capsized paddlers can get back in.

> **TEACHING TIP**
>
> During all rescue procedures, clear and abundant communication is the key to safety and understanding procedures; teach students to talk continuously throughout each procedure.

PADDLES AND STROKES

The first thing students need to know when on the water is how to grip a paddle so it can be used most efficiently. To help guide students, refer back to the earlier discussion on paddle sizing and how to properly hold a paddle. Good paddle strokes are yielded from an appropriately sized paddle combined with an understanding of good stroke mechanics. Begin teaching the paddle strokes by presenting the strokes to be covered for the day on land, covering the key points of each stroke and then checking for understanding before allowing the students to move onto the water. During the first several sessions on the open water, set up your students for success by sequencing your instruction so that you teach the less-difficult maneuvers first and the more-difficult maneuvers later on.

Because one of the most difficult maneuvers paddlers perform in a canoe is traveling forward in a straight line, a novice group of students can quickly become out of control, spread out, and unable to bring themselves back together. For this reason, begin paddle stroke instruction with students as a group, teaching them how to use their paddle efficiently without traveling a far distance. This allows you to demonstrate skills to the whole group and communicate with students easily. Examples of such skills include spinning in circles and moving side to side using draw, pry, and sweep strokes. Other examples include the low brace and high brace for helping to recover from a potential spill and the sweeps used to assist in either spinning or turning a canoe. All of these strokes allow students to get oriented to

being on the water. When exercised with caution, they can be performed near other canoes without danger; they keep the students together as a group for easy instruction and easy access to assistance in case of an accidental spill; and they allow students to experience immediate success.

Once students are comfortable on the water and have a working knowledge of proper stroke mechanics due to practicing in close proximity as a group, you can introduce strokes that allow the students to branch out a short distance. These strokes include the forward stroke, the J-stroke, and the sit and switch. Toward the end of your canoe unit, you can teach students advanced strokes that will allow them to move in reverse, influence steering from the bow, and travel around obstacles or in patterns such as a figure eight. The remainder of this chapter focuses on the key points used to teach a variety of canoe paddling strokes.

Each stroke has in common the general phases of enter, power, exit, and recovery. However, you must steer students' attention away from relying *only* on these general commonalities. For example, these four phases don't tell you anything about body position, grip and thumb placement, paddle placement, torso rotation, or angle.

Pry and Draw Strokes

The pry and draw strokes are useful in a variety of ways while paddling. This section focuses on the application of the pry and draw strokes for the purposes of spinning the canoe in circles in either direction and for moving left to right in a side-to-side fashion. To make the canoe spin in circles, paddlers simultaneously use the pry or draw stroke on opposite sides of the canoe (e.g., the bow on the left side and the stern on the right side), and to move side to side, the two paddlers perform the pry or draw simultaneously on the same side of the canoe. The key is that the paddlers are performing the same stroke at the same time. An example of the steps students could follow to perform the *pry stroke* (see figure 6.5) is the following:

1. The paddlers turn their torsos toward the side of the canoe on which they will perform the stroke (each paddler turns toward her onside), squaring the shoulders so they are aligned with the gunwale.

2. The paddlers place the paddle blade into the water so it is fully submerged with the flat side of the blade parallel to the canoe.

3. Each paddler's grip hand is approximately at eye level, grip-hand elbow is bent about 90°, and shaft hand is low but comfortably above the blade.

4. Being careful not to get fingers caught between the paddle shaft and the gunwale, the paddlers can rest the shaft against the gunwale to create a lever.

5. The paddlers pull the grip hand in toward their body, forcing the submerged blade to kick out slightly and hence making the canoe pry away from its starting point.

6. For an in-water recovery of the stroke, the paddlers turn the blade 90° so it is perpendicular to the canoe and slice the water while pushing away with the grip hand.

7. The paddlers perform the pry aspect of the stroke as well as the recovery in unison.

8. When paddlers perform the stroke on opposite sides, the canoe spins; when paddlers perform the stroke on the same side, the canoe moves sideways in the opposite direction from where the canoe paddles are placed.

9. *Special note:* You can also use the pry stroke to right the canoe when it is tipping over unintentionally; in this case, apply the stroke on the side opposite the direction in which the canoe is tipping. For example, if the canoe is tipping to the right, perform the pry on the left side of the canoe while simultaneously using a slight jolt of the hips to upright the canoe.

An example of the sequence students could follow to perform the *draw stroke* (see figure 6.6) is the following:

1. The paddlers turns their torsos toward the onside of the canoe, squaring the shoulders so they are aligned with the gunwale.

2. Each paddler's grip hand is approximately at eye level, grip-hand elbow is bent about 90°, and shaft hand is low but comfortably above the top of the blade.

3. Keeping the paddle vertical and the paddle blade parallel to the canoe, the paddlers reach out with the paddle approximately an arm's length away from the canoe and fully submerge the blade in the water.

4. Keeping the paddle vertical, the paddlers pull the paddle as a whole unit in toward the canoe.

5. For in-water recovery, the paddlers turn the paddle blade so it is perpendicular to the canoe with the grip hand thumb pointing away from the body and slice the water in the direction away from the canoe.

6. The paddlers repeat the stroke as many times as desired.

7. The paddlers perform the draw aspect of the stroke as well as the recovery in unison.

8. When the draw stroke is performed on opposite sides, the canoe spins; when the draw stroke is performed on the same side, the canoe moves sideways in the same direction to where the canoe paddles are placed.

Figure 6.5 The pry stroke.

9. *Special note:* Beware the suck zone. This is the area immediately next to the sidewall of the canoe and just under the canoe. When a draw stroke is pulled in toward the canoe too far and too forcefully, the paddle will get caught in the momentum of the water and get sucked under the canoe. This most often results in the paddle getting jammed against the gunwale and the canoe sidewall and an unanticipated bath for the paddlers. To avoid the suck zone, stop the draw stroke short of the side of the canoe by about the width of one paddle face.

Sculling Draw

The *sculling draw* is an extension of the draw stroke in which the paddle is left in the water during the entire stroke execution. The motion of the sculling draw is akin to spreading icing on a cake using back and forth motions with the knife—the water is the cake and the paddle is the knife. Generally, the sculling draw is completed by both paddlers simultaneously. If the sculling draw is performed on opposite sides, the canoe spins; if the sculling draw is performed on the same side, the canoe moves sideways in the direction of the onside. The following is an example of the sequence students could follow to perform the sculling draw:

1. The paddlers turn their torsos toward the onside of the canoe, squaring the shoulders so they are aligned with the gunwale.

2. Each paddler's grip hand is approximately at eye level, grip-hand elbow is bent about 90°, and shaft

hand is low but comfortably above the top of the blade.

3. Keeping the paddle mostly vertical but at a slight angle pointing away from the canoe and with the blade mostly flat on the water, the paddlers pull the paddle side to side, back and forth, as if to spread icing on a cake (this is called *sculling*). When the paddlers move the paddle from right to left, the paddle face will be open to the left at a slight angle, and when the paddlers move the paddle from left to right, the paddle face will be open to the right at a slight angle.

4. The two paddlers continue using the sculling draw as long as desired.

Cross Bow Draw

An additional draw stroke that is useful for complex maneuvers, particularly in the bow, is the cross bow draw (see figure 6.7):

1. The bow paddler begins with the paddle set up on his onside. Without changing the position of the grip hand or shaft hand on the paddle, the paddler crosses the paddle over to the offside of the canoe.

2. With a vertical shaft and blade fully submerged, the paddler completes a draw stroke on the offside with in-water recovery (thumb points toward the body during recovery). The paddler does this as many times as desired before returning to the onside.

Figure 6.6 The draw stroke.

Figure 6.7   The cross bow draw.

Low Brace

The next skill students can practice while maintaining close proximity to the group and instructor is the low brace. Paddlers use the low brace to prevent an unintentional spill. Unlike the pry stroke (when it is being used for the same purpose), the low brace is performed on the *same side* as the direction in which the canoe is tipping. The following is an example of the steps students could follow to perform the low brace:

1. The paddlers place the grip hand on the paddle grip and the shaft hand low on the shaft but comfortably above the paddle blade.

2. The paddlers hold the paddle at torso height over the lap, perpendicular to the canoe, with the paddle blade sticking out over the water and aligned with the surface as if to lay flat on top of the water.

3. As the canoe tips in the direction of the onside, the paddlers carefully use the paddle blade to create a modified slapping motion on top of the water while jolting the hips to help upright the canoe.

4. *Key point:* You must place your hands on the paddle such that the thumb on your grip hand is pointing *away* from your body and your hands and arms are *over* the paddle.

High Brace

The counterpart to the low brace is the high brace. Typically, the high brace is used in white-water scenarios where rapids are present and the waves in the water are taller than the sides of the canoe or even the paddler. Although your students are not going on white water during this unit, it is still useful for them to know the high brace so they can compare it with the low brace. Also, from time to time a paddler may be in just the right position to use the high brace even on flat water. The high brace is set up the same way as the low brace, with the exception that the thumb on the grip hand points *toward* the paddler and the hands and arms are *under* the paddle, as if in position to do a pull-up on a bar. The following is an example of the steps students could follow to perform the high brace.

1. The paddlers hold the paddle at torso height over the lap, perpendicular to the canoe, with the paddle blade sticking out over the water and aligned with the surface as if to lay flat on top of the water.

2. As the canoe tips in the direction of the onside, the paddlers carefully use the paddle blade to create a modified slapping motion on top of the water while jolting the hips to help right the canoe.

3. *Key point:* You must place your hands on the paddle such that the thumb on your grip hand is pointing *toward* your body and your hands and arms are *under* the paddle.

Forward Sweep

When performed in the bow, the forward sweep (see figure 6.8) helps turn the front of the canoe in the direction opposite the side on which the sweep is executed. When performed in the stern, the forward sweep tends to also turn the front of the canoe in the direction opposite the side on which the sweep is executed. What is of interest is that the sweep turns the canoe on a wide arc rather than makes the canoe turn sharply. The following is an example of the steps a paddler could use to perform the forward sweep:

1. The paddler places the grip hand on the paddle grip and moves the grip in toward the belly. The shaft hand is low on the shaft but comfortably above the paddle blade.

Figure 6.8   The forward sweep.

2. With the paddle shaft at about a 45° angle to the canoe, the paddler fully submerges the blade in the water near the front tip of the canoe. The blade is positioned so that it is perpendicular to the water and the power face will catch the water during the stroke.

3. Using the cue *tip to hip,* the paddler sweeps the paddle wide from the front end of the canoe to about the hip.

4. The paddler withdraws the paddle from the water and recovers by pointing the thumb of the grip hand forward, keeping the paddle blade near the water during the recovery phase. The paddler is ready to begin again.

Reverse Sweep

In contrast to the forward sweep, the reverse sweep (see figure 6.9) turns the canoe slightly in the direction of the side on which the sweep is performed; for example, if the stern paddler executes a reverse sweep on the right, the bow of the canoe turns to the right. The same steps used to execute the forward sweep are used to execute the reverse sweep with the exception that the cue *tip to hip* means to sweep from the back of the canoe to the hip for the stern paddler and from behind (near the side wall of the canoe) to the hip for the bow paddler:

1. The paddler places the grip hand on the paddle grip. The shaft hand is low on the shaft but comfortably above the paddle blade.

2. The paddler completes the reverse sweep using the key steps from the forward sweep but sweeping in the opposite direction.

3. The paddler sweeps tip to hip: from the back of the canoe to the hip for the stern paddler and from behind (near the side wall of the canoe) to the hip for the bow paddler.

4. *Special note:* When the forward and reverse sweeps are performed in unison on opposite sides of the canoe, the canoe will spin.

> **TEACHING TIP**
>
> Allow students to take their time and experience many practice attempts with pry strokes, draw strokes, braces, and sweeps before moving on to forward travel. More time spent in the canoe practicing basics leads to more comfortable and proficient paddlers later on.

Figure 6.9 The reverse sweep.

FORWARD TRAVEL AND TURNING

Day 6

Day 7

After practicing several strokes on the water within a small area, students should be ready to attempt other strokes that will allow them to travel greater distances and to maneuver in various directions. This next sequence of strokes focuses primarily on forward and reverse travel and on maneuvering in various directions.

Forward Stroke

The forward stroke (see figure 6.10) can be performed in the bow or the stern or in both locations simultaneously and is used to make the canoe move ahead. Stroke mechanics and proper form are especially important for the forward stroke; improper form can make the canoe very difficult to keep under control. A symptom of improper technique with the forward stroke is a canoe that moves across the water in a slalomlike path rather than in a straight line. The following is an example of

the steps students might use to perform the forward stroke:

1. The paddler places the grip hand on the paddle grip, with the shaft hand low on the shaft but comfortably above the paddle blade.

2. The paddler places the paddle vertically in the water, with the blade fully submerged and perpendicular to the canoe (i.e., the power face is set to catch the water). The paddle stays in the vertical position throughout the power phase of the stroke.

3. The paddler completes the power phase of the stroke from a point near the tips of the toes if the paddler is seated in position one or from a point just forward of the knees if the paddler is seated in position two. Using the cue *tip to hip,* the paddler follows through on the stroke until the paddle is aligned with the hip.

4. *Special note:* During the power phase of the stroke, the shaft arm must remain straight. *Do not bend*

Figure 6.10 Forward stroke.

the elbow, as bending the elbow causes lazy and inefficient mechanics.

5. *Special note:* Use significant torso rotation to complete the power phase of the stroke. Do not rely solely on the arms and shoulders.

6. To exit the paddle from the water, the paddler pulls the grip hand from 12 o'clock to 3 o'clock, causing the paddle to be bridged across the lap.

7. The paddler points the grip thumb forward, aligning the paddle blade so that the flat side of the blade is parallel to the water.

8. The paddler recovers to the start position of the stroke and begins again.

Stopping

Knowing how to stop a canoe when a destination is reached is just as important as knowing how to make it go. To stop when traveling forward, students may use the following steps:

1. Both paddlers place their paddles in the water. The shaft is vertical and the blade is fully submerged.

2. Holding the paddle steady in position, the paddlers apply force to the back face of the paddle.

3. When the paddlers work in unison, the canoe will stop.

J-Stroke

Often when the stern paddler performs a forward stroke consistently on one side, the canoe turns in the direction opposite the side of stroke execution. To avoid this, the J-stroke (see figure 6.11) can be used. The J-stroke is used only by the stern paddler. It is very similar to the forward stroke but incorporates one small addition after the power phase and before the exit phase. This small addition is known as the *J.* The purpose of the J-stroke is to keep the canoe on track when paddlers desire to travel forward in a straight line without having to switch the onside. Paddlers should be aware that the J-stroke can create a small amount of drag, and so it may not be the stroke of choice for racing. The following is an example of the sequence paddlers could follow to perform the J-stroke:

1. The stern paddler places the grip hand on the paddle grip. The shaft hand is low on the shaft but comfortably above the paddle blade.

2. The stern paddler places the paddle vertically in the water, with the blade fully submerged and perpendicular to the canoe (i.e., the power face is set to catch the water). The paddle stays in the vertical position throughout the power phase of the stroke.

3. The stern paddler completes the power phase of the stroke from a point near the tips of the toes if the paddler is seated in position one or from a point just forward of the knees if the paddler is seated in position two. Using the cue *tip to hip,* the paddler follows through on the stroke until the paddle is aligned with the hip.

4. To apply the J, the stern paddler points the grip thumb downward toward the water, making the flat side of the paddle blade sit parallel to the side of the canoe. The paddler then pulls the grip hand slightly in toward the centerline of the canoe, creating a slight prying motion to complete the J phase of the stroke.

5. To exit, the stern paddler gently pulls the blade out of the water at an angle with the grip thumb still pointing downward (called "feathering"), pulling the paddle out of the water carefully so as to not slow the boat.

6. The stern paddler recovers to the start position of the stroke and begins again.

7. *Special note:* Do not use the pry stroke in place of the J, as it creates improper mechanics and decreases efficiency.

8. *Special note:* As with the forward stroke, complete the J-stroke with significant torso rotation and a straight shaft arm during the power phase.

Figure 6.11   The J-stroke.

Sit and Switch

When paddlers wish to move forward in a straight line with a smooth cadence and a bit of speed, the sit and switch may be a good stroke choice. To perform the sit and switch, both paddlers execute forward strokes on their onside, in unison, with a slightly quickened pace. When the stern paddler anticipates that the canoe may deviate from its forward course, she calls for a switch. The paddlers then switch their onside, using appropriate hand placement on the paddle for the new onside. Generally the switch is called at the beginning of the power phase of a forward stroke; the paddlers perform one more stroke and then switch their onside. There is not really any rhyme or reason to the number of strokes performed on each side; it is simply up to the judgment of the stern paddler to make the call. The following are the steps students can use to complete the sit and switch:

1. Both paddlers execute forward strokes on their onside, in unison, with a slightly quickened pace.

2. When the stern paddler anticipates that the canoe may deviate from its forward course, he calls for a switch, and the paddlers switch their onside.

3. To call for a switch, the stern paddler yells "Switch!" at the beginning of the power phase of a forward stroke. The stroke made during the call becomes the second-to-last stroke on that side.

4. The paddlers perform one more stroke after the call and then switch their onside.

Cross Forward

Another way the canoe can remain on course is for the bow paddler to perform the cross forward (see figure 6.12). The bow paddler executes the cross forward by moving the paddle from the onside to the offside of the canoe without changing the position of the grip hand or shaft hand on the paddle. The following is an example of the steps a paddler could follow to perform the cross forward:

1. Without changing the position of the grip hand or shaft hand on the paddle, the bow paddler crosses the paddle over to the offside of the canoe.

2. Keeping the paddle vertical, the bow paddler fully submerges the blade in the water so that the power face of the paddle is perpendicular to the canoe.

3. Using the idea of tip to hip, the bow paddler pulls the paddle back to perform the power phase of the stroke.

4. To perform an in-water recovery, the bow paddler points the grip thumb forward, turning the blade 90° to slice the water and recover back to the start position of the stroke. The bow paddler must take care to make sure the blade is not angled so that it does not get jammed against the bow.

5. The bow paddler performs the cross forward as many times as desired to get the bow back on course and then returns the paddle to the onside and continues paddling.

Figure 6.12   The cross forward.

Duffek

Performed by the bow paddler, the Duffek (pronounced "doo-feck"; see figure 6.13) is a stroke that is useful for making a sharp turn, such as when going around an obstacle or when paddling through a figure eight. The Duffek is unique in that it is a static stroke (i.e., the paddle blade is submerged in the water and held in place). The following is an example of the sequence the bow paddler could follow when performing the *Duffek:*

1. The bow paddler places the thumb of the grip hand on the onside shoulder (use the cue "Thumb to shoulder!" when teaching students).

2. The bow paddler places the elbow of the shaft arm on or very near the onside hip.

3. The bow paddler fully submerges the paddle blade in the water, dipping the shaft down at an angle.

4. The bow paddler holds the paddle blade at the desired angle in relation to the bow of the canoe; the wider the angle, the more forceful and sharp the turn. The canoe will turn in the direction of the onside of the bow paddler. Students should use caution: An angle too wide creates so much drag that the canoe may lose its momentum.

Figure 6.13   The Duffek.

Cross Duffek

When the bow paddler wishes to turn the bow sharply in the direction of the offside, the *cross Duffek* (see figure 6.14) is used. As with the forward and cross forward, the positions of the grip and shaft hands do not change between the Duffek and the cross Duffek. The follow-

ing are the steps the bow paddler might use to perform the cross Duffek:

1. The bow paddler places the elbow of the grip hand on or very near the offside hip.

2. The bow paddler extends the shaft arm and holds it strongly in place to create support for the paddle placement in the water.

3. The bow paddler drops the paddle shaft at an angle and fully submerges the paddle blade in the water.

4. The bow paddler holds the paddle blade at the desired angle in relation to the bow of the canoe; the wider the angle, the more forceful and sharp the turn. The canoe will turn in the direction of the offside of the bow paddler. Students should use caution: An angle too wide creates so much drag that the canoe may lose its momentum.

Figure 6.14   The cross Duffek.

REVERSE TRAVEL

There are times when paddlers may wish to travel in reverse, such as when they want to realign with a desired location without having to complete a full 180° turn or when water currents push the canoe toward an undesired obstacle. As with traveling forward, traveling in reverse requires paddlers to take several considerations into account in order to keep the canoe on the desired course.

Reverse Stroke

To propel the canoe in reverse, the bow and stern paddlers may apply the reverse stroke (see figure 6.15) in unison. The following are steps that the paddlers might take to perform the reverse stroke:

1. The two paddlers place the grip hand on the paddle grip and the shaft hand low on the shaft but comfortably above the paddle blade.

2. The two paddlers reach back with the paddle approximately 1.5 ft (0.5 m) on their onside and fully submerge the blade in the water.

3. The paddlers pull the paddle toward the bow of the canoe, applying the force of the water to the back face of the paddle, and rotate the onside shoulder forward.

4. The paddlers follow through the stroke until their paddle is approximately 1.5 ft (0.5 m) ahead of their torso, feather out of the water, recover, and begin again.

Figure 6.15   The reverse stroke.

Reverse J

Like the J-stroke, the reverse J is applied to keep the canoe traveling on course. The difference is that the reverse J is applied when the canoe is traveling in reverse by the *bow paddler* and not the stern paddler. To perform the reverse J, the bow paddler simply completes the steps for the reverse stroke, adding in one step at the end of the power phase before the exit and recovery phase:

1. The bow paddler places the grip hand on the paddle grip and the shaft hand low on the shaft but comfortably above the paddle blade.

2. The bow paddler reaches back with the paddle approximately 1.5 ft (0.5 m) on the onside and fully submerges the blade in the water.

3. The bow paddler pulls the paddle toward the bow of the canoe, applying the force of the water to the back face of the paddle, and rotates the onside shoulder forward.

4. The bow paddler follows through the stroke until the paddle is approximately 1.5 ft (0.5 m) ahead of her torso.

5. The bow paddler turns the grip thumb down toward the water and applies a small amount of force to the back face of the paddle to create the J.

6. The bow paddler feathers out of the water, recovers in unison with the stern paddler, and begins again.

7. *Special note:* When traveling in reverse it is the responsibility of the *bow paddler* to keep the canoe on the desired course.

Compound Back

The compound back offers another choice for traveling in reverse and is slightly more powerful than the reverse stroke. The following is an example of the sequence paddlers might use to perform the compound back:

1. The paddlers place the grip hand on the paddle grip and the shaft hand low on the shaft but comfortably above the paddle blade.

2. While reaching back and behind the body by approximately 1.5 ft (0.5 m), the paddlers turn the grip thumb so it is pointing in toward their body.

3. Fully submerging the blade in the water, the paddlers catch the water with the power face of the paddle.

4. The paddlers pull the paddle forward toward the bow of the canoe.

5. When the paddle blade is aligned with their hip, the paddlers turn the thumb of the grip hand outward and away from their body, causing the paddle to turn 180°.

6. The paddlers finish the stroke with the back face of the paddle catching the water as the paddle continues to move forward approximately 1.5 ft (0.5 m) past their hip.

7. The paddlers feather out of the water, recover, and begin again.

STROKE COMBINATIONS

Once students have practiced the strokes individually and have increased their stroke proficiency, it is time to accelerate the fun and perform the strokes in combination! At this point, you can construct any sequence of maneuvers to help students gain experience combining strokes. For example, you might set up a triangle of buoys for students to traverse around, arrange two buoys to create a station for performing a figure eight, or set one buoy as a target to travel toward in reverse. Each of these exercises requires students to employ a working knowledge of canoe stroke combinations.

It is crucial for paddlers to stay on their original onside when they are performing combination maneuvers. There may be times when it might seem easier to keep the boat under control by switching the onside instead of performing corrective strokes (e.g., the J-stroke) or crossover strokes (e.g., the cross bow draw, cross forward, or cross Duffek). To accommodate proper form and skill execution, however, the various corrective and crossover strokes need to be employed during combination maneuvers.

Triangle

To set up this practice station, set three buoys at the three points of a triangle. The distance between each buoy should be several canoe lengths; if the sides of the triangle are too short, your paddlers will paddle in a large circle, and if the sides of the triangle are too long, you might not be able to set up several practice stations

where you can see and hear all students at all times. The students will traverse the triangle with turns in the direction of the onside or offside of the bow paddler or stern paddler, respectively. The following is an example of the steps paddlers might use when traversing a triangle by turning in the direction of the *bow paddler's onside* and the *stern paddler's offside*:

1. The two paddlers approach the triangle so that the canoe is parallel to a chosen side. Staying on course (e.g., with the bow paddler using the forward stroke and the stern paddler using the J-stroke), they traverse the first side.

2. The paddlers turn the first corner, with the bow paddler using a Duffek or combined reverse sweeping action with the paddle placed in a low brace and the stern paddler using a forward sweep.

3. The paddlers traverse the second side in a straight line (e.g., with the bow paddler using the forward stroke and the stern paddler using the J-stroke).

4. The paddlers turn the second corner (e.g., with the bow paddler using a Duffek and the stern paddler using a forward sweep).

5. The paddlers traverse the third side in a straight line (e.g., with the bow paddler using the forward stroke and the stern paddler using the J-stroke).

6. The paddlers turn the third corner (e.g., with the bow paddler using a Duffek and the stern paddler using a forward sweep).

7. Finally, the paddlers paddle back to their starting point or home base (e.g., with both paddlers using the sit and switch).

The following are the steps paddlers might take when traversing a triangle by turning in the direction of the *bow paddler's offside* and the *stern paddler's onside*:

1. The two paddlers approach the triangle so that the canoe is parallel to a chosen side. Staying on course (e.g., with the bow paddler using the forward stroke and the stern paddler using the J-stroke), they traverse the first side.

2. The two paddlers start the first corner turn (e.g., with the bow paddler using a cross Duffek followed by a cross bow draw and the stern paddler using a light reverse sweep to help the canoe

spin around the corner; momentum will be lost momentarily).

3. The paddlers finish the first corner turn (e.g., with the bow paddler using a forward sweep and the stern paddler using a light reverse sweep followed by a forward paddle).

4. The paddlers follow the same sequence until they have traversed all three sides and turned all three corners.

5. The paddlers paddle back to their starting point or home base (e.g., with both paddlers using the sit and switch).

Figure Eight

Turning corners in a figure eight is similar to turning corners in a triangle except that when completing a figure eight, the paddlers must see the turns all the way through a complete U-turn. When performing the figure eight, each paddler will naturally experience one turn on the onside and one turn on the offside. The following example begins with the first turn being to the bow paddler's onside:

1. The two paddlers enter the figure eight on a straight path, getting ready to make the first U-turn (e.g., with the bow paddler performing the forward stroke and the stern paddler using the J-stroke).

2. The paddlers complete the first U-turn (e.g., with the bow paddler using the Duffek and the stern paddler using the forward sweep).

3. The two paddlers cross the middle of the figure eight on a straight path, getting ready to make the second turn (e.g., with the bow paddler performing the forward stroke and the stern paddler using the forward stroke or the J-stroke).

4. The paddlers complete the second U-turn (e.g., with the bow paddler using the cross Duffek followed by the forward sweep and the stern paddler using a light reverse sweep followed by a forward paddle).

5. *Special note:* To begin the figure eight with the first U-turn in the direction of the bow paddler's offside, simply reverse the order of the steps just listed.

6. The paddlers paddle back to their starting point or home base (e.g., with both paddlers using the sit and switch).

Reverse Paddle to a Target

An effective way to find out if students know how to travel in reverse is to have them paddle in reverse to an established target. The target could be a point seen on the horizon (e.g., the tall birch tree across the lake) or a buoy that you set up. The following is a set of instructions you could give students to teach them how to travel in reverse in a straight line:

1. Each paddler begins with the reverse stroke; the stern paddler stays with the reverse stroke.

2. The bow paddler quickly adds in the reverse J for staying on course.

3. The bow paddler may need to incorporate a draw or cross bow draw intermittently to help keep the canoe on course.

4. When the destination is reached, the paddlers stop the canoe by placing each paddle in the water with a vertical shaft and the blade fully submerged. They then apply force to the power face of the paddle in unison.

Paddling Routine

It is very helpful to students if you can film them with a video camera while they are performing maneuvers in a canoe. Capturing them on video provides them with the opportunity to evaluate themselves as they become familiar with the kinesthetic awareness needed for the various strokes. It also creates the opportunity for classmates and instructors to provide feedback, enhancing learning for all, and it is often fun for students to see themselves on film. An example of a routine that you can film to assess students' knowledge of canoe strokes is the following:

1. Spin to the left, spin to the right.

2. Move sideways right, move sideways left.

3. Paddle in reverse to a buoy and stop.

4. Paddle forward, using the sit and switch, back to home base.

5. Traverse a triangle.

6. Traverse a figure eight.

> **TEACHING TIP**
> Encourage several paddling routine practice opportunities sitting in both the bow and the stern prior to testing students' skills. As with any set of skills, the more practice, the better.

SAFETY

Throughout all aspects of canoe instruction, whether conducted in a controlled environment or an outdoor setting, the number one priority for you and your students is the physical and emotional safety of all. Students should challenge themselves to learn new skills but should also stay within their ability level, especially in open water. As an instructor, you must be sensitive to the needs and abilities of your students, as their experiences in and around water may vary greatly. A good initial evaluation of students' comfort with water is to conduct a simple swim test, asking students to swim the length of a swimming pool. You can assess skills at a basic level and obtain much valuable information from watching students in action during a swim test; if anyone is afraid of the water or cannot swim, you will see it right away in this context. Students who have difficulty moving proficiently in the water should be given adequate time and instruction to overcome their difficulties. As always, you must teach students to hold themselves and each other accountable and to enforce all safety rules, especially those surrounding the use of PFDs.

CONCLUSION

This chapter provides basic information on canoeing as well as in-depth descriptions of a variety of canoe strokes that can be used to construct an effective canoeing unit. If you are using this chapter as a guide for teaching canoeing in your school-based program, you are certainly free to make modifications in order to accommodate individual needs in respective programs. For example, in some cases it may be enough

for students to learn entering and exiting and only a few strokes (e.g., forward, sweep, reverse, stop) to enjoy canoeing at a very basic level. On the other hand, this chapter provides enough information on constructing a full instructional unit that you may lead a course to prepare paddlers to move into more-advanced instruction later on.

REFERENCES

American Canoe Association. (2009). Paddler's safety checklist. www.americancanoe.org/atf/cf/%7B74254DC2-74B4-446F-92BE-547992272AB7%7D/SafetyChecklist.pdf.

Department of Education and Science & the Welsh Office. (1992). *Physical education in the national curriculum.* London: Her Majesty's Stationary Office.

McGuffin, G., & McGuffin, J. (1999). *Paddle your own canoe: An illustrated guide to the art of canoeing.* Ontario, Canada: Boston Mills Press.

National Association for Sport and Physical Education. (1991). *The physically educated person: Outcomes and benchmarks for quality education programs.* Reston, VA: Author.

National Association for Sport and Physical Education. (2004). *Moving into the future: National standards for physical education.* (2nd ed.). Reston, VA: Author.

Qualifications and Curriculum Authority. (2007). National curriculum online: PE. http://curriculum.qcda.gov.uk/index.aspx.

RECOMMENDED READINGS

American Canoe Association. (2009). Resources for ACA instructors and instructor candidates. www.americancanoe.org/site/c.lvIZIkNZJuE/b.4486093/k.98B2/For_Instructors.htm.

Furtman, M. (1992). *Canoe country camping: Wilderness skills for the boundary waters and Quetico.* Minneapolis: University of Minnesota Press.

Gullion, L. (1994). *Canoeing.* Champaign, IL: Human Kinetics.

Mason, B. (1999). *Path of the paddle: An illustrated guide to the art of canoeing.* Buffalo, NY: Firefly.

CANOEING UNIT PLAN

General Lesson Information

Each lesson contains the following seven elements:

1. Objectives—primary learning outcomes
2. Equipment—specific materials and gear
3. Introduction—opening concepts, ideas, and questions that identify the focus of the day
4. Warm-ups—lap swim in pool; swim assessment.
5. Central activities—activity progressions that increase in difficulty and lead to more advanced skills
6. Closure—suggested discussion and reflection items
7. Assessment—examples of evaluation strategies

Day 1

Focus: Equipment and preparation

- PFDs
- Paddles
- Parts of the canoe
- Swim skills assessment

Day 2

Focus: Canoe basic skills and self-rescues

- Entering and exiting dockside or poolside
- Capistrano flip
- Deepwater rock wall rescue

Day 3

Focus: Rescues

- Submerged float self-rescue
- T-rescue

Day 4

Focus: Canoe spins, moving left or right, balance

- Pry stroke
- Draw stroke
- Sculling draw
- Cross bow draw
- Low brace

Day 5

Focus: Spins and balance

- High brace
- Forward sweep
- Reverse sweep

Day 6

Focus: Forward travel and stopping

- Forward stroke
- Stopping
- J-stroke

Day 7

Focus: Racing strokes and bow maneuvers

- Sit and switch
- Cross forward
- Duffek
- Cross Duffek

Day 8

Focus: Reverse travel

- Reverse stroke
- Reverse J

Day 9

Focus: Combination maneuvers

- Compound back stroke
- Routine for skills testing

Day 10

Focus: Tying it all together

- Traversing a triangle
- Figure eight
- Reverse paddle to a target
- Routine for skills testing
- Written exam

chapter 7

Coastal Kayaking

Michael Odberg

Earth and sky, woods and fields, lakes and rivers, the mountain and the sea, are excellent schoolmasters, and teach some of us more than we can ever learn from books.

John Lubbock

Coastal kayaking offers an exciting, intimate experience with the water. The graceful kayak, when combined with a bit of skill, can take you to places nearly unapproachable by any other practical means.

It was a warm, calm, and foggy day on Lake Superior as we headed out toward the sandstone sea caves. It looked as though our group was heading into the abyss, as the fog began to envelop us just a few hundred yards offshore. We kept a tight pod, with all paddlers and the shore within sight. We reached a stretch

of caves and skillfully carved our sleek vessels through the smallest of passages, finishing with a limbo over the aft deck to avoid hitting our heads on the arch of the natural passageway. We laughed aloud as we weaved through the wave-carved paddling wonderland.

Kayak designs have been adapted for many different paddling environments, from flat-water ponds and lazy rivers to huge ocean waves and towering vertical drops down fast-moving waters. Kayaks for each application have their own unique design elements, shapes, and sizes. The three major categories include white-water kayaks, recreational kayaks, and coastal (sea) kayaks. Generally speaking, white-water kayaks are shorter and have more rocker than coastal kayaks have (see figure 7.1). These features make the white-water kayaks more maneuverable in fast-moving rivers. Recreational kayaks are designed for novice use and are a few inches wider and a few feet shorter than coastal kayaks, offering comforting stability and maneuverability for untrained paddlers. Coastal kayaks are long and lean and have less rocker; they are designed for straight tracking and efficient movement over open water. The term *coastal kayaking* has replaced *sea kayaking* in American Canoe Association (ACA) language and will be the form of paddling described in this chapter. Foundational solo, enclosed-cockpit paddling skills associated with flat-water coastal kayaking are the emphasis of this chapter. Emphasizing flat-water skills early on offers a solid foundation and enjoyable paddling experience for beginners. This foundation of competency will allow paddlers to branch off in many directions as they add to their toolbox of skills.

Kayaking has many benefits. It helps paddlers develop balance, skill, and fitness to engage actively in the natural environment. It is a truly beautiful form of travel in which refined skills become artistic movements. In its many forms, kayaking offers enjoyable and beneficial recreation throughout a lifetime.

Inuit cultures of the Arctic established the enclosed, solo sea kayak as a means of hunting walrus and seal. Their kayak designs were based on the need for pursuing their particular prey in potentially hostile weather conditions. These designs were largely skin-on-frame constructions consisting of gunwales, deck beams, and rib frames made of bent wood. This frame was secured and covered tightly with seal skin, and only a small manhole was left open to allow the paddler to sit within. Kayaks and paddles were custom designed for the individual paddler through ingenious systems associated with body measurements. Although the application of coastal kayaking has changed, many of these original kayak designs (particularly those of ancient Greenland) persist and have tremendous influence on modern coastal (sea) kayaks.

INSTRUCTIONAL ENVIRONMENT

Coastal kayak instruction can be successful both in pools and in open water. As the instructor, your access to and use of resources will affect your lesson design as well as the depth and breadth of your instruction. It is recommended that you use a combination of the two teaching environments when leading this kayaking unit.

Pool

To teach introductory lessons, you will need at a minimum a pool that is a standard 82 ft (25 m) long and four or more lanes wide. Larger pool sizes will allow for more paddlers, larger boats, and additional practice space. Zero-entry pools offer additional options for teaching launching and landing, while U-, T-, or L-shaped pools offer defined spaces for a station approach to instruction and practice. You can use the pool deck for equipment demonstration, fitting, and video lessons for some stu-

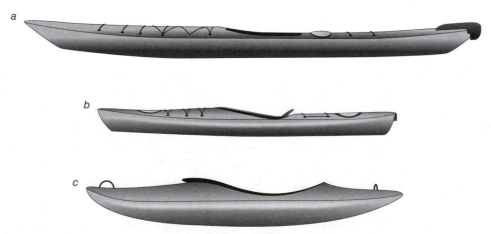

Figure 7.1   Kayak types: *(a)* coastal, *(b)* recreational, and *(c)* white-water.

Reprinted from ACA, 2008, *Kayaking* (Champaign, IL: Human Kinetics), 39.

dents while other students are using the pool space itself. Short, recreational, or white-water kayaks allow room for more paddlers in this confined area, but full-length coastal kayaks also can work. It is helpful to have a few kayaks equipped with flotation or bulkheads for ease of lifting and draining during rescue skill practice. The pool lessons should focus on equipment acclimation, play, and paddling skills requiring minimal travel and warm water temperatures. This process does not follow a perfect progression, but it does emphasize time on task in the most applicable environment.

Open Water

Sessions in open water allow sustained paddling and application of skills introduced in the pool. Locations with a beach or soft, gradual landing are preferred. Low docks or piers can substitute when a gradual entry is not available. If possible, choose calm, protected waterways such as ponds, small lakes, or protected bays. Buoys or other floating markers are useful to define the instructional area and offer targets for directional paddling. Water temperatures should allow students to swim briefly without experiencing substantial discomfort or hypothermia. Avoid areas with submerged obstructions. Good site selection offers a productive learning environment while reducing risks.

EQUIPMENT

Choose durable, adjustable, and affordable paddling equipment appropriate to your paddling environment and instructional sequence. Products designed for institutional use are often the best choices for heavy use by multiple paddlers. Ask retailers for the most durable products.

Coastal Kayaks

Coastal kayaks generally fit into three categories: North American, British, and Greenland style. These styles are further classified as introductory, advanced, and professional models. Construction materials vary widely. All styles and materials have advantages and disadvantages that are beyond the scope of this chapter. Coastal kayaks made of rotomolded plastic survive the abuse of an instructional environment while still offering solid performance.

The boats you use for your class should be designed for introductory success but still offer opportunities for advancement. Hull shapes should allow for initial stability and should maintain secondary stability while moving or leaning on edge. For instruction involving flat-water touring, choose kayak lengths of 13 to 17 ft (4-5 m) with a beam 22 to 24 in. (56-61 cm) wide. Coastal kayaks should be fitted with dual bulkheads for ample flotation and prompt rescue. Choose models with soft and hard deck lines for storage and rescue applications. Rudders or skegs are nice options for touring but are unnecessary for introductory instruction. Most manufacturers offer several models that fit this description.

The language of kayaking begins with the vessel itself. Although many of the terms describing kayaks are common to other watercraft, they are uniquely adapted to each type of vessel. Figure 7.2 illustrates the construction features and components of a coastal kayak.

Dimensional and Positional Terms Used to Describe Kayaks

length—The measurement of the length of the hull from bow to stern.

beam—The measurement of the width of the hull.

rocker—The amount of hull curvature from bow to stern as viewed from the side.

chine—The transition between the sides and the bottom of the kayak. The shape of the chine influences the stability and feel of the kayak when flat or on edge.

fore—The portion of the kayak ahead of the paddler.

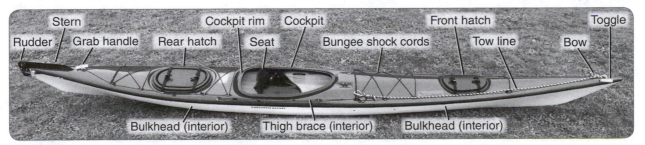

Figure 7.2 Construction features and components of a coastal kayak.

aft—The portion of the kayak behind the paddler.

starboard—The paddler's right side when seated in the cockpit.

port—The paddler's left side when seated in the cockpit.

Coastal Kayak Components

hull—The bottom half of the kayak, and the portion of the kayak designed for primary contact with the water.

deck—The permanent enclosure over the top of the kayak.

bulkheads—Walls that divide the cargo areas of the kayak from the paddler's area of the kayak and offer flotation chambers.

bow—The front end of the kayak.

stern—The back end of the kayak.

cockpit—The seating area for the paddler.

cockpit rim (coaming)—The protruding rim around the cockpit where the spray skirt is secured.

hatch—The opening into the cargo storage.

hard lines (deck lines)—The static cord that generally outlines the outside of the deck and is used for holding onto the kayak during rescues.

soft lines (deck bungees)—Stretchable bungee lines across the deck used for storing gear.

toggles—The handles on the bow and stern used for carrying the kayak.

rudder—A multidirectional fin mounted on the stern that influences the direction of the kayak and that is controlled by a cable system attached to moveable foot pegs.

skeg—A unidirectional fin mounted on the aft of the hull (usually retractable) that aids the kayak in tracking straight, especially in wind and waves.

thigh braces—Padded braces that secure the paddler's thighs to the kayak.

foot pegs—Adjustable pegs on a track that securely brace the paddler's feet.

seat—The part of the kayak on which the paddler sits; usually mounted low in the cockpit to properly position and secure the paddler.

Kayaks are often built to fit a specific body type, height, and weight. Choose a variety of sizes with a broad range of adjustments to provide a good range of fit for your students. A poorly fitting kayak hinders a student's development as a kayaker. Cockpit size should allow for ease of entry and escape but still allow the paddler to brace her thighs in a snug position in the boat. Lower decks generally track better in wind and waves but may cause discomfort for less-flexible or larger paddlers.

Paddles

Paddles are offered in a wide range of construction materials that vary greatly in price, application, and weight. Look for modern paddles designed for touring. Paddles featuring aluminum or fiberglass shafts with plastic or fiberglass blades offer affordable durability. A variety of sizes ranging from 83 to 91 in. (210-230 cm) will fit the majority of paddlers, with smaller paddlers generally using the shorter lengths and larger paddlers generally using the longer lengths.

This chapter focuses on the use of European paddles rather than the traditional Greenland paddles that are amazingly fluid but are not as readily available and require slightly different techniques. European paddle styles (depicted in figure 7.3) often feature spoon-like, asymmetrical, and concave blades. Widths and lengths of these spoon blades vary. Selected paddles should offer a rotating shaft and the ability to secure the paddle blades in an in-line or offset position for either left-handed or right-handed control. These adjustments offer options for a variety of paddling styles and preferences.

Students should be able to identify the parts of the paddle:

shaft—The long, stick part of the paddle and the handle used during paddling strokes.

ferule—The junction of a two-piece paddle shaft that generally marks the center point of the shaft and offers a mechanism for rotating and locking off the paddle shaft at different blade angles and dominant-hand alignments. In some models, the ferule allows for adjustable shaft length.

drip caps—The large, fitted rubber washers on the paddle shaft that discourage water from running down the paddle shaft during stroke work.

neck—The narrow transition from shaft to blade.

blade—The part of the paddle that creates the force to propel the kayak during all strokes.

power face—The concave side of the modern European blade that catches the water when moving forward and performing draw strokes.

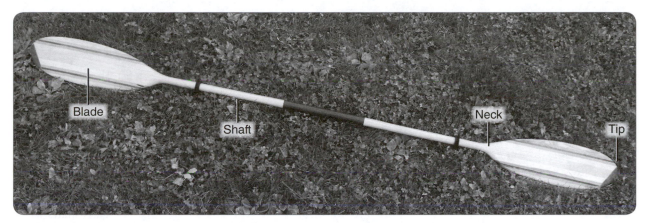

Figure 7.3 Paddle design and components.

back face—The convex side of the modern European blade, often featuring an obvious spine. This secondary surface catches water during reverse strokes.

tip—The sharp edge at the end of the blade. On asymmetrical blades, the most acute angle of the tip marks the top edge of the paddle blade.

Personal Flotation Devices

PFDs should be designed specifically for paddling, properly sized for each student, and worn at all times when on any type of water. A whistle should be lashed to each PFD to relay emergency situations. Type III PFDs approved by the coast guard are required by most governing agencies. Inflatable PFDs are not recommended. Do not substitute other types of flotation devices for ones that are approved by the coast guard. When a student is wearing a PFD, make sure all adjustment points on the PFD are drawn tight for a snug fit.

Spray Skirts (Spray Decks)

Spray skirts cover the cockpit opening and seal in the paddler. Spray skirts are constructed of nylon or neoprene and consist of a tunnel opening for the paddler and a fitted deck attached to the cockpit rim by an elasticized rand (the seamed rim of the spray skirt, which often houses an elastic band). When properly sealed, spray skirts maintain relatively dry conditions inside the cockpit. The tunnel should be sized to fit securely on the paddler's torso below the chest and the deck should be sized to lay flat and snug when attached to the cockpit rim. There must be a convenient and obvious grab loop attached to the skirt where it meets the front of the cockpit rim.

Paddle Float

The paddle float is an inflatable or closed cell foam flotation device that sleeves over and attaches to a paddle blade. It acts as an outrigger for self-rescue and can be used for developing hip snap when students learn braces and rolls. Using the float is considered the most reliable method for deepwater kayak reentry without assistance. Use of the paddle float is described in the lesson plans.

Rescue Sling

The rescue sling is a 12 to 14 ft (3.7-4.3 m) diameter loop of floating rope used to help the capsized paddler in self-rescue or in assisted rescue. The paddler places a foot in the loop, using it like a stirrup to climb back into the kayak.

Bilge Pumps

These hand or mechanical pumps are used to pump excess water out of the cockpit. Hand pumps are small and affordable and can be exchanged easily between two vessels. Use of bilge pumps is described in the lesson plans.

Clothing

Athletic, layered, synthetic, wool, or neoprene clothing provide insulation and a barrier against wind and water and should accommodate water temperatures rather than air temperatures. In cold paddling conditions, consider having students wear wet suits or dry suits to prevent hypothermia. Footwear should be capable of draining water and should protect the heel from chafing. The sole must protect the foot against sharp objects that might be found along the shoreline or underwater, while the upper part should fit over the ankle to keep out sand or rocks. Footwear should fit snugly to allow for proper, comfortable foot positioning on the foot pegs.

Additional Equipment for the Instructor

You should also have some additional safety equipment readily available for students to use at the site. The following safety items are particularly important during sessions on open water and tours. Store them in an accessible location on your kayak.

- **Tow ropes.** At least one instructor in your group should have an accessible tow rope. A tow rope is a releasable rope that attaches to a PFD or belt or a cleat on the aft deck of the towing boat and securely attaches to the bow lines of the vessel being towed. Usually the tow rope is 50 ft (15 m) in length, rigged for adjustable length, and attached via a shock-absorbing pigtail device. It is essential that the device can be released quickly in the event of a vessel capsizing or impending danger to either paddler.

- **Throw bags.** The throw bag typically consists of a 50 ft (15 m) section of floating rope attached to a bag you can toss. In the event you are unable to approach a distressed paddler, you can hold onto one end of the rope while throwing the bag beyond and over the distressed paddler. Keep this device readily accessible.

- **Communication devices.** When touring in patrolled and open bodies of water, carry a portable VHF marine radio to provide access to emergency communication and weather information. This radio allows for sea-to-land, land-to-sea, and vessel-to-vessel communication. Waterproof models with U.S. National Weather Service weather bands and one-touch emergency channel selection are recommended. If you are partnering with another instructor, waterproof two-way radios may be used for instructor-to-instructor communication.

- **Signaling devices.** To help students signal distress, a whistle attached to each individual PFD by a short lashing cord is recommended. When touring, you may elect to bring along signaling mirrors, strobes, flares, and markers that are viewable from overhead.

- **First aid kit.** Carry a comprehensive first aid kit containing all essential field treatment supplies consistent with your medical training, common ailments, and environmental factors. Consider including a hypothermia kit for touring or extended crossings in cold water or weather.

BASIC SKILLS AND TECHNIQUES

Begin instruction with a brief acclimation to the kayak and its associated equipment (as described in the equipment section of this chapter). Then begin fitting the students into suitable kayaks. The deck of the pool offers a suitable location for fitting before launching into the water.

Properly Fitting a Kayak

When in a kayak, the paddler must secure all points of contact for efficient paddling, as secure contact provides the foundation for all stroke work. Much of the kayaker's stroke work is initiated from the lower body. To promote efficient stroke work, have your students

- sit upright with good posture supported by a back band or backrest,
- engage the thighs against the deck or place the thighs in thigh braces with the knees slightly bent,
- position the feet with the heels inward and toes outward and secure the ball of the foot with the foot peg at a neutral angle, and
- secure their position so that movements of the thighs or hips engage the edges of the boat.

Fit like a shoe is often the description of proper fit. Most quality kayaks can be adjusted at all contact points. Figure 7.4 depicts the recommended positioning for paddlers.

Properly Fitting a Paddle

Using a properly sized paddle can have a dramatic effect on kayaking performance and enjoyment of the paddling experience. Take the time to fit each student properly. Use the following steps for fitting a paddle:

1. Have the paddler stand straight while extending an arm overhead.
2. Stand a paddle upright in front of the paddler's outstretched arm.
3. Check to see that the paddler can reach the fingertips of the outstretched arm over the blade of the upright paddle.
4. Consider a slightly longer paddle for wider boats (more than 25 in. or 64 cm).
5. Once students begin using draw strokes and advanced maneuvers in their lessons, adjust paddle length as needed.

Paddle Alignment: Finding Home Position

Proper paddle grip depends on the type of paddle being used. Modern paddles often feature offset blade angles. This allows the blade on one end of the paddle to cut the wind while the blade on the other end engages the water. For traditional in-line blades, neither hand leaves the home position during paddle strokes. With offset blades, the dominant hand stays at the home position while the nondominant hand allows the paddle to rotate freely within its grasp. Each time students practice a new stroke, they should remain in or return to the home position. Proper paddle grip is a foundation for good technique. Encourage the paddlers to maintain a relaxed but secure grip. Figure 7.5 shows the home position for offset blades. Teach students the following tips for aligning the paddle properly:

> **TEACHING TIP**
>
> To label paddles for easy length identification, wrap a short piece of colored electrical tape on both pieces of the paddle shaft. Use different colors for your different lengths of paddle. For example, use blue tape on all 87 in. (220 cm) paddles and red tape on all 91 in. (230 cm) paddles. Students will be better at remembering which color of tape they use rather than which paddle length they use.

Figure 7.4   Paddler positioning.

Figure 7.5   Home position for offset blades.

- **Knuckle alignment.** Align the set of the largest knuckles with the top edge of the paddle blade. This applies to only the dominant hand in offset blades. The opposite or nondominant hand maintains a loose grip that allows the shaft to rotate freely.

- **Spacing.** The junction at the ferule marks the middle of the paddle shaft. Hold the paddle with the paddle blades extended equally when gripped. Position the hands with the palms down and slightly wider than shoulder-width apart.

- **Power face location.** Position the concave side (power face) of the paddle toward the back of your body (on an offset paddle this applies to only the dominant hand).

- **Sharp tip positioning.** On asymmetrical blade designs, the edge that extends the furthest and has the sharpest angle at the blade end is considered the tip. This sharp angle is upward when properly positioned. Often the paddle logo is printed on the blade. Align the blade so that the logo is upright and readable.

Experiential Paddling

Get paddlers into the water early on in the instructional sequence. You can look at a boat and gear for only so long. Students are eager to paddle, and the earlier you engage them, the more productive your instruction will be. Allow time for self-initiated experimentation. Begin with a few playful drills, encouraging paddlers to test the stability of the kayak and its reaction to paddle movements before initiating a formal instructional sequence. Suggestions for playful drills include the following:

- Persuade students to try to turn, go backward, and move sideways using their paddle.

- Encourage students to rock their boat and see how stable it feels.

- Have students test stability by spinning around in their seat, slithering forward on the deck to kiss the bow, and moving back to the cockpit.

- Have students try to trade boats with a partner while floating.

After these drills you are likely to have several tipped boats and wet paddlers. Make sure your students are in waist-deep or deeper water and wearing PFDs. Consider having them use helmets in the pool. Do not underestimate the value of experiential playtime.

Make learning fun! Paddling is not rocket science; it's actually very intuitive. Encourage students to reflect on how different movements of the body and paddle affect the movement of the boat. Use student responses as a springboard into the instructional phase.

Before Learning Paddle Strokes

Before sealing into the cockpit of a kayak and paddling off into the sunset, paddlers need to know how to safely get into and out of a boat in both shallow and deep water. The following sequence of skills (through the wet exit) must be taught before students can begin skirted paddling.

Entering the Kayak

Proper entry and exit may not seem important to new paddlers in shallow, calm waters, but once wind and waves are added, your students will appreciate the skill. Have students practice proper entry every time they enter the kayak. One proven entry technique is to use the paddle to create a kickstand (or outrigger) and to lean slightly onto that side as you enter (figure 7.6):

1. Straddle: Straddle the kayak or sit over the back deck, behind the cockpit.

2. Create a kickstand: Grip the paddle shaft (just in from the neck) and the rear cockpit rim with the inside hand. Extend the remainder of the paddle shaft (power face up) to make firm contact with the shore or bottom of the lake. With the outside hand out over the water, grasp securely down the extended shaft.

3. Slide in: Transfer your weight slightly in the direction of the paddle kickstand. Slide over the backrest and into the seat without raising the hips.

4. Secure: Secure yourself into your braces and pegs. Stash your paddle under multiple soft lines and secure your spray skirt.

Exiting the Kayak

To exit the kayak, reverse the process of entering the kayak.

Launching the Kayak From Poolside or Dockside

Launching from a pool deck can be a challenge for beginning paddlers. Since the kayak is already in rela-

Figure 7.6 Entering the kayak.

tively deep water, the students must lower themselves into the floating boat. Assistance from another student (spotter) may be necessary. The spotter should lie down on the dock or pool deck perpendicular to the kayak and reach across the fore deck with the hand farthest from the cockpit and grasp the front of the cockpit with the near hand. This setup allows the paddler to enter from behind the cockpit in the following manner:

1. Position: Line up the kayak against the pool deck. Place the paddle so that the shaft stretches across the pool deck and the top of the kayak, just behind the cockpit. Sit on the pool deck with the paddle behind you.

2. Brace: Place one hand over the part of the shaft that is on the pool deck and the other hand on the cockpit rim and the part of the paddle that is on top of the kayak.

3. Slide in: Push down on the paddle, lifting your body off the dock, and slide your feet and legs deep into the cockpit as you lower your hips into the seat.

4. Secure: Attach your spray skirt, pick up the paddle, push off from the dock, and away you go!

Surf Launching From a Beach or Shoreline

Launching from a beach or shoreline is referred to as a *surf launch*. It can be performed bow first or stern first (either way the kayak is perpendicular to the shoreline). Bow-first launching offers the opportunity to see oncoming surf and is often the preferred method for new paddlers. Use proper technique for entering the kayak as outlined earlier. Then launch from the beach as follows:

1. Shove off: With your paddle, using both hands, lift and push off of the shoreline or lake bottom, launching the kayak into the water while maintaining a perpendicular orientation.

2. Protect the paddle: Do not use the paddle blade to shove off. It is likely to break under these forces.

3. Avoid bridging: Bridging, or creating airspace between the bottom of the kayak and the water or shore, dramatically increases the chances of capsizing. Avoid bridging by moving the kayak further into or out of the water or relocating to a more gradual slope.

Spray Skirt Attachment

To attach the spray skirt use the following sequence of skills (and see figure 7.7). Instructional cues are in bold.

1. Knot under: While seated in the kayak, secure the back of the spray skirt under the back of the cockpit rim.

2. Rand around: Work forward as you secure the rand around the cockpit until the back half is secured.

3. Elbows secure: Using your forearms to secure the midpoint, stretch the remaining rand over the front of the cockpit. Secure the entire rand under the cockpit rim.

4. Buddy smiling: Make sure the grab (buddy) loop is fully exposed when the skirt is sealed to the cockpit.

5. Take off: Pick up the paddle, push off from the dock, and away you go!

Wet Exit

The wet exit is a technique for underwater escape from a skirted and capsized (overturned) kayak. When teaching students this technique, emphasize the five *Ts:* tuck, tap, tug, trousers, and together.

1. Tuck: While tipping, lean forward as if touching your toes, and secure the paddle in your hand or armpit to prevent it from separating from you during the wet exit.

2. Tap: While capsized, tap three times on the hull of the boat as a distress signal. This also helps to calm you and gather yourself for the final steps. Three taps = "I'm-O-K."

3. Tug: Find the grab loop by running your hands along the combing toward the fore deck. Grab the loop, pull it forward, and release the skirt from the rim and back toward your body.

4. Trousers: Remove yourself from the boat in a manner similar to that of taking off a pair of trousers (pants).

5. Together: Emerge from the water with both the paddle and the boat secure at hand.

After the students successfully execute the wet exit, guide them through draining their boat. Then you can take them through proper deepwater reentry.

Draining a Boat With Dual Bulkheads

Kayaks equipped with dual bulkheads can be drained easily by lifting the capsized kayak at the bow end. To drain the kayak, go through the following steps:

Figure 7.7   Attaching the spray skirt.

1. Drag the bow of the overturned boat to water that is waist or shoulder deep.

2. Squat under the bow in a lifting position.

3. Place the bow end over your shoulder.

4. Wrap your arms around the front of the hull to secure it.

5. Stand up slowly while the seal between the cockpit and the water surface breaks. Use good squatting form (do not lift with your back).

6. Lift the bow high; the stern will float.

7. Allow the water to hit the rear bulkhead and drain out the rear of the cockpit.

8. Carefully return the boat to the surface, turning it upright.

9. Use a bilge pump or sponge out excess water.

Reentry (Deep Water)

The technique for deepwater reentry remains the same whether you are aided by a rescuer or an outrigger device such as a paddle float. To perform a deepwater reentry, hoist yourself belly down onto the aft deck with your head toward the stern. Slide toward the stern until you can place your legs into the cockpit, and then slide in toward the bow until your hips are over the seat. Fluidly, turn your hips into a seated position while facing your support.

Boat Boogie-Woogie and Intro to J-Lean

Early on in the instructional sequence, encourage new paddlers to feel how their hips and legs can control and edge the kayak. Have your students practice the boat boogie-woogie by inviting them to wiggle the boat from edge to edge while keeping their torso upright. Next, invite students to try to hold each edge for a few seconds. This position, when performed with the paddler in an upright posture, is referred to as a *J-lean* (for the J-like shape created by the hips and torso). The J-lean will be useful during stroke refinements taught later in the instructional sequence. It also gives paddlers confidence in the stability that kayaks offer, even when placed on edge.

PADDLE STROKES

You may wish to begin the paddle stroke progression with the sweep stroke, both to emphasize its significance and to emphasize the importance of torso rotation in all strokes. All strokes share three phases: catch, power, and recovery. These terms, as well as others you'll need to know for paddling instruction, are defined in the following section.

General Paddle Stroke Concepts

catch phase—The initiation of the paddle stroke by inserting the blade into the water.

power phase—The phase in which the path of the paddle face is directed through the water.

prehip power phase—The portion of the paddle stroke performed in front of the paddler's hip. This motion causes the kayak to move forward.

posthip power phase—The portion of the paddle stroke performed behind the paddler's hip. This motion causes the kayak to turn in a direction opposite of the water arm.

recovery phase—The phase in which the blade is slid from the water and returned to the catch.

water arm—The arm closest to the inserted blade.

deck arm—The arm farthest from the inserted blade.

pretorque—Prerotating the torso in the opposite direction of the stroke to allow for a more pronounced rotation during the stroke.

paddler's box—An imaginary box in front of the paddler's chest that is outlined by the paddler's arms, the paddle shaft, and the paddler's chest. Maintaining this box requires torso rotation rather than wide arm swings that may encourage injury. The box follows the stroke, therefore necessitating good torso alignment and rotation during paddling strokes.

shaft angle—The angle of the shaft during paddle strokes changes the efficiency of the stroke. Efficient draw strokes require the shaft to be almost perpendicular to the water surface, while efficient sweep strokes demand a very low angle to the water surface. Touring strokes utilize shaft angles in between.

> ### TEACHING TIP
> When teaching paddle strokes, remind students to "watch their work," or to follow the path of their paddle blade with their eyes. Their head and upper torso will follow naturally. This will help them get acclimated to correct torso rotation.

Forward Sweep Stroke

The forward sweep stroke is used to turn or correct the bow of the kayak in the opposite direction of the water arm. Therefore emphasis during the power phase should be behind the hip. Figure 7.8 illustrates a proper forward sweep stroke, which should be performed as follows:

1. Pretorque: Create pretorque by coiling your torso in the opposite direction of the paddle stroke. While maintaining the paddler's box, catch the blade parallel to the side of the kayak near your foot peg.

2. Straight water arm: Maintain a nearly straight water arm throughout the entire stroke.

3. Shallow blade and low shaft: Maintain a low shaft angle by keeping the hand of your deck arm close to the kayak deck. The blade should be just under the surface of the water.

4. Torso guides the big C: Uncoil your torso throughout the power phase, emphasizing the posthip power phase. Guide the paddle blade in a wide C until the blade nearly touches the stern.

5. Recovery: Recover by slicing the blade from the water and returning it to a position for the next stroke.

6. Enhancement: A J-lean toward the paddle stroke dramatically increases the pivot of the kayak, requiring less strokes to complete rotation.

Reverse Sweep Stroke

A reverse sweep is the opposite of the forward sweep. This motion draws the kayak bow toward the water arm. To complete a reverse sweep, use the forward sweep motion with some slight modifications:

1. Coil: Create pretorque over the back deck.

2. Catch: Present the back face of the paddle flat to the water, next to the stern of the boat. The flat face offers a slight brace and keeps the boat steady in this somewhat compromising position.

3. Power phase: Rotate the blade as you initiate the sweep to present the back face of the blade, moving the blade through a wide arc, or C, until the blade is forward of your torso and next to the bow near the location of your foot peg.

4. Recovery: Recover and prepare for the next stroke.

Forward Touring Stoke

This stroke causes the kayak to proceed forward and is the stroke most commonly used for kayak touring (figure 7.9). Since all the emphasis is on forward motion, the power phase should be performed in front of the hip:

1. Tip to hip: Pretorque slightly and catch the paddle blade perpendicular to the kayak just shy of full extension. Recover at the hip and prepare the opposite blade for the catch.

2. Straight water arm: Maintain only a slight bend in the water arm during the power phase.

3. Trunk rotation: Untorque through the prehip power phase.

4. Chin high: The hand of your deck arm should travel parallel to the deck at approximately chin height during the power phase, but it should not cross the midline of the deck.

5. Other side: Repeat on the other side. If using an offset paddle, cock the wrist of your control hand back

Figure 7.8   The sweep stroke.

toward you as you bring the opposite blade forward and into the water.

Reverse Touring Stroke

This stroke is used for reversing direction and stopping forward progress of the boat. The following steps are used to perform the reverse touring stroke:

1. **Reverse:** Reverse the process of the forward touring stroke.

2. **Catch:** Catch well behind the hip.

3. **Apply:** Apply the power phase with the back face (never rotate the paddle out of home position).

4. **Recover:** Recover just forward of the hip.

Draw Stroke

This stroke causes the kayak to travel sideways without progressing forward or backward. Figure 7.10 depicts the draw stroke. An overaggressive draw can cause a quick capsize. To prevent this, release the deck hand if the kayak becomes unsteady.

1. **Rotate square:** Rotate your torso toward the intended direction of travel until your shoulders are square to the side of the kayak.

2. **Perpendicular reach:** Catch the paddle with a reach out from your hip and insert the blade with the edges parallel to the kayak. The shaft angle should be nearly perpendicular. Maintain a perpendicular path through the power phase as the blade is drawn toward the kayak to within a few inches of the boat.

3. **Read your watch:** Maintain your upper hand (deck hand) at a fixed point (just in front of your head) throughout the entire motion, as if you were reading your wristwatch while performing the stroke.

There are two options for recovery during the draw stroke:

1. **Drop to the deck above water:** Drop your deck hand to the deck. This causes the paddle to slice out of the water without encountering resistance. Return the paddle blade to the catch of the next stroke.

Figure 7.9 The forward touring stroke.

Figure 7.10   The draw stroke.

2. Knife away underwater: Rotate your wrist inward until the edges of the submerged blade are perpendicular to the boat. Push the blade straight out in a path perpendicular to the boat. Open your wrist to return the submerged blade to parallel and repeat the stroke.

BRACING

Bracing is a stability technique used to right an unsteady or overturning craft or to secure the boat in wavy conditions. When bracing, you apply a flat paddle blade against the surface of the water to brace the craft.

Low Brace

A low brace, the most common and practical of the two braces, can be performed quickly from home position in the midst of a paddling stroke, should the craft begin to tip. It is a quick and ready way to gain equilibrium. The cues *push-up, slap, snap,* and *slice* describe the four phases of this skill:

1. Push-up: Cock your wrist to present the back face of your paddle blade to the water surface. Move your elbows above your hands, as in a push-up position.

2. Slap: Lay the back face of the paddle blade on the water surface.

3. Snap: Snap your hips against the brace to regain an upright position.

4. Slice: Cock your wrist to slice the paddle (edge first) out of the water.

High Brace

The high brace is a more aggressive bracing technique that is applied against oncoming waves or as the over-turning paddler approaches the water surface. When applied against the upward forces of an oncoming wave, the brace can hold a paddler on the surface of the water while the kayak is pushed by the surf. This technique is commonly used when breached against a wave. The cues *pull-up, slap, snap,* and *slice* describe the four phases of this skill:

1. Pull-up: Drop your elbows, raise your hands, and cock your wrist to present the power face of your paddle blade to the water surface. Hold your elbows down and your hands above your elbows as in a pull-up position.

2. Slap: Lay the power face flat on the top of the oncoming wave or water surface.

3. Snap: Snap your hips against the brace to regain an upright position.

4. Slice: Cock your wrist to slice the paddle (edge first) out of the water.

RESCUES

As paddlers grow more independent, rescue skills become an essential addition to a paddler's repertoire.

Independent paddlers should be competent at both self-rescue and assisted rescue. Though paddlers are discouraged from paddling alone, especially over large, open bodies of water, self-rescue is important when the paddling partner has insufficient assisted rescue skills. In the event of a capsize, assisted rescue is faster and more efficient than self-rescue. The following rescue techniques offer a strong foundation for recreational paddlers. In addition to the paddle-float self-rescue, the bombproof Eskimo roll is the most efficient technique of self-rescue. The Eskimo roll is included in the advanced techniques section of this chapter.

 Day 8

Self-Rescue: Paddle-Float Reentry

Although solo paddling in open water is discouraged, there are times when a paddler may need self-rescue, such as when a paddler gets separated from other paddlers or when paddling partners lack rescue skills. In these situations, a paddle-float self-rescue is a reliable reentry. This reentry is illustrated in figure 7.11. After a wet exit, the paddler should be in the together position, with the capsized boat and paddle in hand. This is the position from which a paddle-float reentry is performed. There are five major phases of the paddle-float reentry: control and create the outrigger, upright the kayak, apply the outrigger, perform deepwater reentry, and secure to paddle.

1. Gain control and create the outrigger by performing the following steps:
   - Using the hard (deck) lines, position yourself so that you are facing the cockpit of the capsized vessel.
   - Hang one leg inside the cockpit to maintain contact with the boat while you use both your hands to create the outrigger.
   - Pull the paddle float from the soft lines on the kayak. Sleeve it over one paddle blade and affix the strap around the shaft.
   - Inflate all the float air chambers and seal the valve.

2. Upright the kayak by performing the following steps:
   - Pull your leg out of the cockpit and grab the boat with the paddle corralled between you and the cockpit.
   - Reach underwater and grab the cockpit rim by both sides.

   - Preventing excess water flow into the cockpit, rock the kayak to break the seal. Pull the far side toward your torso to right the boat.

3. Apply the outrigger as follows:
   - Place the part of the paddle shaft that is near the bare blade on the aft deck just behind the cockpit rim.
   - Make sure the paddle float stretches out over the water at a perpendicular angle to the kayak so it can be used as an outrigger.

4. Perform the deepwater reentry by performing the following steps:
   - Position yourself on the stern side of the paddle shaft, being sure to maintain the paddle position.
   - Maintain a perpendicular paddle while you use a scissors kick to hoist your torso, belly down, onto the aft deck.
   - Keep your center of gravity toward the paddle. Maintain the perpendicular orientation of the paddle as well as paddle shaft contact at all times during reentry.
   - Transfer your inside leg into the cockpit while transferring your outside leg onto the paddle shaft.
   - Transfer your second leg into the cockpit while transferring your outside hand to hold the paddle in position.
   - Keep your belly and hips down as you slide your hips over the seat. Maintain a weighted paddle float.
   - Facing the weighted paddle float, turn your hips upright into the seat.

5. Secure to paddle by performing the following steps:
   - Move the paddle ahead of your body (the paddle should still be perpendicular, as an outrigger).
   - Pump out excess water with the bilge pump. Squeezing the pump between your legs will allow two-handed operation.
   - Affix your spray skirt.
   - Deflate, detach, and stow the paddle float.

TEACHING TIP
A partner's kayak, even when capsized, can be an extremely stable platform to brace against. Any time you feel tippy during a rescue, simply lean toward the capsized boat and use it to regain your balance.

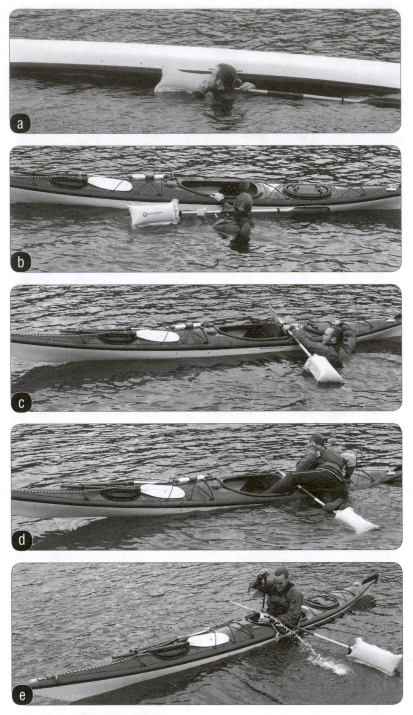

Figure 7.11   The paddle-float reentry.

Assisted Rescue: T-Rescue

Once a capsized paddler performs a wet exit and is in the together position, a T-rescue can commence. There are four major steps to a T-rescue: approach and control, upright the kayak, align for deepwater reentry, and secure the paddler (see figure 7.12).

1. Approach and control by performing the following steps:

- Track a perpendicular approach to the bow of the capsized kayak, reassure the distressed paddler, and grab the bow of the overturned boat. Maintain a perpendicular orientation.

Figure 7.12 The T-rescue.

- Stash your paddle under multiple soft lines and coach the distressed paddler to retain contact as he swims to the stern of the capsized vessel.

2. Upright the kayak by performing the following steps:

- On a clear signal, have the distressed paddler push down on the stern of his kayak while you lift the bow over the deck of your kayak.
- Work the kayak up onto your deck until the cockpit clears the water, and allow the water to drain off of the rear bulkhead.
- Lift and rotate the kayak upright. Use the kayak as an outrigger at any time you feel unstable, so distribute your weight slightly in that direction.

3. Align for deepwater reentry by performing the following steps:

- Align the two boats bow to stern, and grab the front of the cockpit with one hand as you wrap the other over the fore deck to give it a strong hug. Leaning onto the kayak is the most secure position.
- Coach the distressed paddler into a deepwater reentry position, and stash his paddle in your soft lines.
- Have the distressed paddler perform a deepwater reentry as you steady the boat. It is often helpful for the paddler to use your hard lines during the reentry.

4. Secure the paddler by performing the following steps:

- Continue to secure the distressed boat as the paddler pumps excess water, affixes his spray skirt, and returns to paddling position.
- Release the boat once the paddler is secure.

Assisted Rescue: Reenter and Pump

When conditions such as wind, waves, or a heavy tandem kayak make a T-rescue difficult, a reenter and pump may be the best rescue method (figure 7.13). The steps for a reenter and pump are similar to those used for the T-rescue, but they are performed with the two kayaks in a parallel position.

1. Approach and control by performing the following steps:

- Approach broadside to the distressed kayak, preferably in opposite orientation (so the two kayaks are aligned bow to stern).
- Reassure the distressed paddler and coach her to retain connection to the boat as she swims to the opposite side of the kayak near the cockpit.

2. Upright the kayak by performing the following steps:

- Flip the kayak toward you and into an upright position.

Figure 7.13   The reenter and pump rescue.

- Secure the kayak as in the T-rescue.

3. Perform deepwater reentry by performing the following steps:

- Coach the distressed paddler into a deepwater reentry position, and stash her paddle in your soft lines.
- Coach the distressed paddler through a deepwater reentry into the flooded cockpit.

4. Secure and assist the paddler by performing the following steps:

Continue to secure the boat as the distressed paddler pumps excess water, affixes her spray skirt, and returns to paddling position.

Release the boat once the paddler is secure.

ENHANCEMENTS AND ADVANCEMENTS

Once your students acquire the strong foundational skills discussed in the preceding sections of this chapter, the fun has just begun. The following sections describe more-refined skills for advancing paddlers.

Enhancing the Strokes (J-lean)

Holding your boat on edge while performing sweep and draw strokes and making slight corrections during your touring stroke adds a new dimension to your paddling skills. The edge of your boat is more rounded and therefore causes less friction on the water surface. Thus holding on edge can be very advantageous. In the J-lean, you use your hips to tilt the boat while you keep your upper body perpendicular to the water surface. With an upright torso and a tilted hip, your body is in the shape of the letter *J*.

1. Tilt your hips in the direction of your water arm. You should feel your offside thigh engage while your onside thigh relaxes a bit.

2. Maintain an upright posture, with your torso perpendicular to the water surface. Together, tipping your hips and keeping an upright posture will tilt your deck downward in the direction of your water arm and lean your boat on edge.

3. Hold the J-lean through the catch and power phases of each stroke.

4. If you feel unsteady, use a low brace to return your hull to a flat orientation.

Subtle Corrections Against Weather Cocking

Wind and waves usually influence your direction by pushing the stern, causing your kayak to weather cock, which occurs when your bow pivots into the prevailing wind. Rather than using corrective strokes to keep your kayak tracking toward your destination, you can apply a knee hang or an offset paddle grip against the prevailing forces.

- **Knee hang.** This is a sustained J-lean on the opposite side of the direction you wish to correct. For example, meet a wind blowing at the starboard side with a J-lean toward the port side. This allows less friction when paddling on the port side and causes the kayak to arc against the wind and maintain a straighter path.

- **Offset paddle grip.** Slide both of your hands down the shaft of the paddle, toward the source of the wind. Thus, if the wind is coming at starboard, less of your shaft is exposed on the starboard side and more is exposed on the port side. This position offers more paddle leverage to be exerted against the wind.

Advanced Techniques

The following advanced techniques offer more fluid and efficient maneuvers for drawing, turning, and self-rescue. All require extensive practice and comfort with balancing the kayak on edge (J-lean) in order to be safely and effectively applied in open water.

Sculling Draw

The sculling draw is a more advanced and fluid method of causing the kayak to travel sideways. The following steps are used to perform the sculling draw:

1. Rotate your torso and catch in draw position, with the paddle shaft nearly perpendicular to the surface of the water.

2. Angle the power face slightly toward the oncoming water.

3. Swivel your torso toward bow and stern.

4. Direct the paddle blade through approximately a 2 ft (0.6 m) arc across the catch point. As you resist the force against the paddle blade, you will begin to travel sideways.

Low Brace Turn

When the kayak has some forward momentum, it can be turned without stroke work by applying a low brace turn. This graceful maneuver effects a fluid and efficient turning motion that saves energy:

1. Gain forward momentum using several forward touring strokes.

2. Place your paddle blade with the back face down in a low brace position at a 45° angle toward the stern.

3. J-lean toward your water arm; the paddle blade will offer plenty of upward lift. The kayak will turn in the direction of your brace.

Eskimo Roll

The Eskimo roll is probably the most notable skill in kayaking. It is a quick, beautiful, and skillful technique of self-rescue that is used in the event of a capsize. Considerable practice is required to master the counterintuitive motion of the Eskimo roll. Strong bracing and hip snaps are prerequisites. There are many forms and techniques of the roll. The C-to-C roll is a reliable method that offers a foundation for other advanced roll techniques. Although it is not the easiest roll to perform, its steps are distinguishable and can be practiced independently. Most paddlers discover that their brace is stronger on one side of the kayak than on the other. The stronger brace side is often unrelated to the paddler's dominant hand. Students will be more likely to succeed in their roll if they begin learning on their strong side.

The C-to-C roll is named for the body orientation at the beginning and end of the roll. A sideways curl at the beginning of the roll ends in a sideways curl in the opposite direction at the end of the roll. The following steps are illustrated in figure 7.14:

1. **Set up.** Lean forward with your paddle shaft touching the water and directly parallel to the kayak on the opposite side of your strongest brace.

2. **Capsize.** Lean onto your paddle as the boat and your paddle rotate through the capsize, continuing until your hands break the surface of the water.

3. **Sweep out.** Bring your forward hand into a high brace position on the top of the water. Your opposing-side paddle shaft and blade remain over the hull of the boat.

4. **Hip snap and head dink.** Using the power face to brace, snap your hips up to level while trailing with your head. This will force the boat upright.

5. **Follow through.** Maintain a trailing head (head dink) as you stare down the paddle shaft and assume a secure, upright position.

SAFETY CONSIDERATIONS

Venturing into open water requires observation and organization as well as a thorough knowledge of the local hazards. Instructors and paddlers should always consider the following as they explore waterways.

Pod Travel

When touring with a group, it can be difficult to maintain an agreeable pace and close proximity and to keep a rescue instructor in position to identify and respond to a distressed paddler quickly. Pod travel is one method of dealing effectively with the challenges of group touring. The following are recommendations for maintaining a tight pod:

• **Paddler proximity.** Your group members should be tight enough to converse without raising their voices. A tight pod resembles a bunch of grapes.

• **Point.** A pace boat, referred to as the *point,* should lead the way. The point is the navigating kayak and must go slow enough to keep the group intact. Pair the point boat with one of the slower paddlers to set the pace. The point paddler should be patient and have strong navigating skills.

• **Sweep.** The trailing boat, or sweep, should keep the group intact from the rear. The sweep is the rescue boat in the event of a straying paddler or capsized kayak. Choose the paddler who is the most experienced and proficient with rescue skills as the sweep paddler.

• **Rafting.** For instruction, water or snack breaks, rescues, and preventing separation in dangerous seas, raft the kayaks. Bring the boats together, face the same direction, and hold the kayaks together using deck lines or paddles across the bows. Watch for paddle collisions and advise paddlers to keep their hands from between the boats to prevent injury as waves toss the boats about. This raft formation also offers an organized opportunity for instruction.

Figure 7.14 The C-to-C Eskimo roll.

Hazards

Each paddling environment offers a unique set of risks and a different prevalence and intensity of hazardous environmental factors. Paddlers must assess these and other factors and formulate a risk management plan before embarking on their paddling adventures. When formulating your plan, start with the most common factors to consider, which are the five *Ws*:

- **Wind.** Strong winds can make paddling very difficult and can quickly separate paddlers from the group.

- **Waves.** Waves are the most common cause of capsize and are very difficult to maneuver within. Avoid wavy conditions with beginners.

- **Weather.** Thunderstorms in particular offer no easy escape for paddlers. It is particularly important to stay abreast of weather conditions when crossing open water or paddling along shorelines without easy escape.

- **Watercraft.** Although the smaller craft has the right of way when two watercraft meet, paddlers should never assume that they are seen or that other watercraft will avoid them.

- **Water temperature.** Immersion in cold water can initiate hypothermia very quickly, and a distressed paddler can lose motor control, lose consciousness, or face worse in a very short time.

The following bulleted list contains additional hazards to consider:

• **Tide and current.** Do not venture into tidal waters without sufficient training. Strong currents can prevent you from paddling in the desired direction. Know the conditions in which you paddle.

• **Marine critters.** Be aware of potential aquatic wildlife hazards. Know precautions, appropriate reactions, and injury treatment.

CONCLUSION

Coastal kayaking remains one of the fastest-growing outdoor pursuits in the United States. A quality invitation into the world of paddling can launch a lifetime of enjoyment for physical education students. The ACA and British Canoe Union (BCU) offer materials, training, and certifications to increase your confidence in your paddling instruction.

RECOMMENDED WEB SITES

Governing Agencies for Coastal Kayak Instruction

American Canoe Association (ACA): www.americancanoe.org
British Canoe Union (BCU): www.bcu.org.uk

Instructional Book, Video, Technique, Destination, and Product Information

Paddling.net: www.paddling.net
Sea Kayaker Magazine: www.seakayakermag.com
University of Sea Kayaking: www.useakayak.org

COASTAL KAYAKING UNIT PLAN

General Lesson Information

Each lesson contains the following seven elements:

1. Objectives—primary learning outcomes
2. Equipment—specific materials and gear and paddling location suggestions for the lesson
3. Introduction—skill focus and overall emphasis of the lesson
4. Warm-ups—routine to stretch or strengthen muscles and tendons specific to paddling
5. Central activities—activity progressions that increase in difficulty and lead to more advanced skills while considering the most constructive use of the paddling location (e.g., confined but controlled warm water environment of a pool)
6. Closure—suggested discussion and reflection items
7. Assessment—examples of evaluation strategies

Day 1

Focus: Nomenclature, equipment fitting and selection

- History
- Kayak design
- Boat component and accessory identification
- Paddle fitting
- Kayak fitting and customized adjustments

Day 2

Focus: Kayak acclimation

- Experiential paddling
- Boat acclimation drills
- Play

Day 3

Focus: Entry and escape

- Solo entry and exit procedures
- Spray skirt fitting and attachment
- Poolside launches
- Wet exit
- Boat draining
- Deepwater reentry

Day 4

Focus: Introduction to paddle strokes

- Paddle alignment
- Paddle grip home position
- Paddle stroke fundamentals
- Boat boogie-woogie and J-lean
- Forward sweep
- Reverse sweep
- Pinwheel turns

Day 5

Focus: Strokes and bracing

- Draw stroke
- Low brace
- High brace

Day 6

Focus: Skills and strokes for open water

- Launching and landing in open water
- Forward touring
- Reverse touring and stopping

Day 7

Focus: Skills for touring on open water

- Pod travel
- Rafting
- Safety considerations and hazards
- Short tour

Day 8

Focus: Deepwater rescue

- Paddle-float rescue
- T-rescue

Day 9

Focus: Coastal kayak touring

- Sustained paddling over a significant distance for skill application and fitness
- Exploring the natural environment

Day 10

Focus: Written test and expert demonstration

- Advanced skill demonstration
- Hip snap development for the Eskimo roll

chapter 8

Orienteering and Geocaching

Daniel L. Chase

Jeff Steffen

Jim Stiehl

Those who wander aren't necessarily lost.

Jeff Crabtree

For centuries, wanderers searching for adventure have plotted and plodded from point to point, on land and water, using the tools available for their times: sun, stars, astrolabes, gyroscopes, sextants, and radar. These and other means for navigation guided them to their destination and, most importantly, guided them back home again. An old navigational standby has been the map and compass, while a relative newcomer is the satellite.

Children are naturally curious, adventuresome people. This chapter provides a basis for introducing them to two navigational instruments, the compass for orienteering and the GPS device for geocaching, that they can use to satisfy their natural inclination to discover new treasures in the outdoors.

INTRODUCTION TO ORIENTEERING

Orienteering is a sport that involves running or walking while thinking and that usually combines compass use (though not always) with map reading. In orienteering, participants navigate their way through unfamiliar territory, moving from one point to another. Orienteering originated in Scandinavia in the 19th century as a military training exercise. It was not until 1919 that Ernst Killander introduced orienteering to Sweden as a competitive sport. Killander's introduction of competitive orienteering marked a distinction between military training and sport. This distinction earned him the title of *Father of Orienteering*. The sport of orienteering spread throughout Sweden in the 1930s and was later introduced to the United States by one of Sweden's premier orienteering champions, Björn Kjellström (Boga, 1997). Although orienteering has not gained the popularity in the United States that it has seen in some European countries (it is a national pastime in Norway and Finland), introducing orienteering in physical education is one way to promote this lifelong physical activity. Furthermore, the requisite skills, map reading and compass use, can be applied in other outdoor activities such as hiking, backpacking, canoeing, and so on.

Many definitions exist for the term *orienteering*. Often in the early stages of incorporating the activity into the physical education curriculum, the definition of orienteering is overlapped or blurred with map and compass instruction. The principle of orienteering is simple and familiar to anyone who has been on a scavenger hunt: Using a map (and sometimes a compass), students seek out a series of checkpoints, also known as *controls* (sites marked with small flags), that must be visited in a specified order and in the shortest time possible. While there is a distinction between orienteering and learning map and compass skills, this chapter focuses specifically on the latter. The reason for this is threefold. First, map and compass skills are requisite for orienteering. Second, a single chapter in a book cannot begin to fully explain the sport of orienteering. For that, there are a number of orienteering books. Third, many schools are not fortunate enough to have access to great orienteering locales, such as wooded areas, and for these schools teaching basic map and compass skills is more appropriate for their physical education curriculum. Students not only will be able to use these new skills in other outdoor pursuits but also will be ready to pursue orienteering inside and outside of the classroom.

Orienteering, one of the most exciting and satisfying outdoor activities, requires very little specialized equipment, can be supervised by a single teacher, and appeals to both genders and all ages. Orienteering can begin with second graders, who can be taught the basic ideas indoors (this presents a great opportunity to collaborate with the classroom teacher!). Then, using newly acquired skills to navigate easy terrain such as school grounds and local parks, students can progress to more challenging and unfamiliar fields, woods, and hills. Furthermore, by incorporating orienteering into physical education, educators have the potential to address most of the NASPE (2004) standards.

Orienteering is a relatively inexpensive activity with minimal risks. All of the fundamental skills can be taught both indoors and outdoors; however, an outdoor setting offers a more authentic experience. The benefits associated with orienteering include an opportunity to improve physical, psychological, and social well-being through appropriate decision making, problem solving, and cooperating with others while navigating a course. In addition, incorporating orienteering into physical education classes provides the opportunity for

- mental challenge,
- physical challenge,
- increased self-confidence,
- better team-building skills,
- an introduction to lifelong activity,
- fun, and
- well-honed map and compass skills.

The following sections provide detailed information on teaching map and compass skills as well as suggestions on how to create an orienteering course in your school yard. The first section, which is on maps, includes specific information on map features and understanding and reading maps. The next section, the compass section, begins with a brief description of major compass parts, explains how the compass functions, and then concludes with a tutorial on how to teach students to be successful using a compass. The next section, which is on combining map and compass, is a continuation of the previous sections and specifically explains how to use a map and compass together. The final section, which is on orienteering, provides information on how to develop an orienteering course for your school yard and then

- indicates how orienteering aligns with NASPE standards both through instruction and content,
- suggests variations by which you can change activities to match different audiences, and
- provides a reference list (at end of chapter) to help you search for more ideas.

EQUIPMENT

One of the greatest aspects of incorporating orienteering in physical education is that it requires very little specialized equipment, maps, and compasses. In fact, a dozen hand-drawn maps of an outside area alone can provide weeks of exploration and discovery. Adding inexpensive compasses and more detailed maps to your lessons can provide countless opportunities for learning and fun.

Maps

Simply stated, a map is a condensed representation of an area of the earth's surface. Maps are everywhere in our world and when used correctly can be of great assistance. For example, a map of an amusement park can help you determine the shortest route to a favorite thrill ride, a city map can aid you in finding your way through unfamiliar roadways, and a hiking trail map can keep you from getting lost during an outing in the woods. Each of these examples describes a favorable outcome; however, many times a simple mistake can result in a less-than-desirable outcome. Take, for instance, the following story of a child traveling with his family on a road trip from Massachusetts to Delaware one summer.

As a 9-year-old there was nothing more exciting than being on the open road with my parents, brother, and sister. As the youngest child I was usually offered the middle of the front seat, between my two parents. I cannot remember why it felt so great to ride up front. Certainly there was a lot more room in the back of the 1970s station wagon, but I would always jump at the opportunity to be part of the navigational team. This choice to sit up front is one that I would soon regret. As my dad was driving through an unknown area late at night he quickly flung a map over me to my mom and asked her which way he needed to turn at the next block. My mom was barely awake at the time and she ended up making one of the most

common errors in map reading: She held the map upside down. Unbeknownst to her, she gave my dad a number of directions that were wrong. I remember my dad driving around the same area for hours that night and I remember feeling somewhat responsible because I was part of this team. I share this story not to point out my mom's inability to read a map but to point out the fact that this simple, common mistake, one made by many, can have negative consequences. Perhaps if my mom had been given the time to look closely at the map features, such as buildings and street names, our hours of driving in circles could have been avoided.

No matter what type of map you are reading, you must have an understanding of what you are doing in order to be successful. As described in the story, orienting the map correctly is one key to success. The rest of this section explains key map features to assist you in understanding how to read maps.

Although basic maps (of local parks, city streets, school grounds, and so on) can be used for simple orienteering instruction, topographic maps are used in more advanced orienteering. Topographic maps are a special drawing of the terrain or an aerial view of the land (figure 8.1) and use contour lines to portray the three-dimensional nature of terrain on a two-dimensional surface. Contour lines are brown in color and connect points of equal elevation; therefore, contour lines never overlap or touch. Every fifth contour line (an interval contour line) is heavier in color and numbered to show the elevation along that line. Topographic maps also include a contour interval that lets readers know the distance between contour lines. For example, if the contour interval is 16 ft (5 m), you can expect to gain or lose 16 ft (5 m) in elevation for each line you cross.

While contour lines can be helpful for finding the path of least resistance, understanding and reading contour lines is an advanced skill that is perhaps beyond the scope of this book. At this point, beginners should remember that the closer the contour lines are to one another, the steeper is the terrain. Use the lesson plan for day 1 of the orienteering unit (on the accompanying CD-ROM) to help students better understand the abstract concept of contours.

Other key features common to most topographic maps include a compass rose that depicts north, east, south, and west; a map legend that describes what the various colors and symbols represent; the name of the

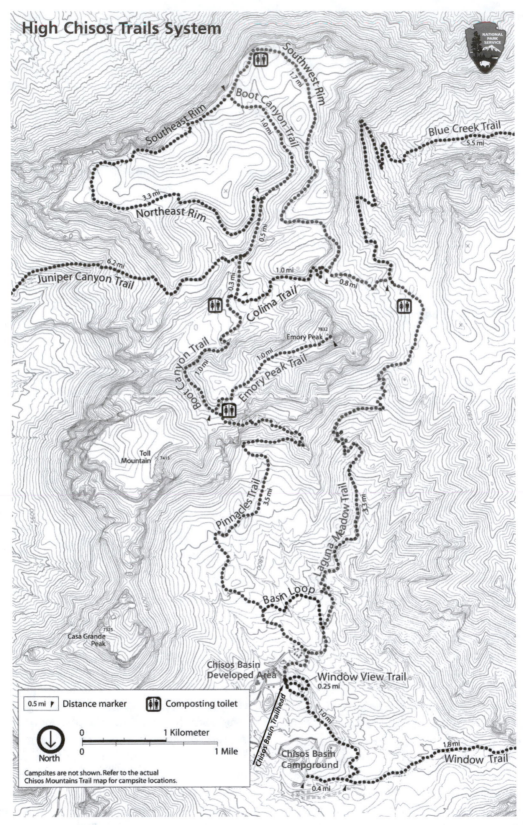

Figure 8.1 A topographic map.

From the USGS.

map; a map scale explaining the ratio between distances on the map and distances in real life; and sometimes a distinction between true north and magnetic north (magnetic declination).

Orienteering maps are simply a specialized type of topographic map depicting a smaller section of the earth's surface in greater detail (figure 8.2). Orienteering maps used in competitions depict a smaller area and show finer details such as big boulders, small hills, slight depressions, and so on. A useful starting point to understand the features on a map is to look at the map legend.

The legend explains what certain features represent. More specifically, the legend describes what common colors represent. For instance, the color black represents manmade features, blue represents water features, green represents vegetation, and brown represents elevation features. Other features, such as a church, cemetery, telephone pole, stream, and so on, are represented by particular map symbols (see the lesson plan for day 1 of the orienteering unit on the accompanying CD-ROM for map symbols). You can also find map symbols at http://egsc.usgs.gov/isb/pubs/booklets/symbols/#4.

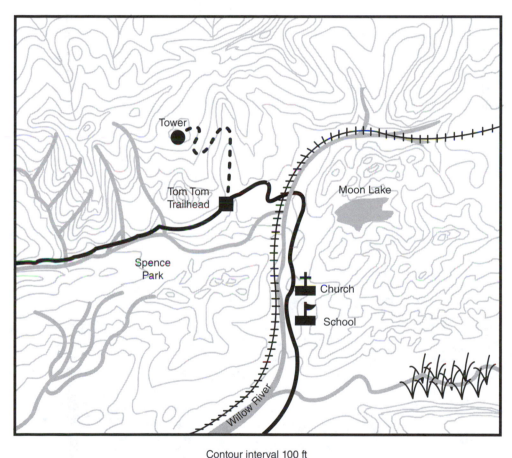

Contour interval 100 ft

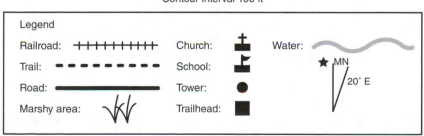

Figure 8.2   An orienteering map.

Reprinted from C. Bunting, 2005, *Interdisciplinary teaching through outdoor education* (Champaign, IL: Human Kinetics), 113.

Compass

The protractor compass is probably the most widely used compass in outdoor pursuits. These compasses are relatively inexpensive ($8-$12 U.S.), last for years, and are common in physical education programs. Although many orienteering competitors may never use their compass during an event, learning how to use a compass is easy and can prove beneficial. For instance, a compass can be used to orient a map when features do not allow for orienting. Learning how to use a compass begins with understanding its basic function and major components (see figure 8.3).

base plate—The transparent rectangular plate that all compass parts sit on and that allows the user to see features on the map. The base plate usually has a ruler on its short and long edge.

magnetic north needle—The magnetic needle inside the capsule that always points to magnetic north when the compass is held flat and away from metal objects.

direction-of-travel arrow—The arrow affixed on the base plate and used to point out the direction of travel.

orienting lines—Also referred to as *north–south lines,* the parallel lines engraved in the bottom of the housing.

compass housing (360° dial)—The dial containing the cardinal directions north, south, east, and west and the numbers representing 360° of a circle.

index mark—The location where the end of the direction-of-travel arrow meets the compass housing. Often it is marked with a triangle and "Read bearing here" notation.

BASIC SKILLS AND TECHNIQUES

The previous sections described the two fundamental pieces of orienteering equipment, map and compass. Having a greater understanding of the specific features on maps and the identifying parts of the compass will assist readers in understanding the basic skills and techniques of orienteering. The next section will fully describe how to orient and follow a map, detail how to use a compass, and end with an explanation on how to use both a map and compass together.

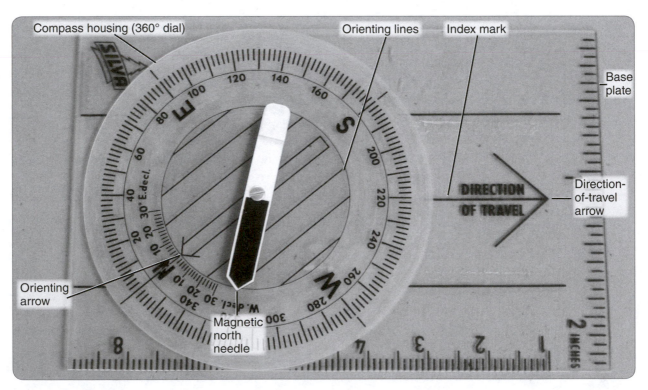

Figure 8.3 Compass.

Reprinted from C. Bunting, 2005, *Interdisciplinary teaching through outdoor education* (Champaign, IL: Human Kinetics), 106.

Orienting and Following a Map

Having a basic understanding of map features (colors and symbols) is the first step in being able to follow or walk a course. The next step is orienting the map. Orienting a map can be done with the features on the land (the lay of the land) or with a compass. Information on orienting a map with a compass is presented later. To orient a map to the lay of the land, the orienteer must line up the map, matching key features on the map to key features on the land. For example, if a student wants to orient a map of his school yard to the lay of the land, he would hold the map in such a way that when he looked down at his map and then out to the school yard, features would correspond. After the map has been oriented to the lay of the land, the student can follow the map, maintaining his location on the map. You should provide students with time to practice following maps to get a better understanding of map features and distances traveled. Two useful techniques, thumbing a map and pacing, can assist students in knowing where they are on the map and in finding controls.

Thumbing a map is a relatively simple technique used in competition and is one that should be introduced to students early. After orienting the map, the orienteer locates her position on the map and places her thumb next to it. Without moving her thumb from the original location, she then moves from destination to destination while using the original location (thumb) as a point of reference. Referencing a small section of the map helps prevent the orienteer from searching all over the map for her location. Another technique for following maps is using handrails. Handrails are linear features such as trails, roads, streams, and fences that are plotted along a given path. Locating handrails on a map can assist the orienteer in finding controls. For instance, an orienteer's next control may be in a direct line with the previous control; however, a closer examination of the map reveals that this direct line will take the orienteer through heavy vegetation (represented in dark green). The orienteer also notices a road (in this case a handrail) farther off to the right that parallels the vegetation. Although taking the road appears to be longer in distance, choosing to walk along the road rather than to walk through heavy vegetation could save time.

Pacing is a technique used to help determine distance traveled. Gaining experience with walking through vegetation, up and over hills, and on flat surfaces is one of the only ways an orienteer can begin to estimate how long it will take to travel a certain distance. Usually distance is represented on a map scale. Encourage your students to become familiar with this scale not only by looking for it on the map but also by knowing the distance it represents. Different maps have different scales. Once students become familiar with the map scale, they need to know how long it takes to travel a given distance. For instance, when an orienteer knows she has to travel 400 ft (122 m) to reach the next control but has been walking for awhile without seeing the control, how does she know how far she has traveled? She may be lucky enough to notice other features on the map that can assist her in locating her position, but using features is tricky when there are many similar features in one location. Pacing, or knowing the distance of each double step taken, can help answer the question of distance traveled. Another technique is to use the length of time spent in travel as an indicator of distance traveled. For example, if the orienteer knows that he can cover 1 mi (1.6 km) on even terrain in roughly 15 min, he could assume he traveled 0.5 mi (0.8 km) after 8 min. Although useful, this technique must be modified for the different terrains covered (uphill, loose gravel, thick vegetation, and so on).

Compass Skills

A solid understanding of the parts of the compass is useful in learning the function of the compass. The names of the compass parts are used to describe the function of a compass and are used throughout the remainder of this chapter. The function of a compass is relatively easy to understand. The north end of the magnetic arrow always points to the magnetic north when the compass is held flat and level and away from metal objects. Magnetic north provides a common reference point (0° or 360°) from which all other angles can be measured. By facing magnetic north, a student can then point to an intended direction of travel; the distance between magnetic north and this intended direction of travel forms an angle measured in degrees. This measured angle is referred to as a *bearing*.

The three uses of a compass without a map are finding directions from a location (taking a bearing), following a direction to a location (following a bearing), and returning to the original location. The following are instructions on how to take a field bearing—that

A student learns how to use a compass.

is, how to find directions to a destination that you can sight off in the distance:

1. Holding the compass flat and level and away from metal objects, point the direction-of-travel arrow to your specified destination.

2. Rotate the compass housing until the north end of the orienting arrow of the compass lines up with the red magnetic needle.

3. Read the direction of travel, or bearing, from the 360° dial at the index mark on the base plate.

The following are instructions on how to follow a bearing:

1. Set the compass dial to the desired degree (this may be given to you or found by taking a bearing) by aligning the desired degree with the compass index mark.

2. While holding the compass flat and level and away from metal objects, rotate your body until the magnetic north needle is aligned with the orienting arrow. Your intended direction of travel will be in line with the direction-of-travel arrow.

3. Site an object ahead of you that is in line with the direction-of-travel arrow and walk toward that object (pick an object that is close to your starting position and then continue to pick new marks as you go).

4. Every few paces, look down at your compass to make certain that your magnetic north needle is still aligned with the orienting arrow. While you may be tempted to continually look down at your compass to make sure you are going in the correct direction, doing so is not recommended. It not only is an inefficient way to follow a bearing but also increases the chances of walking into a tree or tripping over a rock.

The third and final way of using the compass by itself is for finding your direction back to your original location. Returning back to your original location can be accomplished by following this simple step: From the destination you recently reached, without moving the compass housing or the compass, rotate your body until the red magnetic north needle is aligned with the south end of the orienting arrow. You are now pointed in the direction back to your original location.

Combining Map and Compass

The previous sections detailed how to use a map and compass independently of one another. This section illustrates how to combine the two skills. To begin this section, it is important to explore the concept of magnetic declination.

A compass needle is always attracted to magnetic north, while maps are oriented to true north, or the geographic North Pole. The difference between magnetic north and true north is measured in degrees and is referred to as *magnetic declination* (see figure 8.4). Magnetic declination must be considered when combining map and compass. There are a number of ways to account for magnetic declination; this chapter explains only the simplest method. The simplest way to account for magnetic declination is to use a map oriented to north using magnetic north. Although that statement may sound confusing, it is rather simple. The next section shows how to orient a map using a compass while taking declination into consideration.

Using a Compass to Orient a Map

There are two ways in which students can orient their maps: (1) using the lay of the land and (2) using the map and compass. While useful, orienting a map with the lay of the land can sometimes be confusing if there are many similar features in the area. Using a compass to orient the map can reduce or eliminate this confusion. Furthermore, using a map and compass to orient your map is a useful trick to double-check how close you were to correct orientation when you aligned your map with the lay of the land. Use the following steps to orient a map with a compass:

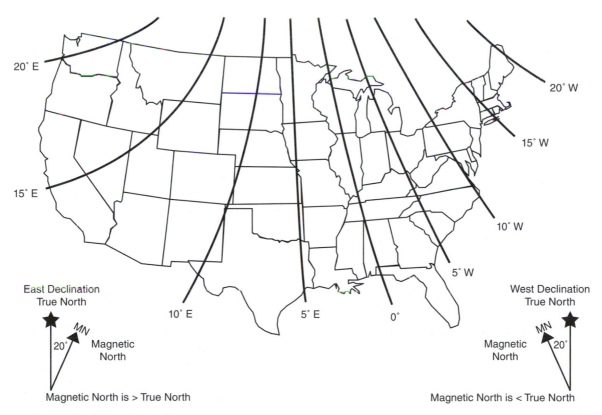

Figure 8.4 Magnetic declination.

Reprinted from C. Bunting, 2005, *Interdisciplinary teaching through outdoor education* (Champaign, IL: Human Kinetics), 111.

1. Set the compass to 0° or 360° at the index mark (you will quickly notice that these are the same).

2. Place the long edge of the compass base plate along the declination arrow on the map with the direction-of-travel arrow pointed toward north on the map.

3. Holding both the compass and map, rotate them together until the north end of the magnetic needle aligns with the north end of the orienting arrow.

Now that the map is oriented to north using magnetic north, bearings can be transferred directly from the field to the map and directly from the map to the field. As long as the map is oriented using the instructions given, users will not have to think anymore about magnetic declination. Orienteering maps usually have magnetic north lines drawn on them, while topographic maps may have only a small magnetic north line drawn in one of the lower corners. In the event that your map does not show magnetic north lines, drawing them in yourself is easy and you may find it useful to do so.

Taking a Map Bearing

The next skill that requires combining map and compass is referred to as *taking a map bearing*. Taking a map bearing is finding a direction from one location on a map to another. The following steps outline how to take a map bearing:

1. Orient the map to north using magnetic north (see previous instructions).

2. Place the long edge of the compass base plate on the map to make a line from your starting point to your intended destination. Make sure your compass is positioned with the direction-of-travel arrow pointing to your ending destination.

3. Holding the base plate steady and making certain not to move the oriented map, rotate the compass housing until the north end of the magnetic north arrow aligns with the north end of the orienting arrow.

4. Read the bearing in degrees at the index mark.

Transferring Bearings

Once you have mastered the skills of orienting a map and finding field and map bearings, you are ready to transfer those bearings from the map to the field and from the field to the map. Transferring a map bearing to the field is easy. If you follow the instructions given

to take a map bearing, your compass will be set to that bearing. To transfer that bearing to the field, you simply pick up the compass off the map, make certain that the magnetic end of the compass needle is aligned with the north end of the orienting arrow, and follow your direction-of-travel arrow.

If you are given a map bearing from a map which was oriented to north using magnetic north but are not standing in the corresponding location in the field, you need to set the compass dial to the desired bearing and then place yourself in the corresponding position in the field. Then your direction of travel will be set once you align the magnetic north arrow with the north end of the orienting arrow.

DESIGNING A COURSE

This final section on orienteering describes how you can design a basic orienteering course in your school yard. In addition, this section provides variations you can use to change the activity for different audiences. Designing an orienteering course begins with creating a map of the school grounds. You can have students draw this map as a way to reinforce map skills. Once the map is created, you must place numbered controls (items marking locations to be visited) out in the school yard. These controls also need to be drawn on the map. Once the controls are established and marked on the map, have the students, in pairs, visit the controls in a specified order. Having students follow a specific set of instructions written on a card located at each control is one way to know whether your students visited each control. Depending on the age of the students, you might incorporate the use of compasses in your course. Students would then have to orient their maps, determine map bearings, and follow bearings in the field. Adding compass skills to the course increases the level of difficulty.

One of the greatest aspects of orienteering is the ease in which you can change your course to meet the needs of various populations or objectives. The key to any activity change is to provide enough choice and challenge to appeal to the needs of everyone. The following are a number of variations on the simple orienteering course for the school yard. The NASPE standards that each variation aligns with are also included.

- Control cards have a number of progressively difficult physical activities in which students might engage (standard 1).
- Students take a given bearing at a control point and identify what they see or provide a sighted bearing to a given landmark (standard 2).
- Students determine personal pace distance in feet on a preplaced measuring unit at the control. Students are directed to measure the distance from the control to an identified object (standards 1, 2).
- Students use pedometers to determine their shortest versus longest route choice (standards 3, 4).
- Control cards have riddles or math problems (ranging from easy to difficult) students need to solve (standard 2).
- Four maps are affixed to the ground, but only one is oriented to the lay of the land. Students use a compass or use identifiable features to select the correctly oriented map (standard 2).
- Students provide a partner with the bearing to the next control and that person guides the other to the next control (standards 1, 2, 5).
- Students determine direction relative to north using a map at a control. For example, when students are at control #1, they must use the map to determine what direction control #5 is from #1 (standard 2).

CONCLUSION

Orienteering is a sport that involves running or walking while thinking and that usually combines compass use (though not always) with map reading. In orienteering, participants navigate their way through unfamiliar territory, moving from one point to another. For many it is best described as a scavenger hunt using a map or using a map and a compass combined. Orienteering is an exciting physical and cognitive activity that requires very little specialized equipment and that offers many opportunities to collaborate with classroom teachers.

INTRODUCTION TO GEOCACHING

Considered by many as a treasure hunt or high-tech game of hide and seek, geocaching is a form of orienteer-ing in which participants use GPS receivers and satellite data to search and find hidden treasures (or caches). In its most basic design, geocaching involves a person hiding a cache and then posting the coordinates (waypoint) of that cache on the Internet. The treasures are placed in waterproof containers and are mostly trinkets such as matchbox cars, golf balls, key chains, and the like. Fellow cachers locate the cache information on a Web site, program the waypoint into their GPS, and then attempt to find the cache. Some caches are nearby and quite visible and thus are easy to find. Others may be tiny, camouflaged, and miles from the nearest road or path. There are caches underneath rocks in city parks or underwater in mountain lakes. Some caches have a theme such as dog goodies or kids' toys. Most contain a hodgepodge of stuff. The rules of geocaching are simple: If you take something from a cache, leave something of yours behind and sign and date the logbook. Geocaching can offer the physical education teacher countless opportunities to combine technology, physical activity, and multidisciplinary learning.

Geocaching is a popular international game that has grown rapidly since its start in 2000 (Groundspeak, 2009). It was then that the U.S. government opened the channels for the public to receive GPS signals from 24 satellites orbiting the earth at a high altitude (11,000 mi, or 17,700 km). Before that time, the U.S. Department of Defense had been using the satellites as a military navigational tool and had jammed the signals on civilian GPS receivers. Several days after the jamming signals were turned off, a computer consultant in Oregon hid a treasure—a black bucket full of prizes, a logbook, and a pencil—in the woods, posted the coordinates online, and challenged others to find it. Within a few days, several people had found it, and the concept of using the GPS to hunt treasure spread quickly through the Internet (Schlatter and Hurd, 2005). Soon others began hiding treasures and posting coordinates online (while there are more than one Web site supporting this game, the most extensive and popular is www.geocaching.com, which is run by Groundspeak), and the term *geocaching* was born (*geo = earth; cache = hiding place*). Today there are more than 800,000 hidden caches around the world (Groundspeak, 2009). Each cache is ranked by difficulty to reach and to locate. Despite the large number of existing caches, it is never hard to find a new place to create a cache. A school playground or a local park can become a great location for hiding a variety of caches. And the joys of caching aren't measured so much in what students find as in the adventure of getting there.

Besides providing the lure of finding hidden treasures, geocaching provides various benefits:

- Opportunities for both able and less-able students to experience genuine success
- Exciting options for improving fitness
- Physical and mental challenges that often lead to increased participation in physical activity
- A means of promoting communication and teamwork while also offering opportunities to engage in problem solving with peers

Geocaching also lends itself well to interdisciplinary activities. Virtually any academic task can be incorporated into geocaching activities, and thus geocaching can facilitate the learning of less-palatable but important academic skills. As explained in several of the accompanying geocaching lesson plans, students can be asked to answer questions and solve problems upon finding a hidden cache. These might range from collecting jumbled letters of the alphabet and rearranging them into words to finding and placing cards into the food guide pyramid to learning about the history of the area by locating various landmarks. Similarly, students can learn about map reading and compass use while discovering new information about geography, geology, archeology, and other academic areas.

EQUIPMENT

Geocaching requires a $100 U.S. GPS unit, a $500 U.S. computer with Internet access (for locating caches that others have hidden), and a multibillion dollar satellite system (compliments of the U.S. government). The GPS unit detects satellite signals that are used to pinpoint the user's location as well as that of a cache using coordinates based on latitude and longitude. The units are useful night and day, rain or shine, and their accuracy depends on the quality of unit purchased (some cost upward of $1,000 U.S., but the basic $100 U.S. units are more than sufficient for school programs). Besides providing the coordinates and elevation of your current position, the GPS device provides additional navigation information such as the direction to a specified waypoint, the distance to a waypoint, the speed of travel, and the direction of travel. Each of these bits of information can be useful when designing learning activities. Additional information about GPS devices is located in the geocaching lesson plans for this chapter (see the accompanying CD-ROM).

Other pieces of equipment that may help you, whether you are geocaching in an urban, rural, or wilderness area, include the following:

- **Essentials.** Geocaching in any environment poses threats common to the outdoors, such as dehydration, annoying insects, sun exposure, and so on. Consider the setting and carry the essential items suggested in chapter 1.

- **Extra batteries.** The GPS unit contains an LCD monitor that displays an icon or message to let you know when batteries are low or depleted. Even when your batteries are fully charged, it is wise to carry spare batteries.

- **Compass.** Listed in chapter 1 as one of the essentials, an old-fashioned magnetic orienteering compass can come in handy when you can't get a GPS signal. Rumor has it that there are some cachers with a substantial number of finds by people who never used a GPS receiver. Knowledge of compass use is essential since a compass does no good to anyone who doesn't know how to use it.

- **Map.** Also listed in chapter 1 as one of the essentials, a map is especially important in geocaching, when you must know where you are and how to get to where you need to be. In the backcountry, a map can assist in locating caches as well as in identifying important features of the area (streams, steep terrain, nearby roads and trails, potential hazards, and so on). In urban areas, GPS signals bounce off large buildings and require a view of the sky in order to function properly. Even if a GPS has mapping software, the amount of detail and guaranteed availability provided by a street map can be helpful.

BASIC SKILLS AND TECHNIQUES

The skills and techniques students will learn during this unit are described more thoroughly in the lesson plans for this chapter and include basic use of the GPS unit, including how to use it when hiding or locating caches. Students will also learn how to locate and record finds on the Internet. In addition, students will learn about the different types of caches.

GPS Fundamentals

The GPS device receives signals that are transmitted from satellites that circle the earth in a very precise orbit. The receivers use triangulation to calculate an exact location.

Although different GPS devices vary in their capabilities (more sophisticated models may come equipped with downloadable maps, color screens, and abundant memory), the basic low-end units are quite adequate for school programs and feature similar characteristics.

Understanding Triangulation

Satellites transmit high-frequency radio waves. By locking onto these signals, a GPS receiver can process these data to triangulate its precise location. If the GPS receiver locks onto at least three satellites, it can calculate a two-dimensional location (basically latitude and longitude). When it locks onto a fourth satellite, it can compute a three-dimensional position that includes latitude, longitude, and *altitude*. To understand how triangulation works, consider the following scenario. Say that one satellite indicates that you are 625 mi (1,006 km) from Boise; that is, you are somewhere on a circle that has its center in Boise and a radius of 625 mi (1,006 km). A second satellite indicates that you are somewhere on a circle that is 690 mi. (1,110 km) from Minneapolis; thus, you are on one of the two points where the two circles intersect. Information from a third satellite reveals that you also are 615 mi (990 km) from Tucson. By determining where the three circles intersect, the GPS receiver calculates your exact location to be somewhere near Denver. Information from a fourth satellite establishes your elevation.

Screens and Pages

There is a set of buttons on the GPS unit that allows users to access several different screens or pages. These buttons also allow users to turn the unit on and off, to access a backlight in dim conditions, to exit or quit a function, to select options (e.g., zoom) on pages, and to confirm data entry. When the unit is turned on, it begins to acquire the satellite signals that it needs to function. Typical screens include the following (for more in-depth information, see the lesson plan for day 1 of the geocaching unit):

- **Main page, or sky view:** Displays the strength of the satellite signals and the degree of accuracy (e.g., within 15 ft, or 4.6 m).
- **Map:** Shows the user's current location and an illustration of where the user is going. Some units depict this as a bread crumb trail showing exactly where the user has traveled on the map.
- **Pointer:** Looks like a compass and helps to guide the user to a destination. Includes a direction arrow and information such as the name of the location and the distance yet to go. The pointer

Some of the essential items for geocaching: cache box, map, compass, whistle, and GPS unit.

is unlike a compass, which uses polar magnetism rather than satellite information, in that the user always walks in the direction that the arrow is pointing.

- **Trip computer:** Provides information on a trip such as distance covered, maximum speed, average speed, time spent moving, time spent stopped.

- **Menu:** Provides access to advanced features such as marking a new waypoint, entering new coordinates, and locating stored waypoints.

Selecting a Waypoint

If a waypoint is already loaded into the memory of the GPS unit, students can select that waypoint from the unit's menu screen. Using commands applicable to the particular unit, the students then access the pointer screen and begin following the pointer arrow. As the waypoint nears, a message such as "arriving at destination" appears. By referring to the degree of accuracy given on the main screen (e.g., 15 ft, or 4.6 m), the students can determine how close they might be to the cache.

If a waypoint has not already been loaded into the unit's memory, the students can enter the coordinates and then proceed. For example, if you have placed some caches and determined waypoints for each, you can have students manually enter those waypoints into their devices. Another option is to have students search for nearby caches on the Web (www.geocaching.com is a good place to start). To do this, students enter a local zip code, select a cache from the list, and then enter the waypoints that are listed for that cache. Each cache is rated on a 5-point scale by difficulty to find and difficulty of terrain.

Finding the Cache

Once it takes you to the general vicinity of the cache, the GPS receiver does not indicate the exact location of the cache. Thus the challenge and excitement of geocaching. Students now must resort to their hunting skills. They may look for something that seems out of place in the area, such as a fake rock or an old box lying in a pile of neatly stacked twigs. Just as hunting for a cache requires some creative skills, so does hiding a cache. Some cachers, for example, once found a cache inside a hollowed-out log on which the bark was removed and then reattached by screws, washers, and magnets. Once students have located a Web site cache, they should exchange some treasure, sign the logbook, and replace the cache exactly as found. After returning home, they should log their experience on the Web site.

As a teacher, you might want to create caches for which students must answer questions to problems once they locate the cache site. For instance, you may wish to use variously colored marbles as caches, with each marble representing a planet. Students must then locate a cache, identify the planet (using a map that presents a scaled-down version of how far each planet is from the sun, which can be defined as the teacher's location), and answer a question that verifies whether they located the correct planet. As you can see, the type of cache students are looking for can have a bearing on what students must do upon finding it.

Types of Caches

Caches come in all shapes and sizes. The following are a few of the many types of caches:

- **Traditional cache.** This is the original cache, which consists of a waterproof container and a logbook. Containers may be as large as an ammo box or Tupperware tub or as small as a film canister (which may be too small to contain anything but a small roll of paper used as the logbook).

- **Multicache.** This type of cache involves two or more locations. The coordinates listed are for the first of several cache locations. Each location contains clues to the next location. The final coordinates are the actual cache.

- **Virtual cache.** The coordinates listed for this type of cache are for a location rather than an object. Often virtual caches are a permanent landmark such as a statue, plaque, or building. They also can be relatively permanent markings such as decals on playground equipment or markings painted on poles at a Frisbee golf course. Because of the nature of these caches, you must actually visit the location and acquire the coordinates there before giving the coordinates to students. But this type of cache is particularly appealing to teachers who wish to spend more time developing activities focusing on locations (e.g., having students answer questions about a historical site) than on continually hiding caches. Virtual caches are now considered waymarks (interesting and useful locations around the world) and are listed on www.waymarking.com.

- **Travel bug.** A travel bug is an item that is moved from cache to cache. The item carries a dog tag with a code on it. This code permits cachers to track the item's progress on www.geocaching.com. Travel bugs usually have a goal destination. For instance, teachers once divided one class of fifth graders into two baseball groups representing the American League and the National League. The travel bug for the American League was a small catcher's mitt on a key chain, and the travel bug for the National League was a small baseball bat. The two teams hid their caches and then posted the coordinates online. The goal was for each travel bug to travel to all of the cities in which its particular league had a baseball team. The students tracked their respective bugs as they moved from city to city. Many cachers even sent digital photos of themselves and the travel bug at the baseball stadium! Another example is a cacher who creates a travel bug that says, "I want to visit every state that begins with the letter *M*." The next person who discovers that cache will note that it includes the travel bug and then leave the bug there or move it to another cache that is closer to or in a state beginning with *M*.

SAFETY CONSIDERATIONS

If students are to search for caches in outdoor settings, they should be made aware of some basic precautions and safety considerations. In addition to teaching your students to safeguard themselves and their environment, encourage them to treat caches delicately and to avoid exposing caches in ways that might spoil the experience for other cachers. When geocaching, consider the following guidelines:

- Let someone know where you are going and when you plan to return. Leave instructions for what to do if you have not returned by a certain time.
- Mark your vehicle as a waypoint to ensure your safe return.
- Note difficulty levels and terrain ratings, and ensure that students possess the skills and fitness necessary to negotiate a geocaching trip.
- Protect the environment by stressing the importance of etiquette. In addition to adhering to the principles of Leave No Trace (see chapter 1), try practicing cache in, trash out, which can be as simple as taking along a trash bag (a recyclable plastic grocery sack fits easily into a small film canister) and picking up the occasional piece of trash you see on the trail or sidewalk. Even this small act can make a huge difference in the cleanliness of the environment.

Students discover the cache.

This last point about protecting the environment is both timely and important. With the surging popularity of geocaching, there has been concern about the proliferation of caches. Getting people, especially young people, into the outdoors is wonderful. But people want to hide and find caches everywhere, even if doing so disrupts wildlife, leaves fire tracks, makes new trails, and damages vegetation. The U.S. Forest Service allows no caches of any kind in wilderness areas. While the Bureau of Land Management allows geocaching in many places, permission must be obtained before leaving a cache. Geocaching is not allowed in wildlife refuges or in national parks unless special permission is obtained. And many cities and counties prohibit or sharply restrict geocaching in their parks, while others require registration of caches and have a long list of geocaching guidelines. Your responsibility, therefore, is twofold: to encourage young people to embrace geocaching while also educating them to practice it responsibly.

CONCLUSION

Geocaching is skyrocketing in popularity. It can be a great activity for kids because it uses their interest in technology to foster a greater interest in the outdoors. It combines physical activity with problem solving while also presenting opportunities for teamwork and multidisciplinary learning. It also offers an excellent platform for making students good stewards of their surroundings.

REFERENCES

Boga, S. (1997). *Orienteering: The sport of navigating with map and compass*. Mechanicsburg, PA: Stackpole Books.

Groundspeak. (2009). Geocaching. www.geocaching.com.

National Association for Sport and Physical Education. (2004). *Moving into the future: National standards for physical education* (2nd ed.). Reston, VA: Author.

Schlatter, B., and Hurd, A. (2005). Geocaching: 21st-century hide-and-seek. *Journal of Physical Education, Recreation and Dance, 76*(7), 28-32.

RECOMMENDED READINGS

Jacobson, C. (1988). *The basic essentials of map and compass*. Merrillville, IN: ICS Books.

Kjellström, B. (1994). *Be an expert with map & compass: The complete orienteering handbook*. New York: Collier Books.

McNeill, C. (1990). *Orienteering: The skills of the game*. Wiltshire, England: Crowood Press.

McNeill, C., Cory-Wright, J., & Renfrew, T. (1998). *Teaching orienteering*. (2nd ed.). Champaign, IL: Human Kinetics.

Randall, G. (1998). *The Outward Bound map & compass handbook*. New York: Lyons Press.

Renfrew, T. (1997). *Orienteering*. Champaign, IL: Human Kinetics.

Renfrew, T., McNeill, C., & Palmer, P. (1993). *Orienteering for the young: Guidelines*. Sollentuna, Sweden: International Orienteering Federation.

Rutstrum, C. (2000). *The wilderness route finder: The classic guide to finding your way in the wild*. Minneapolis: University of Minnesota Press.

SCIGO Learning Products. (1992). *How to use a compass: Using an orienteering compass for fun & exploration*. Colorado Springs: SCIGO.

RECOMMENDED WEB SITES

U.S. Orienteering Federation

www.us.orienteering.org

International Orienteering Federation

www.orienteering.org

ORIENTEERING AND GEOCACHING UNIT PLAN

General Lesson Information

Each lesson contains the following seven elements:

1. Objectives—primary learning outcomes
2. Equipment—specific materials for each lesson
3. Introduction—fundamental concepts and skills pertaining to the lesson's focus
4. Warm-ups—activities that promote cooperation and communication in pairs
5. Central activities—activity progressions from basic understanding to practicing new skills
6. Closure—suggested discussion and reflection items
7. Assessment—examples of evaluation strategies

Lessons are separated into two groups: orienteering and geocaching.

Orienteering Lessons

Day 1

Focus: Drawing and orienting maps

- Common map symbols
- Orienting a map
- Contours and intervals

Day 2

Focus: Pacing

- What is pacing
- How to determine your pace
- When to use pacing

Day 3

Focus: Understanding the compass

- Major compass parts
- How a compass works
- Finding a bearing
- Following a bearing

Day 4

Focus: Combining map and compass

- Magnetic declination
- How to orient a map using a compass

- Taking a bearing on a map
- Transferring map and field bearings

Day 5

Focus: Navigating the school yard orienteering course

- Locating predetermined landmarks
- Orienting a map to the surrounding landscape

Geocaching Lessons

Day 1

Focus: Understanding basic GPS use

- GPS unit description and operation
- Creating and locating a waypoint

Day 2

Focus: Finding a series of waypoints on a playground

- Downloading waypoints
- Locating and documenting caches

Day 3

Focus: Finding waypoints in the local community

- Learning about local lore by discovering virtual caches

Day 4

Focus: Multicaching

- Using clues at one waypoint to discover subsequent waypoints

Day 5

Focus: Using the Internet to identify, locate, and document caches

- Identifying caches online
- Locating and documenting caches
- Tracking travel bugs

chapter 9

Mountain Biking

Jeff McNamee
Stacy Birdsall Claus

The first mountain bike ride we went on we got caked with mud. The students said, "Let's go give Mr. Smith (the school's principal) a hug." We went to the front of the school and they ran into the front office. They had just carpeted the office and the secretaries were trying to get the kids out. There were six other administrators in there from other schools. One of the [other] administrators stood up and said, "I wish our kids were this excited about something."

High School Physical Education Teacher

Bicycling, including mountain biking, is one of the fastest-growing recreational activities in the United States (Cordell, 2004). In 2001, more than 180 million Americans reported that they had participated in bicycling in the past year, and mountain biking itself is the third most popular land-based physical activity in the United States (Cordell, 2004). Mountain biking was born out of human ingenuity and a desire to find refuge in the outdoors. The exact beginning of mountain biking as an outdoor pursuit is difficult to pinpoint. Who among us cannot imagine a young child riding one the first bicycles through farm fields and forests in the middle of the 18th century? There were no paved roads at this point in time, and bicycling required the skills we now associate with mountain biking. The feeling of being connected mentally and physically to a bike and trail is like no other. With the right set of skills, correct equipment, knowledge of safety, and ethical usage of natural places, a winding single track (a narrow dirt path that winds through forests and deserts) and large mountains become places of refuge and enjoyment. As a physical activity leader, you want your students or participants to seek out opportunities for physical activity enjoyment and to lead a health-enhancing life. This chapter presents a course outline that will enable your participants to feel competent and confident on a mountain bike and will inspire them to seek out opportunities to participate in this type of physical activity. More importantly, this overview will provide you with the critical and updated information that you need to present this material, even if the activity is new to you. Specifically, this chapter gives a brief history of mountain biking as an outdoor pursuit and sport, lists the physical activity benefits of mountain biking, describes the basic types of mountain bikes and the general components of most mountain bikes, discusses safety considerations, and teaches sustainable trail use.

EVOLUTION AS A SPORT

Mountain biking can take many forms. Loosely, it can be defined as placing a bike on dirt. This may include pedaling down gravel paths, single track, or steep descents. The skills associated with mountain biking are similar to those covered in chapter 10 but are also distinctly different. Mountain bikers must perform routine cycling skills (e.g., braking, cornering, descending) on quickly undulating and loose natural terrain such as dirt or gravel.

The now Olympic sport of mountain biking has ties to northern California, where local cyclists decided to modify their bikes into "clunkers." The bikes were balloon tired and had inadequate braking or shifting mechanisms (see figure 9.1). Riders used drum brakes and often had to modify the original frames to accommodate the wider off-road tires. The first organized mountain bike events were what are now defined as downhill events. Participants raced the clock down fire roads and dirt trails outside of San Francisco. The sport eventually evolved into the more commonly known discipline of cross-country style racing, in which participants race their bikes over natural terrain, including gravel and dirt roads and single track. As the sport gained popularity, the National Off-Road Bicycling Association (NORBA) was born. With assistance from the organizers of the first clunker races, NORBA formalized the rules of mountain biking, and in 1996 mountain biking was introduced as an Olympic sport in the United States at the Atlanta Games. Currently, cross-country racing is the only recognized discipline of mountain biking in the Olympic Games. However,

Figure 9.1   Pioneer mountain bikers used bikes with balloon tires and inadequate braking and shifting mechanisms.

as many of the gravity disciplines (e.g., downhill, dual slalom, four cross) continue to gain in popularity, they may soon appear in future Olympic Games.

While the evolving discipline of mountain biking (e.g., free ride, downhill, dual slalom) will catch the attention of your students, the skill set used in these disciplines is grounded in the fundamental skills of cross-country riding. Therefore, this chapter and its accompanying lesson plans (found on the CD-ROM) focus on the knowledge and skills most commonly used in cross-country riding.

BENEFITS OF MOUNTAIN BIKING

Mountain biking provides several health benefits that can assist students in meeting the NASPE standards (National Association for Sport and Physical Education, 2004). For example, standard 4 asks students to achieve and maintain a health-enhancing level of physical fitness. In terms of energy expenditure measured in metabolic equivalents (METs), mountain biking at a leisurely pace equates to about 8 METs, which is well above the 3 to 4 METs that define exercising at moderate to vigorous levels. Mountain biking at a more moderate pace equates to approximately 10 METs. If you consider that 1 MET is the rate of energy used while sitting at rest, you can see that mountain biking can be a relatively taxing pursuit. It's important to remember, especially for students considered to be overweight, that energy expenditure varies significantly depending on terrain, pedaling efficiency, and equipment. As you plan your lessons, consider asking students to ride for a designated duration (e.g., 30 s up a campus hill) instead of asking students to perform a designated workload (e.g., everyone ride to the top of the hill).

One of the other major health benefits of mountain biking is muscular strength and endurance. Because mountain biking often takes place on uneven terrain (e.g., steep ascents), it is a wonderful opportunity for participants to increase the strength and endurance of their core, leg, and upper-body muscles. For example, moderate ascents require riders to stand, which engages most of the core muscles and the main leg muscles. However, very steep terrain requires riders to stay seated to keep the back tire in contact with the ground and to bring the chest down toward the front of the bike. This technique requires substantial upper-body strength, as the rider uses the upper-body muscle groups to pull against the pedaling motion. The terms *moderate* and

steep are relative for riders and depend on a rider's experience and level of physical fitness. As a course leader, you should pilot test various terrains with beginning and experienced riders before implementing the activities found in the lesson sections on these terrains so that you have a sense of how difficult your lessons will be for your students. Scouting the hill is particularly important when using activities from the lesson for day 4 (see the accompanying CD-ROM).

Beyond meeting health-related objectives, mountain biking offers several other benefits. For example, the sport requires individuals to know when to use specific movement techniques on the trail, to act responsibly in natural settings, to socialize and interact appropriately with other nature users (e.g., hikers and horseback riders), and to challenge themselves cognitively while repairing their mountain bike or reading and interpreting trail maps. All of these benefits are related to NASPE standards and can assist teachers and students in reaching these goals.

EQUIPMENT

This section describes the various types of mountain bikes, the components of most mountain bikes, the helmets available, and the tools needed in a repair kit. This section is not meant to be an extensive list of equipment; rather, it is an overview of the pieces of equipment essential to conducting a mountain bike unit in an instructional setting.

Basic Types of Mountain Bikes

The evolution of the standard mountain bike is difficult to keep up with. Although there are several types of mountain bikes with specific design features for each type of riding (e.g., downhill, dual slalom, trail, and free ride), this chapter presents an overview of the two main types of mountain bikes used in cross-country arenas: hardtail (figure 9.2a) and full suspension (figure 9.2b). The hardtail mountain bike has several modifications

> **TEACHING TIP**
>
> Partner with local bicycle retailers and other bicycle organizations such as Safe Routes to School, your regional chapter of the International Mountain Bicycling Association, or the Bicycle Transportation Alliance.

when compared with a typical road bicycle. First, the frame geometry places the rider lower to the ground. All mountain bikes are designed this way to increase stability over variable terrain and to significantly increase maneuverability on curvy single track and down descents. The hardtail gets its name from the frame design; the rear triangle of the frame is rigid and does not include active suspension of any kind. In the late 1980s, the hardtail was equipped with a front suspension that allows the rider to ride over uneven terrain and obstacles more efficiently. This technology significantly improves the rider's ability to keep the

Figure 9.2 Basic types of mountain bikes include the *(a)* hardtail mountain bike and *(b)* the full-suspension mountain bike.

front tire in contact with the dirt, a major benefit when trying to turn or apply the brakes. It also decreases a rider's fatigue, as the shock does most of the work.

The full-suspension mountain bike revolutionized the industry. These bikes look similar to an off-road motorcycle with suspension in both the front and the rear. The rear suspension affords many benefits to the rider, the biggest of which is traction. The rear tire of the bicycle stays in contact with the dirt over uneven terrain as the rear suspension absorbs the bumps. The secondary advantage of this absorption is comfort. The rider feels the bumps of the terrain less as the bike actively absorbs these terrain changes. This shock absorption also allows the rider to feel less fatigued after a bumpy ride. Table 9.1 lists the advantages and disadvantages of a hardtail mountain bike compared with a full-suspension mountain bike. If you have an opportunity to purchase mountain bikes for your class, the hardtail is recommended. A hardtail is less expensive to purchase and requires less maintenance over the life of the bike.

Basic Components of All Mountain Bikes

Mountain bike styles and geometry have changed significantly over the past 20 years. The basic components of mountain bikes, however, have stayed relatively the same (refer back to figure 9.2). This chapter does not intend to cover all of the various components on a mountain bike. Rather, it discusses the components directly related to efficiency on the trail and compo-

nents that need the most attention in terms of repair. You are advised to review one of the many mountain bike repair manuals available (see the recommended readings section at the end of this chapter).

As mentioned, suspension (front, rear, or both) is one component you will find on all new mountain bikes. Suspension is not mandatory, but it does significantly improve the rider's ability to control the bike when cornering, braking, and descending. Another set of components found on all mountain bikes is the front and rear derailleur. The derailleur acts as a guide for the chain and derails the chain onto a different gear when the rider shifts. Finally, the wheels and tires of a mountain bike are unique from those on other styles of bikes. Most mountain bike tires are 26 in. (66 cm), but the 29 in. (74 cm), also known as the *29er,* has gained significant popularity over the past decade. The wheel of a mountain bike is built to sustain the direct and side-wall pressures of natural terrain. Mountain bike tires also include either a Schrader valve (see figure 9.3*b*) or a Presta valve (see figure 9.3*a*). It is important to inspect the wheels and tires on a regular basis. Wheel and tire inspection, including a full preride inspection for the bike, are included in the final section of this chapter.

Helmets

Helmets are a mandatory piece of equipment while mountain biking. Do not teach a bicycling unit without having each participant wear a properly fitted helmet. New bicycle helmets are lighter, stronger, and more comfortable than their predecessors were. In 1999 the

Table 9.1   Hardtail Versus Full-Suspension Mountain Bikes

	Pros	Cons
Hardtail mountain bike	• Lighter option • More active energy gets to pedals • Fewer parts to maintain • Cost effective (you can upgrade to higher-quality parts with the money you save on the frame)	• Less comfortable over uneven terrain • Greater rider fatigue, since the rider's body has to absorb bumps
Full-suspension mountain bike	• Most comfortable over uneven terrain • Less rider fatigue	• Heavier option • Energy to pedals lost as the rear end bobs (many manufacturers have designed a lockout feature to create a rigid frame) • More parts to maintain • Less bike for your dollar

Figure 9.3   *(a)* Presta valve and *(b)* Schrader valve.

Consumer Product Safety Commission (CPSC) began certifying bicycle helmets. Only helmets certified by the CPSC should be used in your program. Today's helmets are engineered to use less material to withstand an incredible amount of force. Most helmets are made from expanded polystyrene (EPS) foam, and more-advanced helmets combine carbon fiber technology with the foam. These helmets offer wonderful comfort and superior ventilation. Recently, the cost of a basic helmet has dropped significantly. Riders can purchase a helmet at their local store for around $10 to $20 U.S. There are several national organizations that offer helmets at less than this amount. Please review the list of resources for helmet safety in the Web resources section of this chapter. Do not purchase used helmets, as internal damage to the foam is not visible to the naked eye. Most manufacturers recommend that a helmet be replaced if it is older than 5 years or it is involved in a crash where you hit your head. Many manufacturers have a crash replacement policy that allows the user to return the helmet and purchase a second helmet at a reduced rate.

Proper fit of the helmet is probably the most critical point to emphasize to your participants (see chapter 10, figure 10.5 for a photo example). Helmet design and fit have changed substantially over the last 5 years.

For this reason it is difficult to review how to properly fit each brand and type of helmet. Therefore, this section focuses on general guidelines that apply to most helmets. You should become acquainted with specific fit instructions from the manufacturer. These are usually available via the Web (look up helmets in the Web resources at the end of this chapter). Table 9.2 outlines the most critical points to consider when reviewing helmet fit with your participants.

Tool Kit

Each of your participants should carry a tool kit secured to the rear of the bike's saddle. Since you are the instructor you may want to include additional items (e.g., first aid supplies) in your tool kit, but the basic tool kit for participants should include the following:

- Extra tube
- Patch kit
- Mini pump or CO_2 (can be used with a Schrader or Presta valve)
- Tire levers
- Multitool with chain tool and a set of hexes (4, 5, 6, and 8 mm)
- One dollar bill (for sealing a blown-out tire)

BASIC SKILLS AND TECHNIQUES

Good cyclists, including mountain bikers, have cardiorespiratory endurance, muscular strength, and agility. However, these attributes will take a beginning mountain biker only so far. Skilled mountain bikers must ride efficiently and thoughtfully if they are to progress. Not unlike a successful rock climber, a successful mountain biker moves effectively through terrain transitions while

attempting to conserve energy. The unfortunate fact is that muscles tire, and learning to ride efficiently helps the rider to enjoy the experience fully. The list of techniques that follows includes the most critical and basic skills that your participants need to refine to succeed at mountain biking. These skills and techniques are summarized here and then discussed in greater detail in the lesson plans for this chapter (see the accompanying CD-ROM).

Braking

Braking with purpose (i.e., braking intentionally given the terrain) is a prerequisite skill that needs to be refined before participants begin working on other skills. This section discusses braking in general terms and does not distinguish between disc braking and rim braking (see figure 9.4). Most of today's mountain bikes include disc brakes. This type of brake provides superior stopping power under all conditions but is essentially the same as a rim brake when it comes to use. Many beginning riders do not understand the importance of applying

Table 9.2 Helmet Checklist

When I place the helmet on my head and tighten the rear adjustment, the helmet *does not turn* on my head.
The front rim of my helmet is at the brow line and is just visible.
The buckle of the strap is snug against the bottom of my chin.
The side straps form a Y below my ears.

Figure 9.4 *(a)* Disc brakes versus *(b)* rim brakes.

both front and rear brakes simultaneously. About 75% of the stopping power is generated from the front brake; the rear brake serves as the assistant. Participants must apply even braking to the front and rear brakes so they do not unweight the rear of the bike (by applying too much front bake) or put the bike into a skid (by applying too much rear brake). Participants should also practice applying the brake before entering a corner instead of applying the brake through the corner. In order to keep traction on the dirt, the tires should be allowed to roll through corners; this is especially true when cornering through loose or soft dirt or gravel.

Pedal Motion and Shifting

Being able to pedal efficiently significantly increases the enjoyment of bicycling. There is debate among cyclists concerning the most efficient pedal stroke. When working with beginners, try to help them to understand the importance of pedaling circles instead of pedaling squares. Most beginning cyclists think of pushing down on the pedal but do not think of also pulling through the pedal stroke. When participants

begin to pull through the pedal stroke, they begin to make a circle with their feet. It is challenging, however, to pull through the pedal stroke without the use of a toe clip or a clipless pedal (see figure 9.5). Toe clips are relatively inexpensive and provide an enormous mechanical advantage. Clipless pedals are more expensive, and few beginning participants are ready for such equipment. If you cannot provide toe clips (try removing the cloth strap and using only the plastic toe basket), you'll need to instruct your participants to do the following:

1. Place the front portion of the foot over the pedal.
2. Flex and extend the ankles though the pedal stroke.
3. Attempt to place even pressure on both pedals throughout the pedal stroke.

Shifting

Directly related to pedaling is shifting. Without a fluid pedal motion, it's difficult to shift properly or smoothly. Mountain bikes come equipped with either a twist shift or a thumb or finger trigger (see figure 9.6). The shifter on the right *always* controls the rear derailleur and the shifter on the left *always* controls the front derailleur. Both types of shifters work well and are a significant improvement over the original friction shifters found on the first mountain bikes. Today's shifters are indexed,

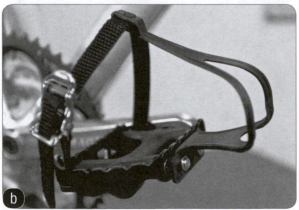

Figure 9.5　*(a)* A clipless pedal or *(b)* toe clip.

Figure 9.6　*(a)* A twist shift and thumb or *(b)* finger trigger.

meaning that, when the bike is well adjusted, each click equals one change in the gear.

Mountain bikes are equipped with three gears (chainrings) in the front and typically eight or nine gears (a cassette of cogs) in the rear. The larger front chainrings are used on flat terrain and sometimes on downhill terrain, while the smallest chainring is used to create a mechanical advantage when ascending steep hills. Advise beginners to use the middle chain most of the time unless they are approaching a steep hill. The critical point when using the front and rear gears together is to not cross the chain. For example, when using the largest front chainring, it is ill advised to be in the largest cog in the rear. Doing so causes the chain to cross and thus places undue pressure on the chain (see figure 9.7), sometimes causing the chain to break. When you need to shift to the smallest chainring in the front, be sure not to shift into the smallest cogs in the rear cassette. The same is true when using the large chainring in front. In this case, use only the smallest cogs in the rear cassette so you can keep the chain parallel to the bike's chainstay (rear frame). Many beginners are concerned about shifting and choose to avoid it. This is unfortunate because using the appropriate gear substantially eases a participant's workload while on certain terrain. The critical points for proper shifting are the following:

- Anticipate the need for a different gear and shift before you think you need it.
- Shift while the drivetrain (i.e., cranks, chainrings, and chain) is under the least amount of pressure.
- Take advantage of shifting technology and don't be afraid to dump the gears, which means to shift through several gears at once (this is particularly important when shifting through the rear cogs to prepare to ascend a hill).

TEACHING TIP

Stay on campus! You don't need mountain and miles of single track to inspire students.

Figure 9.7   *(a)* A parallel chain or *(b)* crossed chain.

Cornering

Cornering is guiding your bike through sharp turns such as those on a switchback (a section of trail that zigzags down a hill). Cornering can be one of those skills that inspire the most fear in your students. The fear and subsequent anxiety can create an unsafe situation. Once you can get your riders to loosen up and relax, they will take corners, even with some speed, with ease. The following is a list of teaching hints to help your students corner through even the toughest of terrain:

- Be sure to brake before the corner.
- Keep your elbows and knees flexible (i.e., keep knees and elbows bent so your body serves as the suspension of the ride).
- Keep the cornering side pedal up and apply pressure on the noncornering pedal to create counterbalance (do not pedal through the corner).
- Look through the corner, and not at it (where your head goes your body will follow).

Climbing

If you're working with beginners you'll want to limit the amount of climbing at first. There are very few of us who enjoy going uphill under our own power. However, climbing is part of cross-country mountain biking and is difficult to avoid. To ease the process and make climbing more enjoyable for your participants, consider the following suggestions:

- Shift into an easier gear before you anticipate needing it and avoid shifting while on the climb.
- Pedal in circles as described in the pedaling section.
- Stay seated (to keep your rear tire in contact with ground) most of the time.
- Sit back on the saddle and bring your chin lower (on very steep climbs, bring your chin very close to the stem to keep the front of the bike down).
- When the terrain allows (such as when climbing a moderate hill), switch from standing to sitting to allow some muscles to rest.

Descending

Students usually seize opportunities to go downhill and sometimes go down faster than they should. Most mountain bikers inherently want to go downhill fast! And most mountain bikes are made for just this purpose. A few tips will help your participants to be proficient and safe downhill riders:

- Get in control (i.e., use your braking technique) before the hill gets steep or the bike begins to move too fast.
- Place your pedals in a neutral position (with both crank arms parallel to the ground).
- Keep the knees and elbows bent.
- Lift yourself off the saddle 2 to 3 in. (5.1-7.6 cm).
- Keep your eyes on where you want to go (look 8-10 ft, or 2.4-3.0 m, ahead of your front wheel) and not on where you are.

Weight Transfer (Bunny Hop)

The bunny hop is probably one of the most useful techniques mountain bikers can add to their skill repertoire. In a bunny hop, the rear wheel and front wheel come off the ground either simultaneously or in succession (first the front wheel followed by the rear wheel). This skill allows the rider to move over small objects (e.g., log or water bar) found on wilderness trails. It also allows the rider to traverse over water cutouts and rocks. Essentially, the bunny hop is weighting and unweighting the front and then rear of the bike. In most instances it is best to lift the front and then the rear rather than lift the front and rear off the ground at the same time. To initiate a bunny hop, the rider must be able to get the front wheel off the ground. You can teach students to accomplish this by taking the following steps:

1. Move the pedals to a neutral position and stand slightly off the saddle.
2. Compress the front (elbows bent) of the bike by quickly weighting and unweighting the suspension fork.
3. After compression, pull up on the front of the bike and picture yourself lifting your saddle with your body.

Once students are able to unweight the front of the bike, they are ready to attempt a bunny hop. In order to get the rear wheel off the ground, they should shift their weight forward after the front of the bike has initiated its flight.

SUSTAINABLE TRAIL USE AND TRAIL ETHICS

Mountain biking, like many outdoor pursuits, has the potential to affect the natural landscape unless participants consciously follow a few basic principles to avoid doing so. Utilizing the natural world for recreational purposes is a privilege you must take seriously, and you must instill this ethic in your students. The International Mountain Bicycling Association (IMBA) has outlined principles for sustainable trail use (see figure 9.8). IMBA's mission is to protect, create, and enhance quality trail experiences for all mountain bikers.

> **TEACHING TIP**
> Find a local mountain biker, hopefully a family member of a student, to assist with lesson planning, bike maintenance, and supervision.

IMBA RULES OF THE TRAIL

1. Ride on open trails only. Ask a land manager for clarifications if you are uncertain about the status of a trail. Do not trespass on private land. Obtain permits or other authorization as required. Be aware that bicycles are not permitted on areas protected as state or federal wilderness.

2. Leave no trace. Be sensitive to the dirt beneath you. Wet and muddy trails are more vulnerable to damage than dry ones are. When the road is soft, consider other riding options. Stay on existing trails and do not create new ones. Don't cut switchbacks. Be sure to pack out at least as much as you pack in.

3. Control your bicycle. Inattention for even a moment can put yourself and others at risk. Obey all bicycle speed regulations and recommendations, and ride within your limits.

4. Yield to others. Do your utmost to let your fellow trail users know you're coming—use a friendly greeting or bell ring. Try to anticipate other trail users as you ride around corners. Yield to all other trail users unless the trail is signed clearly for bike travel only. When traveling downhill, yield to bicyclists headed uphill unless the trail is signed clearly for one-way or downhill-only traffic. Strive to make each pass a safe and courteous one.

5. Never scare animals. Animals are easily startled by an unannounced approach, a sudden movement, or a loud noise, so give animals enough time and room to adjust to you. When passing horses, use special care and follow directions from the horseback riders (ask if you are uncertain). Running cattle and disturbing wildlife are serious offenses.

6. Plan ahead. Know your equipment, your ability, and the area in which you are riding—and prepare accordingly. Strive to be self-sufficient: Keep your equipment in good repair and carry necessary supplies for changes in weather or other conditions. Always wear a helmet and appropriate safety gear.

Figure 9.8 The sustainable trail use guidelines provided by the IMBA are important concepts to share with your students.

Reprinted, by permission, from International Mountain Bicycling Association.

SAFETY CONSIDERATIONS

There a few items you and your students should attend to in order to manage the risk involved with mountain biking. Mountain bikes are ridden off road and on uneven ground. This means that a mountain bike takes an enormous amount of punishment (which it is designed to do) every time it is ridden. Much of the risk involved in mountain biking can be reduced significantly with a preride inspection of the bike and other critical equipment such as the helmet. These inspections should be performed after, or before, each ride. Performing inspections before each ride provides the rider with the time to address areas of concern and be prepared for the next ride.

Helmet

Visually scan the inside and outer shell of the helmet for any cracks. If the helmet is cracked in any way, replace it. Be sure the straps are in good condition and the material is intact. Engage the strap fastener and pull on both sides of it to be sure it is working properly.

Bike

Get into the routine of inspecting your bike the same way each time. Begin with the frame and inspect the bike from the front to the rear. Consider having a 4 and 5 mm hex wrench with you as you inspect the bike.

1. Check all allen bolts to ensure they are tight (use two fingers and a thumb on the hex; these bolts are not made to be cranked down like a typical bolt).

2. As you visually inspect the frame for cracks, pay attention to the points where the frame is joined together, typically with a weld. Look for paint chips, as these can be a sign of a deeper crack in the frame's material.

3. After inspecting the frame move to the front wheel. Lightly grab two spokes at a time to be sure all your spokes are secure. Pound on the top of your wheel with your fist to ensure the wheel is on the fork tightly. Check the tire pressure in the tire.

4. Squeeze the front brake and rock the bike back and forth. If the bike moves back and forth, your headset, fork, or bars may be loose. Many suspension forks have some play in them, so don't be concerned if you see the fork stanchions rocking forward and backward (by 0.08-0.12 in., or 2-3 mm).

5. Visually inspect the brake cables and look for cracks in the housing; look for fluid leaks if you are using disc brakes.

6. Position the front wheel between your knees and turn the wheel from side to side. If the headset or stem is loose the entire front end might turn even though the wheel is stationary.

7. Visually inspect the brakes and look for debris or loose bolts. Grab the brake mechanism and wiggle it to check for looseness.

8. Move to the middle of the bike and visually inspect all cables and housing. Look for cracks in the housing and splits in the cables. Wiggle the front derailleur and be sure it's tight.

9. Gently step on the drive-side pedal to ensure the cranks are tight (you might hear a creak if the cranks are loose). Grab the crank arms and pull them together to check for tightness.

10. Inspect the chain and look for bent or damaged links. Grab the saddle and check for tightness of the saddle itself and the seat post.

11. Move to the rear triangle of the bike and perform the same brake, wheel, housing, and cable inspection you performed on the front of the bike.

12. Inspect the rear derailleur for tightness and any broken components such as the pulley wheels.

CONCLUSION

As mountain biking becomes more popular, a reduction in access to natural areas is a concern. All mountain bikers share the responsibility to preserve natural areas by minimizing their environmental effects, practicing sustainable mountain biking principles, and respecting public and private property. Bikers can also help to ensure that these areas remain open to mountain biking by volunteering for trail-building and maintenance projects (e.g., see IMBA), participating actively with forest rangers and rescue teams, and finding other ways of demonstrating that they are responsible users of shared outdoor resources.

REFERENCES

Cordell, K. (2004). Outdoor recreation for the 21st century America: A report to the Nation. State College, PA: Venture Press.

National Association for Sport and Physical Education. (2004). *Moving into the future: National standards for physical education* (2nd ed.). Reston, VA: Author.

RECOMMENDED READINGS

Lopes, B. (2005). *Mastering mountain bike skills.* Champaign, IL: Human Kinetics.

Trombley, A. (2005). *Serious mountain biking.* Champaign, IL: Human Kinetics.

Zinn, L. (2005). *Zinn and the art of mountain bike maintenance.* (4th ed.). Boulder, CO: Velopress.

RECOMMENDED WEB SITES

Helmet Fit Information

Bicycle Helmet Safety Institute: www.bhsi.org

Competitive Mountain Biking (National)

USA Cycling: www.usacycling.org/states/new/

Competitive Mountain Biking (Regional)

South: www.sorba.org
www.ntmba.org
Midwest: www.worba.org
Northeast: www.nemba.org
West: www.swimba.org
Northwest: www.obra.org

Trail Ethics and Mountain Bike Advocacy

International Mountain Bicycling Association: www.imba.com

MOUNTAIN BIKING UNIT PLAN

General Lesson Information

Each lesson contains the following seven elements:

1. Objectives—primary learning outcomes
2. Equipment—specific materials and gear
3. Introduction—opening concepts, ideas, and questions that identify the focus of the day
4. Warm-ups—some on-the-bike warm ups that encompass health related physical activity
5. Central activities—activity progressions that increase in difficulty and lead to more advanced skills
6. Closure—suggested discussion and reflection items
7. Assessment—examples of evaluation strategies

Day 1

Focus: Braking and shifting

- Bike fit
- Helmet fit
- Balance
- Braking
- Shifting

Day 2

Focus: Braking and shifting

- Bike inspection
- Braking
- Shifting
- Squeeze box
- Snail race

Day 3

Focus: Turning and cornering

- Tight turns
- Finding a turn

Day 4

Focus: Climbing and flat repair

- Introduction to hills
- Climbing practice
- Flat tire Olympics

Day 5

Focus: Descending

- Going down hills

Day 6

Focus: Riding over obstacles

- Wheelie
- Riding over obstacles practice
- Balloon pop

Day 7

Focus: Advanced skills and stunts

- Clearing the back wheel
- Wheelie practice
- Bunny hop

Day 8

Focus: Bike rodeo

- Creating a bike rodeo station
- Bike rodeo

Day 9

Focus: Ethics and trail riding

- Yielding to other users
- Group riding etiquette
- Passing
- Leave No Trace

Day 10

Focus: Indoor activities (inclement weather possibilities)

- Interviews
- Create posters to promote National Walk or Bike to School Day
- Work with the art teacher and design collages from bike magazines
- Work with the visual arts teacher to create a mountain biking "trick" video
- Find a local trail advocacy group and perform trail work or maintenance
- Have students research and compile a list of local and state trails

chapter 10

Cycling

Gay L. Timken
Amy Lutz

Nothing compares to the pleasure of a bike ride.

John F. Kennedy

Why teach cycling in schools? Why not! Cycling is a great way for students to get to and from school, and it can help encourage youths to include physical activity as part of their daily living. As a lifetime physical activity, cycling has great carryover into adulthood, and so the effect of cycling as part of the physical education curriculum far outweighs that of many traditional sports. Riding bikes to and from school helps young people meet the guidelines for physical activity established by the Centers for Disease Control and Prevention. Cycling delivers health-related fitness, increasing muscular strength and endurance and improving cardiorespiratory health. Cycling improves skill-related fitness components, including balance, coordination, agility, and power. The positive effect of physical activity on elevating mood and decreasing stress, anxiety, and depression is no longer a debate. Youths can be encouraged to ride a bike on their own as well as with friends and family members, so there is clearly a social dimension to cycling. The social and environmental benefits of cycling to and from school or work, such as conserving energy and reducing emissions, should not be overlooked. Though not an immediate outcome, the potential economic rewards of cycling

Example of a Successful Middle School Cycling Unit

Sarah Coffman and Jordan Scoggins teach cycling to eighth graders at Wood Middle School in Wilsonville, Oregon. The administration has been very supportive; they and the district have an emphasis on teaching lifetime activities. The cycling unit consists of 16 lessons that help students learn how to ride bikes safely on the roads. Beginning lessons are safety related and include helmet and bike fit. Several lessons are taught on the track oval before the class heads off campus to ride on the roads. Sarah Coffman and Jordan Scoggins offer the following suggestions:

- Find alternative sources of funding. A physician interested in the cycling unit gave a donation to get started, and the local hospital donated helmets.

- Find ways to make it work within the schedule. Students have physical education 3 days per week for 43 min, with one 90 min class each week. The 90 min class allows for longer rides.

- Send letters home to parents to communicate about the cycling unit. Ask for volunteers and help for the culminating ride.

- Have enough volunteers to help supervise on rides and even during on-campus lessons.

- Always carry a first aid kit, bike tools, a cell phone, and walkie-talkies to communicate between teachers who may be at the front and back of the pack.

- Help students learn the routine of getting bikes and helmets out of storage as well as returning them to storage. Following the routine allows for smoother transitions and a much longer time to ride.

- Include a segment on how to use gears. This may be the difference between success or no success while cycling.

- Use student coaches to help with accountability. Students are put in groups of four, and each group member has a role: coach, sentinel (helps others know where to go), safety police, and lead rider. The coaches wear something to distinguish themselves from the others and they are in charge of their group. This has worked very well in that students become accountable for each other and what happens on rides.

- End with a culminating ride off campus. The Wood Middle School cycling unit ends with a culminating ride to a local park approximately 2 mi (3.2 km) from school. A few parents meet students at the park with snacks, and students get to play at the park for about 20 min before returning to school. A volunteer with a bike trailer carries soccer balls, basketballs, and skateboards to the park.

include reduced health care costs for individuals and for the whole of society. And who can now deny the benefits of physical activity, including cycling, on cognitive functioning, particularly in improving student readiness to learn (Ratey, 2008)?

The following is a list of benefits that result from including cycling in the physical education curriculum:

- There is much that can be learned while cycling, some of which is perfect for integrating science (identifying flora and fauna of the local area), mathematics (calculating distance and speed), geography (mapping), social studies (studying the historical significance of cycling in different societies), language arts (reading and writing about cycling), environmental science (reduction of emissions by cycling), and more.

- Cycling helps students to meet each and every NASPE standard for physical education. Table 10.1 provides only one example of how cycling meets each standard; the cycling lessons on the accompanying CD-ROM include more on how cycling helps students to meet NASPE standards.

- There is a natural fit between cycling and learning about health-related fitness. During cycling, students learn how to determine their target heart rate zone,

how to stay in the target heart zone while riding, how to keep track of calories burned, and how to develop muscular endurance.

- Connecting a cycling unit to a local cycling event can provide students with physical activity opportunities outside of school. For example, students can complete 40 to 45 mi (64-72 km) of the 50 mi (80 km) of a half-century ride during the cycling unit in physical education and then complete the last 5 to 10 mi (8-16 km) at the event itself.

- Learning basic principles of biomechanics and physics, such as center of gravity (seat position), force production (standing versus sitting while climbing), optimal joint angles (saddle height), gear ratios (optimizing gears on a climb), and bike design (why the seat is positioned behind the crankset), provides depth to the topic.

- Some teachers have students who become trained as bike mechanics and establish their own bike shop in the school.

- Students can become proactive citizens for personal, community, and environmental health while engaged in a cycling unit. Conducting a bikeability survey of the local community or area surrounding the

Table 10.1 Cycling Through NASPE Standards

Standard	Standard description	Cycling example
1	Demonstrates competency in motor skills and movement patterns needed to perform a variety of physical activities	Students demonstrate the ability to ride in a paceline and to use the correct hand signals for debris, slow, stop, and right and left turns.
2	Demonstrates understanding of movement concepts, principles, strategies, and tactics as they apply to the learning and performance of physical activities	Students identify basic biomechanical principles of cycling related to power, ascents, descents, and braking.
3	Participates regularly in physical activity	Students are physically active while cycling during class.
4	Achieves and maintains a health-enhancing level of physical fitness	Students can describe how cycling benefits health-related physical fitness.
5	Exhibits responsible personal and social behavior that respects self and others in physical activity settings	Students demonstrate respect for other cyclists and drivers by obeying traffic laws, including using correct hand signals.
6	Values physical activity for health, enjoyment, challenge, self-expression, and social interaction	Students express what they value about being physically active, including what they derive from cycling.

From *Moving Into the Future: National Standards for Physical Education,* 2nd ed., 2004 (Reston, VA: National Association for Sport and Physical Education), 11.

school can encourage students to become more aware of the needs of cyclists and to become more civic minded. Students can encourage people in the community to cycle more during National Bike Month, which typically is May and includes the designated Bike to School or Work Week.

• Middle and high school students can buddy up with and mentor elementary school students through a cycling education program. This program might include helping the younger students to travel safely between home and school.

• And, of course, just learning about bikes, bike maintenance, and riding safely and efficiently provides a good deal of learning material!

Clearly there are many benefits to incorporating cycling into a physical education curriculum. So what are the potential challenges, and how might a teacher overcome such challenges? First and foremost, it is a teacher's knowledge, attitude, and willingness to accept and surmount challenges that make implementing outdoor activities possible. In a recent study of 10 physical education teachers who implemented various outdoor activities at secondary schools, McNamee and Timken (in review) found that each teacher faced multiple barriers when offering nontraditional outdoor pursuits (e.g., mountain biking, rock climbing, backpacking, cycling). Funding, space (including storage), time, and scheduling were common barriers. Nonetheless, these 10 teachers forged ahead, most often because of the benefits to students, but also for themselves. Various tips on getting started for teaching cycling are provided in figure 10.1. No doubt there are more challenges to teaching cycling than there are to teaching badminton in physical education, but the motivation to continue teaching outdoor activities often comes from the positive reactions the students have to learning something new.

CYCLING TERMINOLOGY

The following is a small selection of cycling terminology. You should decide which of these terms are most appropriate for your learners.

aerodynamic—Creates less wind resistance. A bike design or rider can be aerodynamic.

bead of a tire—A bead found on each edge of a tire's inner circumference. It fits into the rim of the tire.

bike friendly—An environment or area that features safe design for cycling, such as wide curb lanes and drain grates that are safe for bicycles, but does not feature roadway signs, pavement markings or striping, or directional and information markers.

bike lane—Part of a roadway specifically designated for cyclists, which includes striping, signs, and pavement markings to indicate the bike lane.

bike route—A route that features informational and directional markers but no striping, signs, or pavement markings.

bonk—When a cyclist runs out of energy (i.e., hits the wall), which typically occurs after riding longer distances.

brain bucket—A helmet.

braking—When the cyclist applies the brakes in order to slow or stop the momentum of the bike.

cadence—A cyclist's revolutions per minute (rpm), or the rate at which a cyclist pedals. The optimal cadence for road cycling is 70 to 90 rpm.

century—A ride of 100 mi (161 km).

chainring—The front sprockets on the crankset. Bikes may have 1, 2, or 3 sprockets.

cleats—Pieces that fit the bottom of specialty cycling shoes that fit into clipless pedals.

clipless pedals—Pedals that are specially designed to fit a particular cleated shoe system.

cog—The sprockets on the rear wheel. There may be anywhere from 1 to 9 rear cogs.

components—The braking and shifting systems.

crankset—The cranks and chainrings (front gears) together.

derailleur—The mechanism that shifts the gears; the front derailleur shifts the front gears and the rear derailleur shifts the back gears.

downshift—To shift to a lower gear, which might include shifting to a larger cog (rear sprocket) or a smaller chainring (front sprocket).

drafting—When one cyclist rides very close behind another, creating an air pocket, to conserve energy. It is estimated that the front rider expends about 30% more energy than the rider behind expends.

drivetrain or power train—The components that make the rear wheel turn, including the chain, crankset, and cassette.

TEACHING CYCLING: TIPS FOR GETTING STARTED

- There are lots of creative ways, including seeking donations and grants, to obtain bikes and other equipment. Police departments and bus transportation systems may be willing to donate bikes from their lost and found, and community members may be willing to donate unused bikes to schools.

- Teachers can look to local Boys and Girls Clubs of America, YMCAs, and park and recreation entities to develop community partnerships to share funding, equipment, and storage.

- Bike shops often make deals with schools and may sell their rented bike fleet or last year's models for reduced prices.

- Resorts have fleets of bicycles they turn over every few years, and these bicycles can be purchased at a fraction of the original cost.

- Through fundraising, one teacher sent a few students to bike mechanic school for the purpose of helping maintain their fleet of bikes.

- There are often smaller grants available to schools and organizations looking to increase physical activity levels of youths or to prevent injury.

- Teachers who feel less confident in their content expertise can find a local bike shop employee, local police officer, community member, or cycling club member to help teach at least a portion of a cycling unit.

- Asking for names of local cyclists at a nearby bike shop or cycling club can assist teachers in finding much-needed help to supervise students on off-campus rides. Educators teaching in small communities without a bike shop or cycling club can look to the nearest city or ask the school's parent organization for help.

- Time and scheduling conflicts are real issues in schools, but with some effort teachers can convince administrators to move a class or integrate a class with another subject to increase class time. Don't be afraid to ask for extended time when teaching something new in physical education.

- It is still possible to teach cycling when time is limited; teachers can use the track just outside the school doors in a 43 min class and ask for 1 or 2 classes where the time is doubled for an off-campus ride.

- Using a numbering system for each bike and helmet can help students find a bike and helmet that fit. It is good to have a variety of sizes of bikes and helmets to fit a variety of students.

- Local cycling clubs or shops may volunteer their time to maintain school bikes on an annual basis.

- Storage tends to be a difficult problem, particularly for bikes. Having temporary storage for bikes (such as the showers in locker rooms) during a cycling unit and long-term storage (such as a shed or corner of the bus barn) when bikes are not in use may prove helpful.

Figure 10.1   Consider these tips when contemplating integrating biking into your curriculum.

endo—When a cyclist crashes by going head over heels (end over end) over the handlebars.

fixed gear—When there is one chainring and one rear cog on the bike such that shifting is not possible.

flat—When the tire loses air.

frame—The frame of the bicycle.

granny gear—The lowest gear ratio or the combination of gears used to make pedaling the easiest; typically the smallest front chainring and the largest in the back.

hand signals—Signals used for left and right turns, passing, road debris, slow, and stop.

high gear—When the gears are shifted to the larger front chainrings and small back cogs. On flat ground, pedaling becomes more difficult in higher gears and there are fewer revolutions per minute.

honking—When a cyclist stands up to pedal, be it for climbing, sprinting, or stretching the legs.

hybrid—A bike combining the features of mountain bikes and road bikes.

low gear—When the gears are shifted to the smaller front chainring and larger back cogs. On flat ground, pedaling becomes easier when shifting to lower gears and there are more revolutions per minute.

metric century—A 100 km (62 mi) ride.

on your wheel—When one cyclist rides closely behind a front rider's back wheel.

overgear—When a rider is riding in a gear ratio that is too big (hard) for the terrain or fitness level.

paceline—A group of riders who ride single file, taking their turn at leading while those behind have protection from the wind. The front rider pulls and then drops to the rear position as the next rider takes a turn at pulling.

pedaling circles—Thinking of bicycling in terms of how many parts of the bike move in circles. This helps a rider focus on pedaling smoothly and efficiently by thinking of the feet as moving in circles (instead of just pushing or pulling).

pedaling squares—When a rider becomes so fatigued that the smooth and efficient pedaling motion is lost.

pinch flat or snakebite—When an internal pinch or puncture creates two small holes (hence the term *snakebite)* in the tube; caused by the tube being squeezed against the rim.

Presta valve—A long, thin valve on a tire.

psi—Pounds per square inch of air pressure in the tire.

pull—When a rider in a paceline takes a turn at the lead, creating a slipstream or air pocket for the other riders.

pull off—When the lead rider in a paceline moves to the side after taking a turn in the lead.

quick-release skewers or levers—Levers that allow the tires to be released from the hub quickly.

rails to trails—The creation of nonmotorized trails from old railways. See the Rails-to-Trails Conservancy Web site for more information (www.railstotrails.org).

reach—The distance between the seat and the handlebars, or the rider's reach. Includes the length of the top tube and stem.

rim—The part of the wheel where a tire attaches.

road rash—An abrasion of the skin due to a fall.

saddle—The seat of the bike.

scanning—A quick and frequent look over the left shoulder (or right for those in the UK) to check for traffic.

Schrader valve—A short, fat valve on a tire.

shift—When the cyclist changes gears.

shifter—What the cyclist uses to change gears.

slipstream—The air pocket created when one rider rides closely behind another rider.

snakebite—See *pinch flat.*

soft pedal—Pedaling without actually applying any power to the pedals.

spin or spinning—Pedaling at a high cadence. This is often seen when the bike is in a low gear, which then causes the pedals to spin more easily and there to be more revolutions per minute. Spinning can also refer to an indoor cycling class that is similar in concept to aerobic dance.

ultra cycling—Long endurance cycling events, similar to ultra marathons.

upshift—Shifting to a higher gear, which might include shifting to a smaller cog (rear sprocket) or a larger chainring (front sprocket).

wheelbase—The distance between wheel axles.

wheel sucker—A rider who doesn't take a turn at pulling in a paceline.

EQUIPMENT

Cycling can be rather equipment intensive, but this should not dissuade you from including it in your physical education curriculum. You absolutely must have bikes that fit students and are in good working condition as well as helmets approved by the CPSC that are in good condition. It is best if helmets are no older than 5 years. Helmets that have been involved in a crash must be replaced, regardless of visible damage. Structural damage can result from a helmet being dropped (not involved in a crash) repeatedly by a student, so use great care with regard to helmets. Regardless of state helmet laws, you, your students, and any community members who work with students should always wear a helmet. In addition to bikes and helmets, you need at least one good-quality floor bike pump, but more than one is recommended for a class of students. At least one bike stand is helpful for maintenance work as well as demonstrations. At a minimum, each adult supervisor should carry the following equipment for rides off campus: a smaller hand pump for the occasional flat tire (can be attached to the bike), at least one set of bike tools, tire levers for changing tires, tubes and a patch kit, a cell phone, a first aid kit, and a class list with emergency contact numbers. A small backpack can carry much of this equipment, although bike bags (see figure 10.2) work nicely for some equipment.

Sport-specific shoes (cleated shoes) and clothing are great but certainly are not a necessity to delivering a cycling unit in physical education. Typical physical education clothing (shorts, sweats, T-shirts, and sweatshirts) is appropriate as long as it isn't baggy or loose fitting. However, in the event of cycling on the roads, it is critical for students to wear a brightly colored and highly visible shirt, sweatshirt, jacket, or vest. You can purchase the bright orange, yellow, or pink vests typically worn by road construction crews for your students. Another safety precaution is to attach reflective tape to each student's clothing and helmet.

Bikes

The goal of a cycling unit is to enable students to engage safely in cycling regardless of the type of bike they ride (see figure 10.3). A road bike, mountain bike, hybrid bike, or coaster or cruiser all work in a cycling unit, although coasters or cruisers may have only one speed (if they are a fixed-gear bike), which may be less desirable for middle school and high school students. Fixed-gear bikes don't allow students to become familiar with shifting. If the cycling unit is geared toward competitive road cycling, then a road bike is most desirable. If mountain biking is the unit and the students will be riding off road, then mountain bikes or hybrid bikes are more desirable (see chapter 9).

Purchasing cheap bikes typically is not the answer to saving money on equipment given long-term wear and maintenance. The expensive parts of the bike tend to be the components, which include the shifting and braking systems. If you are able to purchase a fleet, consult a bike specialist for guidance.

Helmets

Helmets, or *brain buckets* as they are commonly called, are a necessity! Properly fitting helmets are critical to head protection. Helmets must be tight fitting and are useless if the chinstrap is not buckled (a common occurrence among youths). Helmets can be adjusted with the chinstrap and internal fitting devices, and they must be adjusted to fit each student's head. Proper fit is when the helmet is snug on the head (so that shaking the head does not cause the helmet to shake) and the chinstrap is tight. A tight chinstrap pulls the helmet down slightly during the open jaw test (see figure 10.4). The helmet should be level to maximize front and side coverage; in other words, the helmet should cover the forehead rather than sit back on the head (see figure 10.5). For more instructions about helmet fit, see the Bicycle Helmet Safety Institute Web site at www.bhsi.org.

Helmet prices start between $10 and $20 U.S. and climb from there. The key to a helmet purchase is making sure the helmet is new, approved by the CPSC,

Figure 10.2   A bike bag.

Figure 10.3   Different types of bikes include *(a)* road bikes, *(b)* mountain bikes, *(c)* hybrid bikes, and *(d)* coasters and cruisers.

and easily adjustable. Students tend to be more motivated to wear helmets that they deem to look cool, so appearance might be a consideration when purchasing helmets. Helmets should be no older than 5 years and if any part of the helmet is cracked, including its internal foam, it is rendered ineffective. If a helmet is dropped its foam may crack, so checking helmets on a regular basis is an important safety precaution. The Bicycle Helmet

Safety Institute Web site provides more specific information on helmet use for teachers, including activities and games for youths.

Bike Pumps

Both floor pumps and travel or hand pumps are necessary in a cycling program. Some bikes have a more

Figure 10.3   *(continued).*

traditional Schrader valve while others have a Presta valve (see figure 10.6), so you should purchase bike pumps that adapt to both types.

Bike Tools

The bike tools you might want for your program depend on the goals and intent of the program. Part of learning about cycling is learning about basic bike maintenance, such as changing a tire, cleaning the chain and gears, and making minor adjustments to the braking system. Changing a tire requires tire levers, a tube, and a patch kit (see figure 10.7). Patch kits may be more practical for physical education classes given the variability in bikes (and tube sizes) that might need repair if students are bringing their personal bikes to school. Cleaning the chain and gears requires chain cleaner, lube, and brushes

Figure 10.4   The open jaw test.

Figure 10.5   Proper helmet fit.

(old toothbrushes work relatively well but are not good for deep cleaning). Making minor brake adjustments doesn't require a set of tools, but learning to make major adjustments to brakes and derailleurs and to fix chains and spokes requires a completely different set of tools and skills. Consult a local bike mechanic to determine which tools you need in order to meet your programmatic goals and to gain expertise in basic bike maintenance before delivering a cycling unit.

Shoes

Usually sneakers or other shoes designed for physical activity work for a cycling unit in physical education, so there is no need to purchase specialized pedals or shoes. Some pedals come with a toe clip or strap (see figure 10.8) in which a shoe can be inserted. These straps allow both the quadriceps and gluteal muscles and the hamstrings and hip flexors to move the pedal;

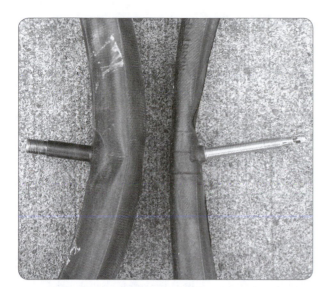

Figure 10.6 A Schrader valve *(left)* and a Presta valve *(right)*.

Figure 10.7 Changing a tire requires *(a)* a patch kit, *(b)* tire levers, and *(c)* a tube.

without the toe clip the quadriceps and gluteal muscles do the majority of the work. Students will quickly feel their quadriceps muscles working while riding, and this affords an excellent opportunity to reinforce anatomy and basic biomechanics. Shoes specifically designed for cycling (i.e., cleated shoe and pedal systems) are more biomechanically efficient than sneakers are due to their

rigid soles. Rigid soles are more efficient at transferring power into the pedal when compared with flexible soles, which allow energy to disperse throughout the shoe instead of go directly into the pedal. As with using the toe clip or strap, being secured into the pedal via a cleated system activates the multiple lower-body muscles for greater work efficiency. There are shoes designed specifically for mountain biking, road cycling, cyclo-cross, touring, and spinning (indoor cycling). The shoes and cleats in figure 10.9 are designed for road cycling.

Clothing

As with shoes, specialty clothing is not a requirement for cycling. However, specialty clothing can enhance the experience by providing physical comfort and protection. To reiterate, students who are riding on the roads should wear brightly colored shirts or jackets to increase their visibility.

Figure 10.8 A toe clip.

Figure 10.9 Cycling shoes and cleats.

- **Shorts and tights.** Padded tights make longer rides that require increased time in the saddle more enjoyable. For people who dislike tights, there are padded shorts available. While designed for comfort, padded shorts and tights are also designed with function in mind, such as whether you are taking a short versus long ride. Shorts or pants with a substantial seam in the crotch will decrease cycling comfort. Encourage students to wear shorts or pants that have little seam.

- **Jerseys.** Jerseys are formfitting and specifically designed to improve aerodynamics. They typically come in bright colors and include pockets in the back for storage. Cyclists store food, money, keys, cell phones, identification, and the like in these pockets, as well as gloves and arm and leg warmers. Jerseys can have long or short sleeves and are made of breathable fabric that wicks away moisture, which increases comfort. Wearing a cotton T-shirt on a long ride is discouraged, but for shorter rides a cotton T-shirt should be fine.

- **Jackets and vests.** Water-resistant, waterproof, and windbreaker jackets and vests come in bright colors and, like jerseys, often have back pockets for storage. Cycling jackets are designed for warmth and protection and are necessary when riding in mild or cooler weather. If students need to wear their own jackets for warmth, have them also wear brightly colored construction vests and reflective tape to increase their visibility.

- **Gloves.** Gloves serve multiple purposes. They provide comfort and protection (from falls), improve grip (less sweat), absorb shock (padding in all the right places), provide warmth, and even come with fleece in just the right spot for wiping your nose. Gloves aren't a necessity, but they certainly make a difference on longer rides.

- **Eyewear.** Eye protection is important for students, particularly when they are cycling on the roads. Dirt, rocks, insects, and sun are all potential hazards for students. Special cycling sunglasses are available and are desirable due to their wraparound protective fit. Encourage students to have some type of eye protection.

Bike Stand

Bike stands are great for maintenance work as well as in-class demonstrations. Though a bike stand isn't a necessity, its benefits far outweigh its nominal cost. A bike stand suspends a bike in the air, allowing the wheels to turn freely. A bike stand is of tremendous help if bike maintenance skills are part of the student learning objectives. Bike stands are also of great help for demonstrating shifting.

Accessories

The following accessories are not essential for cycling, but they can make the ride more safe and enjoyable, especially when riding in rainy weather:

- **Bike lights.** Students should learn all the safety precautions and rules of the road required to be a safe and competent cyclist. One rule of the road is to light the bike when commuting in the early morning or late evening. Riding a bike in the dark, including at dawn and at dusk, requires a front light. Cyclists can be ticketed for failing to have their bike lighted properly. Using blinking lights for night riding is also beneficial. Using bike lights during the day is not required, but it does increase a cyclist's visibility to motorists.

- **Cycle computers.** The computer is a permanent fixture on each individual bike because it is calibrated to wheel size. The basic bike computer gives the distance, time, and intensity of a ride. The distance can be logged in miles or kilometers, the time can be logged in minutes, and the intensity can be logged in speed, including the average speed of the ride. Computers allow students to know more about any given ride, and information gleaned from computers potentially could be integrated into another class.

- **Water bottles, water bottle cages, hydration systems.** Hydrating before, during, and after a ride is an important habit for students to develop. Some bikes may come with attached water bottle cages. On the other hand, students may rather carry a hydration system such as a Camelback. There is some skill involved in removing the water bottle from the cage, drinking, and returning the bottle while riding. Have students practice this skill before riding on the road.

- **Bike locks.** Securing bikes, particularly a fleet of bikes, requires a significant security system. Schools should have adequate bike racks, and teachers should encourage students to purchase and use a lock for their own personal bike. If your school is able to purchase a fleet of bikes for physical education classes, then a cable system is a more practical solution, even if the fleet is secured in an indoor space. Do not overlook a secure locking system.

- **Fenders.** Though not a necessity, fenders make cycling in wet weather a little more enjoyable. Fenders keep the water, dirt, and grime off clothing. If your school purchases bikes, it might be wise to purchase fenders as well.

- **Bike trainer.** A bike trainer is designed for stationary cycling with a road bike. Many cyclists train on a trainer during the nasty winter months. A trainer can also be useful for fitting a bike to a rider. Bike trainers can be expensive, but sometimes it is possible to purchase a used trainer for less (e.g., when local cyclists upgrade to a new model).

BIKE FIT

Knowing how to fit an individual to a bike is an important skill for teachers and students alike. Body position on the bike determines power and efficiency as well as comfort, and improper positioning can lead to injury and poor bike handling due to instability. The key to bike fit is compromise—compromise between power and comfort. The final outcome of the compromise depends on each individual's cycling goals. For example, cyclists who race short distances are more concerned with power and less concerned with comfort. Conversely, individuals who engage in touring, or riding long distances, are more concerned with comfort, especially when their rides place them in the saddle for 5 to 12 hours each day.

The advice provided in this chapter for fitting bikes for physical education classes is basic and practical, given the logistics of working with groups. There are many good books and Web sites that offer more detailed information, and bike shop owners and cycling enthusiasts are excellent resources as well. It might prove beneficial to have a few cycling experts on hand when teaching classes on bike fit and when fitting students to bikes. As a cycling instructor, you must balance the time required to fit bikes properly with the time you want to engage students in physical activity. Many cycling experts suggest using a bike trainer to fit bikes. While a trainer works well for individuals, it is not necessary when working with an entire physical education class. Instead, you can have students complete a peer checklist in groups of three: one student sits on the bike to find a proper fit, one student acts as the peer assessor and evaluates the fit, and the third student straddles the front wheel to hold the front of the bike steady (see figure 10.10).

There are three points of contact between the body and the bike: the hands, the feet, and the seat. Adjust-

ments based on these three points of contact make for more efficient and comfortable rides. Take a fine-tuning approach to bike fit. Minor adjustments are more desirable than major ones, and fine-tuning over time works better in the long run. For example, if you make a substantial adjustment to saddle height in order to fix a seat that is way too low, the student may complain. Adjusting saddle height in small increments over a few days seems to be a better approach.

Saddle height, saddle fore and aft positioning, saddle tilt, and handlebar adjustments are the most important adjustments for efficiency and comfort. These are addressed in the following sections.

Saddle Height

Saddle height is important for getting the most out of each pedal stroke. The height of the saddle determines the angle at the knee, which affects the efficiency and power of the leg muscles. The saddle should not be too high or too low. If the saddle is too high (so that the knees are fully extended), the hips rock side to side with each stroke. This creates inefficient pedaling and extreme discomfort in the buttocks. If the saddle is too low (leading to a smaller knee angle), the quadriceps fatigue quickly and there is greater potential for knee pain. While the method outlined here for fitting a bike is slightly time consuming, it is precise and worth the effort. Using this process will help students understand efficient saddle height more clearly.

The most efficient saddle height is determined by sitting on the saddle with the heel of one foot resting on the pedal at the bottom of the pedal stroke (6 o'clock position; see figure 10.11*a).* At this position the leg should be fully extended with the knee straight or nearly straight. Once the saddle height is positioned so that the leg is fully extended when the heel is on the pedal, it is time to move the ball of the foot onto the pedal; now the knee should be slightly bent (figure 10.11*b).* At this point you should use your best judgment and your knowledge of a student's skill level to adjust the saddle height. Sometimes the saddle needs to be lower if a student is still learning or young. When adjusting the seat, take note of the mark on the seat post that indicates maximum height; raising the seat beyond the mark (or leaving less than 3 in., or 7.6 cm, of seat post in the frame) decreases the strength and stability of the seat post. At a minimum, take time to adjust saddle height to make the cycling experience more enjoyable.

Day 2

BIKE FIT PEER ASSESSMENT

Cyclist: _____

Assessor: _____

Students should complete the bike fitting in groups of three. One person assesses; one person tries out the bike for proper fit; and one person holds the bike steady. Each student should have a bike fitted and turn in an assessment form to the teacher.

Use a check mark to indicate that each task was completed correctly and to indicate that the bike is fitted to the rider.

Fitting the bike	Completed and fitted	Not completed or fitted
Saddle height		
Cyclist sitting on seat, one pedal up, one down		
Right heel on pedal at bottom of pedal stroke		
Ball of right foot on pedal, slight bend at right knee		
If moved, seat post is not higher than the mark (or there are 3 in., or 7.6 cm, of seat post in the tube)		

Problems with saddle height: _____

Fitting the bike	Completed and fitted	Not completed or fitted
Saddle position (fore, aft)		
Cyclist sitting on seat, pedals parallel to ground		
One foot in forward position, plumb line falls from knee to right over pedal axle		
If seat was moved forward or backward, saddle height was adjusted again		

Problems with saddle position, either fore or aft: _____

Fitting the bike	Completed and fitted	Not completed or fitted
Saddle tilt		
Cyclist sitting on seat, hands *not* on handlebars		
Cyclist is able to sit on seat (while pedaling backward) without sliding forward or backward (adjust seat if needed)		
Saddle is adjusted so it is level or the nose is slightly higher		

Problems with saddle tilt: _____

Figure 10.10   Students use this checklist to learn how to properly fit a bike (this form can also be found on the accompanying CD-ROM in the day 2 lesson for the cycling unit).

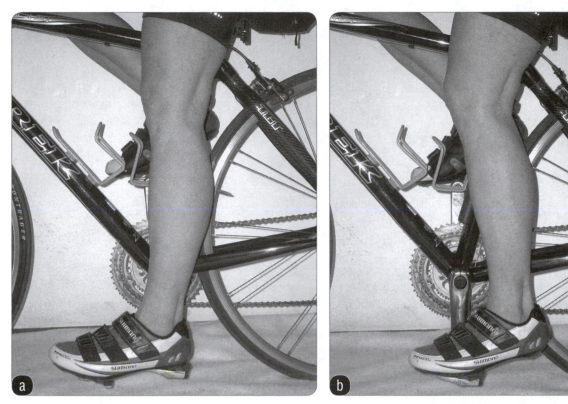

Figure 10.11 Determining saddle height: *(a)* saddle is at the correct height if the leg is fully extended (heel of the foot is on the pedal at the 6 o'clock position), and *(b)* the knee should be slightly bent when the ball of the foot is placed on the pedal.

Saddle Fore and Aft Positioning

Fore and aft positioning is the forward or backward positioning of the saddle on the seat post. A saddle that is positioned incorrectly can cause knee, back, shoulder, and neck pain. Once you establish the fore and aft positioning, you will likely need to make another adjustment in saddle height. This is because moving the saddle forward has the effect of lowering the seat height. Use the following method for determining the best fore and aft positioning (neutral position) for the saddle. You may need to make minor adjustments depending on your cycling goals (power versus comfort). Start with the student sitting properly on the saddle, with the balls of the feet on the pedals, the feet level (no heel or hip drop), and the pedals at horizontal (parallel to the ground). Drop a plumb line from just below the kneecap (at the tibial tuberosity) of the forward knee. For the most efficient pedaling, the plumb line should fall directly over the pedal axle (see figure 10.12). Adjust the seat position forward if the plumb line falls behind the pedal axle; adjust the seat position backward if the plumb line falls in front of the pedal axle.

Saddle Tilt

The saddle must be level. If there is too much forward tilt in the saddle, the rider will continually push against the handlebars to keep the body positioned back on the seat, and if there is too much backward tilt in the saddle, the rider will experience pain on the sit bones (ischium). Some experts suggest positioning the nose of the saddle slightly higher than the rear, while others recommend keeping the nose a degree or two lower than the rear. Whichever the case, students should be able to sit upright on the saddle without feeling like they are about to slide off in either direction. The students must pay close attention to how they feel on the saddle, and minor adjustments should be made accordingly.

Handlebar Adjustment

Adjusting the handlebars is the next step to fitting the bike. Again, handlebar position depends on the cyclist's goals. Some cyclists may desire or require a more upright position (e.g., for touring) while others need more aerodynamic positioning (e.g., for racing). The upright position is less stressful on the back but creates greater wind resistance. For better control and

Figure 10.12   Finding the correct fore and aft position of the saddle.

shock absorption, the best position is one in which the elbows are slightly bent at all times. As a general rule, road riders and mountain bikers should position the handlebars 1 to 2 in. (2.5-5 cm) below the seat height, while touring cyclists should position the handlebars at the saddle height. Positioning the handlebars closer to the seat establishes more of an upright position, while moving the handlebars farther away creates more forward lean. Again, your students must pay close attention to how they feel. Making minor adjustments and fine-tuning the handlebars are the best method of determining bike fit.

Fitting a bike requires some science and art, but it also has a practical side. Younger children and children who have less cycling experience may have more difficulty balancing a bike and so may require the seat to be lower than what is considered biomechanically advantageous. In some cases children may be riding a bike that is slightly large for them, which again requires a lower seat height. Safety is more important than cycling efficiency; efficiency comes with time and practice as long

as students have the opportunity to practice under safe conditions.

BASIC SKILLS AND TECHNIQUES

Being a confident and predictable bicyclist is essential for riding safely. Traffic laws are the same for both cyclists and motorists, so learning cycling safety skills will help students become better drivers as well as better cyclists. Knowing how to ride safely is the key to both feeling safe and being safe. An understanding of proper road positioning and emergency response enables riders to more safely coexist with traffic. Therefore, before cycling for fitness, students need to demonstrate knowledge of the following skills. Reviewing these skills is also good for cyclists who consider themselves proficient, as you can always learn something new. Practice will lead to proficiency and increased confidence and a greater ability to cope with hazards encountered on the road.

Figure 10.13   A group of middle school students demonstrating riding in a straight line.

- **Riding in a straight line.** This is the first skill all riders need to learn. No matter where your students ride, they must be able to handle a bike in order to ride in a straight line (figure 10.13). This is necessary when riding with traffic, as riding in a predictable manner allows drivers to have confidence in the rider's ability. This confidence often leads drivers to give riders more space on the road.

- **Starting.** The correct position for starting, in which one pedal is in the 2 o'clock position, is referred to as the *power position*. Ideally the dominant leg is in the 2 o'clock position in order to provide the most power when starting.

- **Stopping.** One of the leading causes of cycling accidents is the failure of the bicyclist to stop. Both the front and rear brakes should be applied concurrently when stopping, as cyclists who use only the front brakes can be flipped over the handlebars. When stopping with the hand brakes, cyclists should apply three times as much pressure to the rear brake. Cyclists should also maintain their balance when stopping by not skidding the back tire.

- **Scanning.** Cyclists ride with—not against—traffic. Riding in the bike lane or where the bike lane would be is the safest. This is the position where the slowest traffic, which is normally the cyclist, should be. However, there are occasions when cyclists want to turn or to avoid hazards that lie in their path and so need to move into the road. Before moving, cyclists should scan over their left shoulder to ensure that the road is clear and that there is room to move. Cyclists must maintain a straight line while scanning so they don't accidently swerve into traffic. This means that cyclists need to be comfortable with taking a quick look over their left shoulder (if riding in the United States) while keeping their right hand on the handlebars.

- **Arm and hand signaling.** This signaling is the primary method for cyclists to relay their intentions to motorists and other cyclists. Proper signaling prevents surprises. Signals should be conducted with the left arm and hand, as they are the closest to traffic and the most visible to cars (assuming the cyclist is riding properly with traffic). Figure 10.14 depicts arm and hand signals for cyclists.

- **Turning.** Left and right turns should be conducted the same way. Cyclists should use appropriate arm signals when approaching the turn. Before beginning the turn, cyclists should place both hands on the handlebars. They should also look where they want to go when making the turn. When learning how to turn, riders should slow down. The inside pedal should be maintained at the 12 o'clock position to prevent it from catching on the road. A rider may need to pedal through a left-hand turn, as left-hand turns are longer than right-hand turns, and so keeping the inside pedal fixed at the 12 o'clock position may not always apply.

Figure 10.14 Arm and hand signals: *(a)* left-hand turn signal, *(b)* right-hand turn signal, *(c)* slow and stop.

• **Cadence.** Maintaining a correct cadence makes cycling more enjoyable for every level of cyclist. Cadence is measured by the number of revolutions the pedals make each minute. An ideal cadence should be between 70 and 90 rpm.

• **Shifting.** Shifting allows riders to adjust pedaling difficulty to maintain a good cadence. For example, pedaling uphill usually requires shifting to make the pedaling easier. When going down a hill, a rider might want to shift to a higher gear in order to go faster. The shifter on the right handle is for the gears (cogs) in the back. The shifter on the left handle is for the chainrings connected to the pedals. Depending on the number of cogs and chainrings, there could be many gear combi-

nations. Choosing a gear depends on the fitness of the cyclist and the terrain.

• **Lane positioning.** Cyclists are considered vehicles on the road and must follow traffic laws. This includes riding in the same direction as other vehicles. Since cyclists are often the slowest vehicle on the road, they should ride in the farthest right-hand lane that travels in the direction they want to go. Cyclists can be in one of three different positions in a lane. Sometimes they have to cross lanes of traffic to get in a left-hand turning lane. For intersections, cyclists should position themselves in the same place they would if they were in the car. For example, if they want to turn left, they should be in a left turning lane. However, in order to end up in the bike lane after making a left-hand turn, cyclists should position themselves on the right-hand side of the left turn lane.

- **Rock dodging.** Sometimes there are obstacles on the road that need to be avoided at the last minute. These may be rocks or potholes that appear so suddenly there is neither time nor room to comfortably ride around them. To perform the rock dodge, cyclists should turn the handlebars quickly just before hitting the obstacle. Just as quickly, they should then turn the handlebars back the other direction more than feels comfortable. The key to this skill is being quick. The front wheel will avoid the obstacle but the back wheel may ride over it—doing so is acceptable.

- **Quick turn.** When cycling on the road, a sudden turn might be necessary to avoid crashing. This turn is performed differently than a planned turn, in which the cyclist leans in the direction of the turn. For a right-hand quick turn, the cyclist turns the handlebars to the left, which forces the bike to lean to the right. The cyclist then turns the wheel back to the right to complete the turn. The initial turn of the handlebars to the left unbalances the cyclist, which causes the turn to happen more quickly.

- **Sudden stop.** This stop is used when no other alternatives are available and a cyclist is trying to avoid a crash. If the sudden stop is done incorrectly, however, it also can cause a crash. When braking, it is common to grab both brakes as hard as possible and hold on. However, doing this can cause a cyclist to lose control and skid or somersault over the handlebars. To perform the sudden stop, cyclists should use both brakes at the same time but should put more pressure on the front brake (up to three times as much pressure) while sliding the body (center of gravity) back over the rear wheel. This prevents the rear wheel from skidding and the cyclist from going over the handlebars.

- **Bunny hop.** Although used more often by mountain bikers and BMX riders, the bunny hop can be a useful skill when riding on the road. Sometimes an obstacle might be too large to avoid by using the rock dodge. The bunny hop allows the rider to get over the obstacle without crashing. The first step in performing the bunny hop is to lift the front wheel up over an obstacle. To do this, the cyclist should ride up to the obstacle and pull up on the handlebars while shifting the weight back. Riders using clipless pedals will need to pull up on the pedals with the feet at the same time. Pulling up brings the bike slightly off the ground to get

over the obstacle. Students should practice until both wheels can get off the ground. The bunny hop can be useful for crossing railroad tracks.

- **Drinking.** What seems like a simple task can quickly spell disaster if a cyclist is unable to safely remove the water bottle, take a drink, and then return the bottle. Drinking while cycling is a skill and should be practiced while riding in a safe area such as on a track or bike path. Riders must be able to maintain their line of travel; pay attention to traffic, including other cyclists; and look for obstacles on the road all while trying to take a drink.

- **Track stand (stationary standing).** Although not essential for cycling on the road, the track stand can be useful when a cyclist must wait at a traffic light but does not want to clip out of the pedals (when using a cleated pedal system). To perform the track stand, the cyclist holds the pedals at the 3 and 9 o'clock positions. The dominant foot is forward, and the front wheel is turned at a 45° angle away from the dominant foot. Initially it might be best to practice the track stand on a slight uphill.

SAFETY

As with any outdoor activity, cycling has its own set of safety issues. There are risks associated with bicycling, but many of these can be reduced by following safety procedures. Students should be expected to always follow the safety rules and should not be allowed to participate if they cannot exhibit responsible behavior.

- Helmets should be worn and buckled at all times during class. When helmets are worn, the severity of head injuries is greatly reduced.

- Students should always perform a safety check before they begin riding. This includes checking the tire pressures, brakes, chains, and quick releases. Any issues can be addressed before riding to prevent an accident.

- Appropriate spacing is essential. Students should be at least one bike length behind the cyclist in front of them. This allows them to be able to stop safely.

- Students should wear appropriate clothing, including footwear. Although students may not want to wear cycling clothing because of style or cost, they need to wear clothing that will not cause accidents. Any baggy pants or untied shoelaces need to be secured, as these may get caught in a chain or gear and cause an accident. Students should wear brightly colored clothing to be more visible to motorists.

- There should be well-established and clear signals and procedures for students to use while on campus. Students should know how to move bikes from the storage area to the riding area. Clear signals for starting and stopping should be established and practiced.
- Students must follow traffic laws when on the road. This is essential for the safety of cyclists and motorists. Students should know they can receive tickets for violating traffic laws.

In addition to following the safety rules, teachers, parents, and students can work together to establish safe routes to school. Bicycling to school can be a great opportunity for students to increase their daily physical activity. However, the routes that students must travel may be neither safe nor practical. Teachers and schools can implement the Safe Routes to School program to assist communities in increasing the number of students walking and bicycling to school. Every community is unique and has different concerns and safety issues. The Safe Routes to School program can be individualized to address the specific needs of a community. The major areas of emphasis in the program are the five *Es:* engineering, enforcement, education, encouragement, and evaluation. Ideally, your Safe Routes to School program should address all five, but the mix may vary depending on the needs of the community and school. Consult www.saferoutesinfo.org for more information on starting a Safe Routes to School program.

CONCLUSION

Although there are some challenges to teaching cycling in physical education, they are far outweighed by the benefits. Students enjoy participating in a new activity, one that may have more personal relevance in their life than a traditional sport. Learning to cycle can encourage youths to be more active throughout their day by riding their bike to and from school, and there is great potential for bicycling to become a lifetime activity. A multiple-lesson cycling unit in physical education gives students the time and safe location in which to learn the various skills associated with cycling. These skills help students feel more comfortable both as cyclists and as future motorists. Each NASPE standard is met in a cycling unit, and being able to demonstrate that students are learning meaningful and relevant content and skills in physical education is important for program success. Cycling provides an opportunity for students to be physically active and improve their fitness *during* physical education and have a good deal of fun in the process. Hopefully this chapter convinced you to give a cycling unit a go despite some of the challenges. Students will be happy you did!

REFERENCES

McNamee, J., & Timken, G.L. (in review). Motivations for teaching outdoor pursuits in physical education: Changes, challenges and benefits. *Journal of Teaching in Physical Education.*

Ratey, J.J. (2008). *Spark: The revolutionary new science of exercise and the brain.* New York: Little, Brown.

RECOMMENDED READINGS

Haynes, C. (2009). *The practical cyclist: Bicycling for real people.* Gabriola Island, BC, Canada: New Society Publishers.

Hewitt, B. (Ed.). (2005). *Bicycling magazine's new cyclist handbook : Ride with confidence and avoid common pitfalls.* Emmaus, PA: Rodale.

Zinn, L. (2009). *Zinn and the art of road bike maintenance.* Boulder, CO: Velopress.

RECOMMENDED WEB SITES

Bicycling **Magazine**

www.bicycling.com

Bike Helmet Safety Institute

www.bhsi.org

League of American Bicyclists

www.bikeleague.org

National Center for Safe Routes to School

www.saferoutesinfo.org

Pedestrian and Bicycle Information Center

www.bicyclinginfo.org

Safe Routes to School National Partnership

www.saferoutespartnership.org

CYCLING UNIT PLAN

General Lesson Information

Each lesson contains the following seven elements:

1. Objectives—primary learning outcomes
2. Equipment—specific materials and gear
3. Introduction—opening concepts, ideas, and questions that identify the focus of the day
4. Warm-ups—routine to prepare students for cycling
5. Central activities—activity progressions that increase in difficulty and lead to more advanced skills
6. Closure—suggested discussion and reflection items
7. Assessment—examples of evaluation strategies

Day 1
Focus: Introduction to safe riding
- Video
- Preassessment

Day 2
Focus: Introduction to bicycling
- Bicycle fit
- Helmet fit
- ABC quick check

Day 3
Focus: Basic skills
- Riding in a straight line
- Braking
- Mounting, starting, stopping, and restarting with whistle
- Scanning while riding
- Turning right and left
- Changing gears
- Scramble drill

Day 4
Focus: Bike handling
- You go first
- Squeeze box
- Riding in a small circle
- Figure eight
- Slalom

Day 5
Focus: Bike maintenance and additional challenges
- Changing a flat tire
- Water bottle pickup
- Snail race

Day 6
Focus: Traffic laws
- Yielding
- Lane positioning
- Lane changing
- Intersections
- Turns
- Bike lanes

Day 7
Focus: Emergency safety skills
- Rock dodge
- Sudden stop
- Quick turn

Day 8
Focus: Riding for fitness
- Heart rate
- Timed ride

Day 9
Focus: Riding in a group
- Etiquette
- Positioning
- Signaling

Day 10
Focus: Group ride or station work
- Group ride with focus on safety, etiquette, positioning, and signaling
- Station work to review various cycling skills

chapter 11

Snowshoeing

John T. Saunders

A journey of a thousand miles begins with a single step.

Lao-tzu

Traveling on snow presents a unique challenge. If the snowpack is just right, you can easily walk on this seemingly solid surface. Many times, though, the snowpack is variable in both density and depth. Anyone who has tried to walk in deep snow unaided can attest to the difficulty of moving through this medium. Thus, to travel efficiently on top of the snow, you need to utilize equipment that will keep you at or near the snow's surface, facilitating an efficient means of moving through the snow. Today there are many types of equipment for traveling on snow. These range from simple snowshoes to complex setups such as backcountry skis and split boards (snowboards split down the middle that behave like really wide skis). For school curriculums, snowshoes offer a simple, elegant, and relatively inexpensive means to explore traveling in snow.

Snowshoeing is simply the art of walking on snow with snowshoes attached to your feet. Snowshoes are pieces of gear, worn on the feet, which keep you from sinking into the snow by increasing the surface area of your foot. Archaeologists have found evidence of foot extenders in central Asia that date back to 4,000 BC

(Osgood & Hurley, 1975, p. 11). The earliest designs of such equipment are thought to be solid slabs of wood strapped to the feet. These eventually fostered ski designs in Asia and Europe and snowshoe designs in North America. In the Altai region of China, there are people using 2,000 year old curved plank designs to ride on the snow while using a single long pole to control their speed (Marquand, 2006).

While the ski dominated Asia and Europe, North America was where the snowshoe became a rich part of the cultural heritage. Evidence suggests that the peoples who migrated over the Bering land bridge brought the snowshoe design with them into North America. Early snowshoe designs reflected the local materials and terrain. The shape of snowshoes was determined by the demands of the terrain (Prater, 1997, p. 15). Indigenous peoples of North America developed hundreds of patterns of snowshoes (Osgood & Hurley, 1975, p. 29). Modern snowshoe designs are the result of these time-tested patterns being handed down generation after generation and then incorporated with modern materials to make them lighter and sturdier.

Snowshoeing provides numerous benefits to those who strap on a pair and head out into winter. Unlike many other winter pursuits, snowshoeing is simple, easy to learn, and fairly inexpensive. As a relatively low-risk activity, snowshoeing can accommodate a wide range of participants who can challenge themselves on a wide variety of terrain. Recreational snowshoeing is an activity that engages the whole body (especially if poles are used). Studies have indicated that the low-impact, aerobic activity of snowshoeing can enhance and maintain cardiorespiratory fitness (Tarallo, 2004). Given our children's diet and lifestyle issues, which are described in a plethora of other studies, our youths need more exercise year round. Often winter is associated with inactivity and poor nutrition patterns (Tarallo, 2004). Snowshoeing can be an excellent way to stimulate activity and exercise during the winter months. Families can enjoy snowshoeing together due to the sport's quick learning curve and accessibility. The benefits of walking are well documented, and as snowshoeing is basically walking in snow, the physiological and psychological benefits of walking can be experienced while on snowshoes. With its elegance and simplicity, snowshoeing is a relatively safe winter activity. As with any winter pursuit, snowshoeing comes with its own elements of risk. In general, though, snowshoeing is a low-risk, affordable, and fun activity for all ages.

EQUIPMENT

Equipment needs for snowshoeing are relatively simple. Snowshoes, trekking poles, and appropriate clothing are all you need to get started.

- **Snowshoes.** There are many varieties of snowshoes and snowshoe patterns. There are generally two groups of snowshoes, traditional wooden snowshoes and modern aluminum or plastic snowshoes. The traditional wooden snowshoes are an art unto themselves and still enjoy popularity in a variety of user groups. Wooden snowshoes are categorized according to size, intended terrain, and the presence or absence of vegetation within that terrain. Their names reflect the regions from which they emerged (such as Yukon, Maine, or Michigan), the indigenous people who utilized them (such as Ojibwa or Algonquian), or the animal they imitate (such as bear paw or beaver tail; for detailed information regarding traditional designs see Prater, 1997; Osgood & Hurley, 1975). For most modern recreational programs, aluminum or plastic frame snowshoes work well due to their low weight, easy attachment systems, and low cost. These modern snowshoes can weigh up to one-third less than a traditional wooden design (Walter, 2004, p. 24). They consist of a frame, a deck, a pivot system, binding, and traction devices, which typically consist of some form of metal crampon underneath the binding and underneath the heel (see figure 11.1). Snowshoes come in pairs, and today many are designed specifically for the right or left foot to improve fit and performance.

TEACHING TIP

Asking students to describe in their own words the shapes and parts of the snowshoe can help you to understand how the students perceive these tools.

- **Trekking or hiking poles.** While not essential for snowshoeing, poles can enhance the experience by improving stability when walking on variable snowpack. They can assist in getting up from a fall off of the track into deeper snow. And poles can provide an increased range of muscle motion and training. Pole designs range from single-piece, fixed-length poles resembling ski poles to multiple-section trekking poles that can be adjusted to various heights to accommodate variable terrain or different body sizes.

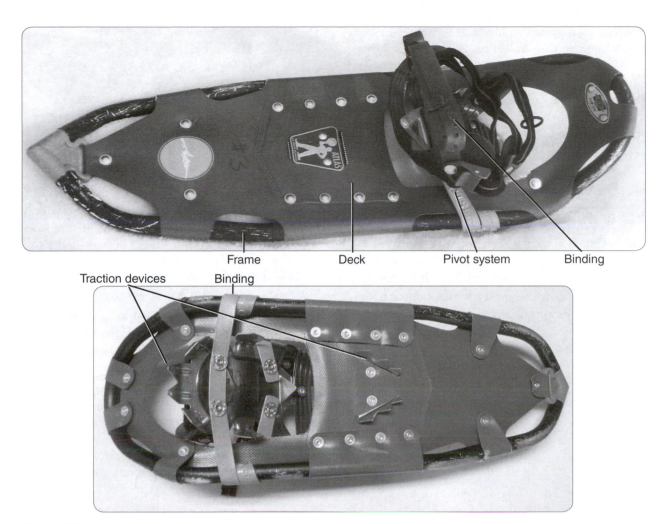

Frame   Deck   Pivot system   Binding

Traction devices   Binding

Figure 11.1 Snowshoes.

• **Clothing.** Clothing for snowshoeing is based on wearing layers that will allow you to enjoy a wide range of temperature and weather conditions. While moving, you may need only a base layer (long underwear) and a wind layer (wind jacket, soft shell, rain jacket). When resting, you may need to add an insulating layer (down or synthetic jacket) depending on the conditions. Hats and gloves are essential. Neck gaiters protect the neck and lower portions of your face. Gaiters are great for covering the junctions between boots and pants to keep snow from getting into your footwear. Footwear for snowshoeing ranges from running shoes to heavy winter boots depending on the application. For example, running shoes are appropriate for a morning jog on your favorite snow-covered trail or in other conditions where a lightweight snowshoe does not penetrate the snowpack very deeply. However, if you are snowshoeing in deep snow (possibly carrying a backpack), you may choose heavy-duty footwear such as insulated leather boots. Protect your eyes with goggles or sunglasses and be sure to utilize sunscreen thoroughly. Conditions can change rapidly in winter environments, so make sure you are prepared for such possibilities.

BASIC SKILLS AND TECHNIQUES

While snowshoeing may seem as simple as walking, there are a variety of techniques you can learn to enhance your experience, gain a sense of accomplishment, and increase your fun! The following techniques are the basics for entering the world of snowshoeing.

Stance and Alignment

Standing on snowshoes requires a slight adjustment to your stance to accommodate the size of the snowshoes underfoot. Your feet should feel level on the snowshoes (not canted to the outside or inside), and your feet should be parallel to each other when you are standing with the snowshoes on. If the snowshoes are rotated either inward (pigeon toed) or outward (duck footed), they could strain the knees and ankles, leading to discomfort. Additionally, the toe of your shoe should be aligned within the snowshoe so that the end of your shoe clears the deck and rotates in the binding without catching on the deck while you are snowshoeing.

Stride

Snowshoes increase the dimensions of your personal footprint. Hence, you will need to adjust your stride when incorporating snowshoes into walking. Stride is your walking technique, and it varies individually (in pace gait). Typically, depending on the design of the snowshoes, you will need to adjust your stride so that your snowshoes clear each other and do not bang the lower portions of your legs. You can adjust your stride by stepping in slightly longer increments until the snowshoes clear each other when you are moving forward.

Breaking Trail

This skill involves establishing a path in untracked snow. Depending on the depth and characteristics of the snow, breaking a trail requires significantly more work than following a trail. When you are snowshoeing in a group, you should rotate the person breaking the trail as often as needed to maintain an adequate pace and prevent exhausting the individual breaking the trail. For example, when you are leading a class, have students rotate every 40 steps when in heavy or deep snow. This encourages focusing on the task and allows everyone to enjoy the experience of breaking trail and following.

Falling Down and Getting Up Gracefully

Falling is part of snowshoeing. Snow can provide a cushion. However, depending on the characteristics of the snowpack, snow can also present interesting challenges to getting up. Anyone who has wallowed in deep snow can attest to how difficult getting up can be. If the snowpack is hard, then getting up can be as simple as standing up. The deeper and softer the snowpack, the more challenging standing up becomes. There are several techniques that can help you get up out of the snow and back onto your snowshoes.

> **TEACHING TIP**
>
> When teaching these techniques, state the technique, demonstrate the technique, explain the technique, and then have students practice the technique. Doing this anchors the technique visually, reinforces it auditorily, and then anchors it kinesthetically.

Technique 1

This technique may be appropriate if the snow pack is shallow or the snow surface is firm enough to support your movements.

1. Roll onto your belly and pull one knee up to move into a partial kneeling position.
2. Bracing your hands on your knee, push yourself to a standing position.

Technique 2

For snow conditions that are somewhat softer in the upper layers of the snowpack, yet firm enough for you to stand and not fall into the snow too deep, this technique may suffice.

1. Roll onto your side and position your snowshoes parallel to each other in the snow.
2. Push yourself over your knees and snowshoes and into a kneeling position.
3. With both feet under you, stand up.

Technique 3

If the snow is very soft and deep, you may not be able to use the resistance of the snowpack to push yourself up. As you push up in deep snow, you may just sink deeper. In this instance poles can be very helpful.

1. If you have one pole, grab it in the middle and lay it flat on the surface of the snow.
2. Push down on the middle of the pole to provide some resistance to help you stand up.
3. If you have two poles, make an X out of your poles, grab both poles at the intersection (middle of the X), and place the poles on the surface of the snow.
4. Push down on the middle of your poles to create a platform of resistance that you can use to push up out of the deeper snow.

Technique 4

Another very valuable technique is the helping hand.

- If you are with someone else, ask for a helping hand.
    1. Position yourself so that your legs and snowshoes are underneath you, or at least in such a position that your snowshoes can get a purchase in the snow. This is important because when your helper pulls upward on your hand, you need to be able to get your legs under you and stand up, without falling in a different direction or pulling your helper down.
    2. Make sure your knees are in a position that points in the direction of the helping pull. This will avoid falling to either side when being helped.
    3. Gently pull on the offered hand increasing strength as needed so that you do not jerk the helper down or place undue stress on either you or your helper.
- If you are providing the helping hand, make sure your stance is stable. Place one leg forward with the knee flexed over the toe and the other leg behind with the knee slightly bent (as if you were performing a shallow lunge). This prevents the person you are helping from pulling you over into the snow.

Changing Direction

While the previous techniques can get you moving forward and help you right yourself after falling in the snow, they can't help you change direction. Snowshoes, by adding to the size of your feet and having a tendency to pivot on the binding when you lift them up, can be challenging to turn. If you have the space and vegetation, and trail considerations allow it, you can simply walk in a tight semicircle to turn.

When this is not a possibility, you may need to perform a step turn or a kick turn. To complete a step turn to the left, turn your left snowshoe to the left and set it in the snow so that it is perpendicular to the right snowshoe. Then, move the right snowshoe so it is parallel to the left. Now you are facing directly left of where you started. Repeat the same moves again (turn your left snowshoe perpendicular and then match the right foot to the left) to face the opposite direction (see figure 11.2).

If conditions are very tight and you need to turn in the trail or on a steep traverse, you should use a kick turn. Pick one foot up and turn it to the outside 180° before setting the snowshoe down facing the opposite direction. Then pick up the other snowshoe and swing it around to make it parallel to the first (see figure 11.3). When learning kick turns, turn counterclockwise if you are switching from traversing left across the slope to traversing right across the slope (or turn clockwise if

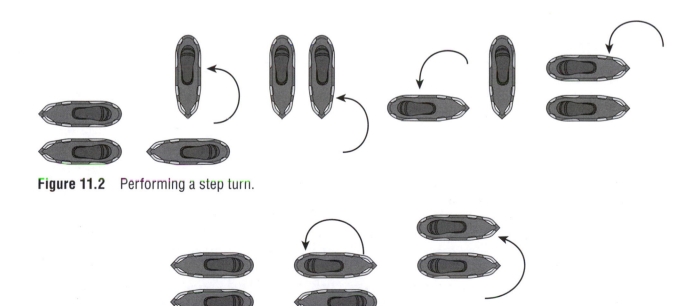

Figure 11.2 Performing a step turn.

Figure 11.3 The kick turn.

switching from a right traverse to left traverse). Doing so puts you in a position to fall backward into a sitting position on the slope if the kick turn becomes difficult. Falling onto your rear provides a much safer option than falling forward down the slope (potentially allowing for a long tumble down the slope). The kick turn takes a bit of practice and is easier to accomplish with a set of poles. Again, the kick turn works well in a very tight situation (turning around in the trail or in dense vegetation) or when traversing steep slopes.

Ascending Techniques

At some point, snowshoeing will take you up. Ascending techniques include stepping up, herringboning, sidestepping, kick stepping, switchbacking, and traversing. When **stepping up** (figure 11.4a), face the hill and step forward into the snow while weighting your toes and engaging the crampons. Keep your body weight over your toes and continue stepping up the hillside. As the terrain steepens, you may wish to **herringbone** (figure 11.4b). This is classic duckwalking, in which you turn both your snowshoes out so that your toes point out at a 45° angle. This technique increases effectiveness because the angles of the snowshoe edges across the fall line create a better purchase in the snow. By putting pressure on those edges, you gain the needed traction to move up moderately steep terrain.

As the terrain becomes more challenging, you may need to **sidestep** (figure 11.4c) up a slope. This technique provides more traction and puts less strain on your knees and legs. Sidestepping is when both snowshoes face the same direction across the fall line and your body is oriented perpendicular to the fall line (so your shoulders point up and down the hill). The fall line is the path of natural descent down a slope (you can visualize the fall line by imagining the line that a rolling ball would take if turned loose at the top of a slope). Step up with your uphill snowshoe, which is the snowshoe that is closer to the top of the hill, and stomp it into the snow to create a platform to stand on. Then weight the uphill snowshoe, bring the downhill snowshoe up to the space vacated by the uphill snowshoe, and put your weight onto the downhill snowshoe. Repeat this process slowly and steadily as you climb.

Kick stepping (figure 11.4d) is a technique used for climbing when the snow is deep and steep. Facing uphill, kick your toe into the slope and weight that leg. This creates a platform for you to step up on. Repeat the process with the other foot. Kick stepping is like climbing stairs and stomping your foot onto each step as you ascend. It is a more aggressive form of stepping up and is used in steeper terrain.

While the techniques just described work well for ascending directly up a slope, there are times when your route, terrain, and natural obstacles might dictate a less-than-direct route. In this case, traversing and switchbacking are two valuable skills to know. **Traversing** means moving across a slope at an angle that ascends the hill across the fall line. The angle at which you ascend will vary depending on the steepness of the slope, your physical conditioning, and the shape of the slope. When utilizing this technique, be cognizant of the uphill edge of each of your snowshoes. You need to kick that edge into the slope to engage your edges and crampons (some authors refer to this as *edging*) and prevent the snowshoes from slipping downhill as you traverse. **Switchbacks** are simple turns in an uphill traverse. You may come across trees, rocks, ledges, and so on and need to turn a different direction while still maintaining the angle of ascent up the slope. When switchbacking, you may use a step turn or a kick turn to negotiate the change in direction. Switchbacking can significantly decrease the amount of effort required to ascend a steep hill by helping you to use the terrain efficiently to climb.

Descending Techniques

Having climbed up, you now must go down. Techniques that snowshoers can employ to descend include down hilling, sidestepping, glissading, and straight lining. **Down hilling** is a technique in which you descend a hill by keeping your snowshoes level with the horizon, flexing your knees, and keeping your weight over your snowshoes (Joque, 2009). Basically, it is walking down the hill and making sure your snowshoes are level while keeping your balance. Depending on the conditions, it works well in easy to moderate terrain. Be careful not to lean too far back, which will cause your snowshoes to lose traction and slip out in front of you, or to lean too far forward, which will send you into a tumble. As the slope becomes steeper, you may wish to **sidestep** down the slope, which is just the reverse of sidestepping up a slope. **Glissading** is as much fun as it sounds. The

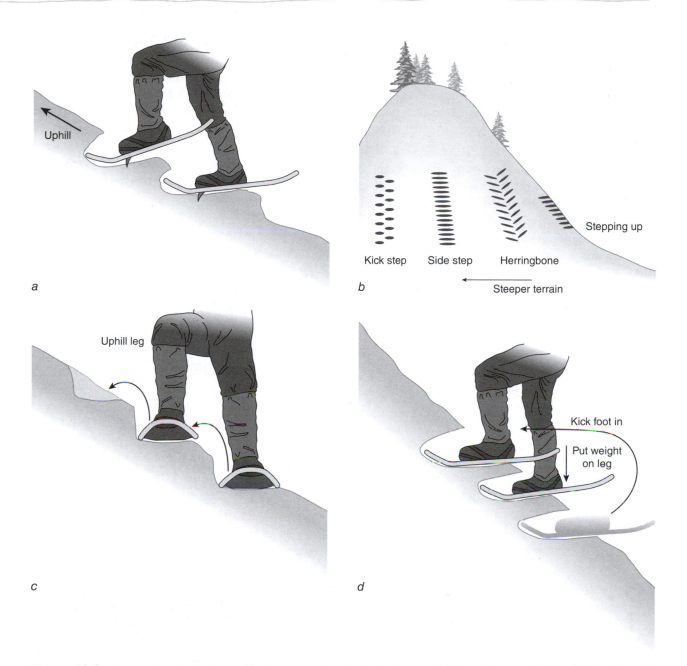

Figure 11.4   Ascending techniques that you can teach students are *(a)* stepping up, *(b)* herringboning, *(c)* sidestepping, and *(d)* kick stepping.

word *glissade* comes from the French word *glisser,* which means "to slide." Basically, you lean onto the backs of your snowshoes and let gravity do its thing. Point your shoes straight down the hill, lean back, and glide down the slope. Be careful not to lean far enough forward to engage your crampons, as this will project you into a dramatic tumbling act. If the snow is deep and powdery and the consequences of a fall are minimal, conditions are perfect for a fast run straight down the fall line, with your snowshoes churning up clouds of snow as you go! This is called **straight lining.**

SAFETY CONSIDERATIONS

Any time you enter the backcountry, you are accepting a certain level of risk for you and your group. In the winter environment, snowshoeing may include risks such as weather, exposure, injury, getting lost, and snow-related dangers. Even though snowshoeing is relatively low risk, is easy to learn, and can be enjoyed in a variety of terrain and winter conditions, you should still take care to plan your excursion to minimize risk.

Weather, Exposure, and Injury

Winter weather can be constantly changing and you must be prepared to handle such changes. Plan according to the weather forecasts, and know your local weather patterns to avoid being caught unprepared in a winter storm. Make sure you have the proper gear for your intended adventure and know how to use that gear. Bring multiple layers of clothing and extra food to handle rapid changes. Exposure to cold, windy, and snowy conditions can have a deleterious effect on both your body and your mind. Watch yourself and the members of your group for signs and symptoms of exposure. The skin is one of the body's largest organs and needs to be taken care of in the winter environment. Use sunscreen and lip balm to prevent sunburn. In windy conditions, cover exposed skin to prevent windburn and chafing. White patches that develop on the nose or cheeks may be a sign of superficial frostbite and need to be covered up and taken care of immediately. If you are snowshoeing hard and sweating but then stop to enjoy the view while the wind picks up, you could quickly become hypothermic. Effective layering of clothing can minimize exposure-related dangers. For example, when you are moving, take off layers to prevent excessive sweating. When you stop, pull on a puffy jacket or add a wind layer to stay warm while you take a break. Additionally, snowshoes can tear or bruise your lower extremities, so be aware of this when moving and resting. Gaiters work well to protect your snow pants against tearing by the snowshoes, which seems to happen more often when you get tired and your dexterity and coordinaton deteriorate. Take breaks accordingly and watch for signs of tiredness. If you are taking groups into winter conditions, be sure you have the appropriate first aid training for the conditions you may encounter.

Route Finding

Snowshoeing can be a wonderful way to travel into the heart of the winter world. In Colorado, for example, many trails are clearly marked, allowing the winter recreationist a chance to enjoy a variety of terrains and challenges. In addition, snowshoes provide flexibility

---

TEACHING TIP

Bring in a duffel bag full of clothes and arrange them on the floor to make a layered visual of a well-dressed recreational snowshoer. Start with base layers and place them on the floor to represent a person. Then build up with snow pants, upper layers, a shell, a hat, gloves, goggles, and so on until you have a visual representation of a clothed body on the ground. Add snowshoes for effect.

These students are well-prepared for whatever risks they may encounter.

for leaving the trails and exploring the unknown. Whether venturing onto marked trails or exploring unmarked territory, you should have knowledge of the terrain and carry a map and compass. Storms can come in suddenly, and a clearly marked trail can become a strange and unknown place when visibility is reduced by blowing snow. Making a wrong turn or wandering off of a marked trail during a heavy snowfall can pose a serious threat to the casual recreationist. Thus, a basic knowledge of route finding can greatly enhance the safety of entering the backcountry on snowshoes.

Snow-Related Dangers

While you may love to play in the snowbound environment, you need to be aware that the snowpack is dynamic. It is always moving, shifting, and settling. Snow tends to be less dense around trees, buried shrubs, and rocks. The reason why snow is less dense in these spots is related to temperature gradients (changes in temperature either vertically or horizontally across a given distance) and water vapor movement within the snowpack. Snow crystals called *depth hoar* (or *sugar snow)* form in these areas near trees, around buried vegetation, and near rocks. Depth hoar can be potentially dangerous to the casual recreationist because the snow crystals do not bond together well and the snow has a sugary consistency that is very difficult to stand up in should you fall into a patch. Thus be cautious around trees (or tree wells; see figure 11.5), shrubs, and rocks. In addition, in country where there is steep terrain and enough snow, avalanches can occur. Be knowledgeable about the terrain that you go into. If the terrain is prone to avalanches, make sure you take all the necessary precautions and have the appropriate training for entering such country.

Food and Hydration

In order to produce enough energy to stay warm and enjoy a day or more of snowshoeing, you need to eat nutritious food and hydrate well. A 2% reduction in hydration is enough to influence your decision making. Be aware of your students and make sure they are hydrating and eating in order to stay warm, have enough energy, and enjoy the experience.

Gear

Snowshoes are relatively simple but can present some sharp points and abrasive edges. Be careful of the crampons on your snowshoes. Also be mindful of the points on your poles if you are carrying them.

Figure 11.5   A tree well.

Reprinted from M. Wagstaff, 2009, *Technical skills for adventure programming: A curriculum guide* (Champaign, IL: Human Kinetics), 659.

ENVIRONMENTAL AND ETHICAL CONSIDERATIONS

More recreationists flock to the winter backcountry every year, and even though you are on top of the snowpack, there are ways to mitigate the potential impacts of your activity. Students should be aware of the environment and others when they go snowshoeing. When you take rest breaks, make sure that the area is clean when you are finished to ensure there are not any pieces of trash or food left behind. Practice proper sanitation when on such adventures. Leave No Trace has excellent guidelines for minimizing human impacts in a variety of environments. Respect others who you meet in the backcountry. In places where snowshoeing and skiing are popular together, snowshoers and skiers set a separate snowshoe track and ski track so that everyone can enjoy a quality experience. Many winter trails are well marked and it is advisable to stay on the trails. If you break trail make sure it is in an appropriate area and that you are familiar with the area and with route finding. And respect the wildlife that you may encounter on a winter excursion. Aggravating the wildlife can stress those organisms and reduce their chances of surviving in a winter environment.

CONCLUSION

Snowshoeing is an increasingly popular sport that people are embracing as part of a healthy lifestyle of exercise and recreation. A snowshoeing curriculum embraces the NASPE national standards for physical education. Snowshoeing demonstrates competency in motor skills and movement patterns needed to perform a variety of physical activities (standard 1); a varied snowshoeing curriculum will demonstrate understanding of movement concepts, principles, strategies, and tactics as they apply to the learning and performance of physical activities (standard 2). By being in the outdoors and involving the students in a program centered around movement and exercise, snowshoeing provides students with an opportunity for participating regularly in physical activity (standard 3). Snowshoeing provides students with a foundation upon which they can achieve and maintain a health-enhancing level of physical fitness (standard 4). Utilizing the group activities and dynamics associated with this curriculum, snowshoeing provides a medium in which students can exhibit responsible personal and social behavior that respects self and others in physical activity settings (standard 5). Finally, participation in snowshoeing and modeling the virtues associated with this activity promotes and values physical activity for health, enjoyment, challenge, self-expression, and social interaction (standard 6). While having fun and recreating in the winter environment, it is our personal and our social responsibility to take care of ourselves and others and to promote and model good habits while enjoying ourselves and the environment in which we live.

REFERENCES

Joque, J. (2009). Snowshoeing 101: Techniques with a short learning curve. *Snowshoe Magazine*. www.snowshoemag.com/pdfmag/snowshoeing101.pdf.

Marquand, R. (2006, March 15). Before Scandinavia: These could be the first skiers. *Christian Science Monitor*, p. 1. www.csmonitor.com/2006/0315/p01s01-woap.html.

Osgood, W., & Hurley, L. (1975). *The snowshoe book.* (2nd ed.). Brattleboro, VT: Stephen Greene Press.

Prater, G. (1997). *Snowshoeing.* (4th ed.). Seattle: The Mountaineers Books.

Tarallo, M. (2004). Bring snowshoes into your physical education program. *Strategies: A Journal for Sport and Physical Educators, 17*(3), 11.

Walter, C. (2004). *The snowshoe experience.* North Adams, MA: Storey.

RECOMMENDED READINGS

Griffin, S. (1998). *Snowshoeing.* Mechanicsburg, PA: Stackpole Books.

McDougall, L. (2000). *The snowshoe handbook.* Short Hills, NJ: Burford Books.

Olmsted, L. (1998). *Snowshoeing: A trailside guide.* New York: WW Norton.

Osgood, W., & Hurley, L. (1975). *The snowshoe book.* (2nd ed.). Brattleboro, VT: Stephen Greene Press.

Prater, G., & Felkley, D. (2002). *Snowshoeing: From novice to master.* (5th ed.). Seattle: The Mountaineers Books.

Zwosta, M. (1998). *The essential snowshoer: A step-by-step guide.* Camden, ME: Ragged Mountain Press.

RECOMMENDED WEB SITES

Snowshoe Magazine

www.snowshoemag.com
Dedicated articles and information regarding snowshoeing.

Winter Feels Good

www.winterfeelsgood.com/
An initiative by SnowSports Industries America (SIA) dedicated to bringing awareness of snow sports to a wide audience. General information about snowshoeing can be found under "Learn A Sport & Gear Up." Educators can find excellent information under "Educators & Rec. Pros." A very helpful curriculum guide for grades K-12 can be found with Dr. G. Linda Rikard's snowshoe instructional unit, *Introduction to Winter Sports: Snowshoe Curriculum Outline*, which can be found at www.winterfeelsgood.com/downloads/helpful/fairfax_curriculum.pdf.

DVDS

Ilg, S. (2007). *Flight Without Wings: Sport Snowshoeing Basics* [DVD].

There are very few DVDs that explore the art of snowshoeing. Steve Ilg had been a trainer for many years and has compiled this DVD that highlights snowshoeing basics. This DVD can be found at www.wholisticfitness.com/Merchant2/merchant.mvc?Screen=PROD&Product_Code=VT-SNOWSHOE1&Category_Code=DVD.

SNOWSHOEING UNIT PLAN

General Lesson Information

Each lesson contains the following seven elements:

1. Objectives—primary learning outcomes
2. Equipment—specific materials for each lesson
3. Introduction—fundamental concepts and skills pertaining to the lesson's focus
4. Warm-ups—routines to stretch and strengthen muscles and tendons related to snowshoeing
5. Central activities—activity progressions from warm-ups to core activities
6. Closure—suggested discussion and reflection items
7. Assessment—evaluation strategies for checking understanding

While some of the following lessons are presented in a sequential arrangement (e.g., ascending and descending techniques), you may find that you can rearrange the lesson days to meet your program needs (e.g., you might use the day 10 lesson toward the beginning of the unit).

Day 1

Focus: Introduction and gear

- History and use of snowshoes
- Snowshoe description and parts
- Attaching snowshoes
- Removing snowshoes
- Walking forward and backward with basic turning
- Moving randomly and as directed in open space
  - Follow the leader
  - Freeze tag

Day 2

Focus: Finding your stride

- Introduction and demonstration of stride
- Finding your stride in 25 steps
- Walking clockwise and counterclockwise in a group
- Paired walks

Day 3

Focus: Falling down, getting up, and turning around

- Maintaining balance while snowshoeing
- Snowshoeing while juggling an object
- Falling down
- Getting up (without poles)
- Turning techniques
  - Circle turn
  - Step turn
  - Kick turn
- Obstacle course on flat area

Day 4

Focus: Breaking trail

- Areas to avoid while snowshoeing
- Creating a snowshoe trail
- Snow write
- Coyote trail

Day 5

Focus: Ascending techniques

- Scrambling
- Stepping up
- Herringboning

Day 6

Focus: Ascending techniques

- Sidestepping
- Kick stepping
- Heart rate checks

Day 7

Focus: Ascending techniques

- Switchbacks
- Kick turns
- Traversing
- Obstacle course on varied terrain

Day 8

Focus: Descending techniques

- Down hilling
- Lynx and hares on varied terrain

Day 9

Focus: Descending techniques

- Sidestepping
- Glissading
- Straight lining
- Red light, green light, caution

Day 10

Focus: Route finding and winter precautions

- Choosing a path
- Basic exposure precautions
- Being prepared

chapter 12

Nordic Walking

Malin Svensson

In every walk with nature one receives far more than he seeks.

John Muir

Nordic walking is basically walking with poles, though not just any poles will do. Nordic walking requires specifically designed Nordic walking poles. Why you have to use special poles and what makes these poles special are covered later in this chapter under the discussion on equipment. Walking with poles is an ancient phenomenon. Even Jesus used a pole, though he mainly used his for support. Using the poles for Nordic walking makes a huge difference in your walking results

by burning more calories and strengthening your upper body. Just taking your poles for a walk is better than sitting still. Just tapping the poles and using them for support while walking is a step up. However, if you want to work your stomach, chest, back, and arms while walking, you have to learn how to create resistance with the poles (this technique is covered later in this chapter during the discussion on basic skills and technique). Thus the purpose of Nordic walking is to get a full-body workout outdoors to improve aerobic capacity and to improve muscular endurance. It provides the benefits of the best cardiorespiratory exercise—cross-country skiing—without requiring you to wear skis or be out in the snow. Though Nordic walking is somewhat based on cross-country skiing in the sense that they both work the upper body and the lower body simultaneously in a sagittal plane, the Nordic walking technique used today has evolved to be more of an enhancement of regular walking.

Teaching Nordic walking to students can have a positive effect on their present and future health. Once you teach them the basics, the students can practice Nordic walking on their own for the rest of their lives. Any age and any fitness level can benefit from Nordic walking, which makes it a perfect family sport. If you are able to teach a class for students and parents together, you will introduce the whole family to a lifetime family activity. When you teach Nordic walking to students, you will also be equipping them with a sport they can practice all year around. All they have to do is add snow baskets to Nordic walking poles, add snowshoes to their shoes, and apply the same pole technique and suddenly they are Nordic snowshoeing, which is such a fun and healthy activity. Other benefits you can share with students are cost efficiency (a onetime investment in a pair of good Nordic walking poles provides year-round physical activity) and time efficiency (Nordic walking provides more health benefits than regular walking provides in the same amount of time). Nordic walking also saves the environment, since you can start Nordic walking right outside the front door—no more driving to exercise! This is possible due to the asphalt paw on the bottom of the pole. Keep it on and you can walk on asphalt and cement. Take it off (expose a spike tip) and you can walk on grass, sand, snow, and dirt. If you can teach students at an early age to exercise without getting into the car and driving to a gym, you have taught them a gem lesson for life.

This chapter describes the history and benefits of Nordic walking and explains what equipment to use. The emphasis is on learning basic Nordic walking, including uphill and downhill techniques. Since Nordic walking is an enhancement of regular walking, this chapter provides key pointers for making a smooth transition from walking without poles to walking with poles. As with anything in life, Nordic walking comes with risks, and thus tips on how to safely handle the poles are also included. On the accompanying CD-ROM you will find a unit plan that includes 10 lessons and suggested assessments to give you a good start in teaching basic Nordic walking. However, this is only one chapter on Nordic walking, and thus only the basics are covered. To learn more, check out the recommended resources at the end of this chapter. A good follow-up to this chapter is *Outdoor Adventures: Nordic Walking* (Svensson, 2009).

HISTORY

Trying to determine how Nordic walking came about has always been a tricky subject within the Nordic walking community. The following story is taken directly from *Outdoor Adventures: Nordic Walking* (Svensson, 2009). Every Nordic person probably has a version or two on how Nordic walking came about. One common story is that in the 1930s, Finnish cross-country skiers tried to come up with a way to stay in shape year-round. Two names come up regarding the start of this fitness movement of walking with poles. One is a gentleman named Tuomo Jantunen, who brought Nordic walking into the spotlight by accident. On the day of a ceremonious cross-country skiing event in Finland from Suomen Latu to Helsinki on January 5, 1988, a sudden rain melted all the snow. Instead of canceling the occasion, all participants walked with only the ski poles—the idea of Tuomo Jantunen, the managing director of Suomen Latu. He made it his mission to continue developing this "ski-walking" idea into a sport to be performed by anyone, not just athletes. The method was to become known as *Nordic walking*. It was refined in the mid 1990s by Risto Kasurinen and Marko Kantaneva, who worked for Matti Heikkilä at the Finnish Sport Institute (Vierumäki) and by Sirpa Arvonen, who worked for the (Finnish) National Association for Recreational Sports (Suomen Latu). In 1997, Exel Oy, a Finnish sport equipment manufacturer, produced the first Nordic walking poles, and the concept of Nordic walking became a real fitness activity and sport. Just 10 years later, in 2007, approximately 8 million people worldwide were Nordic walking (Svensson, 2009).

According to another legend, a man in the United States named Tom Rutlin started the walking-with-poles movement in 1985. Like any other successful fitness movement, such as Pilates, Feldenkrais, or the Alexander technique, Nordic walking came about due to a need. In the previous story, the Finnish cross-country skiers needed to stay in shape throughout the year, so they explored training with poles during the dry seasons. In this story, Rutlin was a competitive runner and Nordic skier who became injured but refused to stop training because of the philosophy of the time—no pain, no gain. Out of despair and persistence, he grabbed his ski poles and added them to his painful running routine. For the first time, he felt some relief from the pain. As he tried to coax his wife, Wendy, into using the poles, he agreed to just walk instead of run with the poles. Rutlin not only found it more pleasant to train with his wife but also had a mind–body experience that made him realize the potential of walking with poles: He felt more benefits from walking with the poles than from running with them. Thus Rutlin developed walking with poles (called *Exerstriding*) into a fitness exercise in the United States (Svensson, 2009).

In 2000, Exel Oy founded the International Nordic Walking Association (INWA) in Finland to provide enthusiasts with proper and safe instruction for using the Exel Oy Nordic walking products. Today INWA, an independent association, focuses on education, providing the latest research and offering an international network of instructors promoting Nordic walking to improve health and quality of life. INWA has member organizations in more than 20 countries. Over the years, several other educational organizations have sprung up, as have variations of the original Nordic walking technique, such as the INWA technique, the Exerstriding technique, the Fittrek technique, and the ALFA technique, to name a few. The average person might not even notice the differences among these techniques. There are various ways to learn Nordic walking, depending on the instructor. The original breakdown of the INWA technique into 10 steps was created by Malin Svensson (Svensson, 2003). It has been revised over the years by the INWA Educational Committee. As in any sport, the technique and teaching methods continue to be polished and further developed.

Nordic Walking North America (NWNA) is the umbrella organization for all Nordic walkers and Nordic walking activities throughout North America. NWNA provides a sense of community and sharing. To learn about most of the various teaching methods, techniques, and poles for Nordic walking, visit www.NordicWalkingNA.com.

BENEFITS

People often ask, "Why do you use the poles?" To respond to these people, you can encourage them to experience the reasoning for Nordic walking by doing the upper-body muscle test.

Tell them to hold your hand in a handshake position, and then ask them to put their left hand on their stomach and leave it there. Next, have them push down on your hand as you provide resistance against their force. Right away they will feel how the stomach muscles activate. Ask them to move the left hand to the chest, the back, and finally the back of the right arm. Every time they apply pressure on your right hand, the muscle that their left hand is touching will activate. Now they understand why Nordic walkers use the poles: to engage the muscles in the upper body! Nordic walking strengthens and creates muscular endurance in the upper body. If you Nordic walk uphill, you can achieve even greater muscular strength. People who do not like to work out indoors (or at least want a variation on working out indoors) are very happy when they realize they can do a full-body workout by Nordic walking outdoors.

So if you are looking for a sport that works the whole body and that brings everyone—regardless of fitness level—together outdoors, you have come to the right place. Adding two poles to regular walking drastically increases the health benefits of walking (assuming you use the poles correctly). According to a study by The Cooper Institute (Church, Earnest, & Morss, 2002), caloric expenditure and oxygen consumption increase by about 20%, while heart rate increases by about 10 beats/min. Individuals who used advanced techniques during the study increased as much as 46% in oxygen consumption and increased about the same (46%) in caloric expenditure. Interestingly, the rating of perceived exertion (RPE) stayed pretty much the same when the participants walked the *same* distance at the *same* speed *with or without poles*. In other words, even though the body works harder while Nordic walking, Nordic walking feels as if it requires no more effort than regular walking! That is the secret to this successful sport. Consider the following personal experience:

> In early 2002, when I tried out Nordic walking for the very first time, I thought something was wrong with my heart rate monitor. Living close to the beach in Santa Monica, I decided to Nordic walk in the deep sand, which intensifies the workout. However, even in the sand I never thought my heart rate would go as high as if I was running. When I realized the heart rate monitor was working, I was sold on Nordic walking.

The study from The Cooper Institute confirms this experience. Compared with regular walking, Nordic walking increases the heart rate as well as the caloric expenditure. This is due to the fact that during Nordic walking the heart has to deliver more oxygen because more muscles (i.e., the muscles of the whole upper body) are working and thus demanding oxygen. The heart has to pump more blood in order to carry the oxygen to the additional working muscles. The study at The Cooper Institute recorded an increased heart rate of 10 beats/min on flat ground. Some Nordic walkers have experienced an increase by 30 beats/min when walking uphill. In the day 9 lesson of the Nordic walking unit (see the accompanying CD-ROM), students will experience the difference in the intensity of walking up a hill with poles and without poles.

One of the best benefits of Nordic walking is the extra calorie burn, which makes you never want to leave the poles behind. On average, basic Nordic walking can burn 20% more calories than regular walking burns. Adding advanced techniques can burn as much as 46% more. This extra calorie burn is based on science: The more muscles you engage simultaneously, the more energy they burn to do the required work. In addition, the more muscles you engage simultaneously, the more oxygen the heart has to pump to be used in the energy-producing process. This is the reason why the study from The Cooper Institute (Church, Earnest, & Morss, 2002) showed an increased oxygen consumption (20%-46%) similar to the increased caloric expenditure (20%-46%).

The fact that the increase in caloric expenditure does not correspond to an increase in the perceived effort (RPE) could have a very important and positive effect on the public health—especially when it comes to people who do not enjoy exercising. Imagine telling somebody that they can burn more calories without feeling like they are putting in the extra effort. It sounds like a dream come true. This less-effort, better-burn benefit can be a great incentive for people to try Nordic walking. It is not until people actually *try* Nordic walking that they are sold on it.

Do you have students who are injured and cannot participate in physical education? If it is their ankle or knee that is injured, you can ask their physician about the possibility of using Nordic walking as a rehabilitation tool. They might be able to participate, although they will have to walk much more slowly and carefully and will require more personal attention from you. Do you have students who are overweight or even obese and

who hurt while walking? If their parents are concerned, you can explain to them the benefits that Nordic walking can have for their children. It not only increases caloric expenditure to help participants lose weight but also diminishes wear and tear on the joints. Walking with two poles is like adding two extra legs. Your body weight is now distributed among four pillars instead of only two. This helps anyone who needs to take weight off their joints. This benefit is especially noticeable when going downhill. If you see students limping due to a lower-body injury, teach them Nordic walking to at least correct their gait. Once they begin using the two poles, you will most likely see the limp disappear or at least diminish. Thus Nordic walking can prevent future injuries caused by muscular imbalances that occur when healthy muscles are forced to work overtime to assist injured muscles.

Many parents wish their kids would learn to move and sit with a better posture. Increased awareness of good posture and form builds good habits and provides a strong foundation for life. The next time you see your students, watch how they walk. Are the tall students trying to appear shorter by slouching? Are the shy students rounding their shoulders? Are the confident students walking with good posture? Teaching your students Nordic walking gives you an excellent opportunity to teach them the basics of good form and regular walking. You can begin to do this via some fun character exercises (see the day 1 lesson plan for the Nordic walking unit on the accompanying CD-ROM). Nordic walking also improves gait, which is a person's walking pattern. Relearning how to walk with awareness of good form and posture is very rewarding. It is amazing the effect that planting the center of the heel first versus the outside of the heel first can have on your gait. It is like a chain reaction. Landing with a strong foundation prevents wear and tear on the joints that are a part of the landing action, including the foot, knee, and hip. Sometimes teenage kids have to give up their favorite sport due to repeated injuries that result from muscular imbalance and weakness in certain joints—imbalance that could be prevented with correct walking mechanics and good form. By Nordic walking, you will also feel your posture naturally improve because you are constantly pushing the upper body away from gravity. As a teacher, you can augment the natural benefits Nordic walking has on posture by specifically teaching good posture, including core activation.

You may not laugh out loud when Nordic walking, but Nordic walking does enhance your mood. Part of the fun comes from learning a new activity. However, part of the good feeling is inherent to the sport itself. There are plenty of people who don't think walking is fun but who do think Nordic walking is fun because it gives them something to do while moving. Anyone who has been Nordic walking knows what I'm talking about. You get into a rhythm that is very meditative and calming. Connecting with the earth with both your legs and your arms (since your poles are an extension of your arms) gets you grounded.

Every Monday evening in Santa Monica, California, you can find groups of Nordic walkers who belong to the Nordic Walking Club. Most people enjoy Nordic walking together; Nordic walking in a group provides both health benefits and social benefits. Nordic walking is more fun when performed with friends and family. Any age, any fitness level, and any gender can perform this sport and fitness activity. Due to the coordination challenge of Nordic walking, 10 years may be a good age for kids to start learning it, though younger children have handled the poles just fine.

Another benefit of Nordic walking is that it is not an expensive sport. All you need is a pair of good Nordic walking poles and a pair of good Nordic walking shoes. Depending on how often you walk on asphalt, you may have to purchase a new asphalt paw 2 to 4 times a year; an asphalt paw costs $10 to $15 U.S. for a pair. Nordic walking is a low-maintenance fitness activity that saves you money in the long run. It may be one of the best investments you ever make considering all the health benefits it gives you in addition to regular walking.

You often hear from adults that back when they were in school they used to play this sport and that sport and were in great shape. Nordic walking is different—it is an activity your students can do for the rest of their lives regardless of their age and fitness level. The range of people who can benefit from Nordic walking is huge. Almost anyone can do Nordic walking (or at least a variation of it), including the patient fresh out of rehabilitation who needs to put as little weight as possible on an injured leg, the elderly person with balance problems looking for stability, the pregnant woman who needs to take the pressure off her achy lower back, the person who is overweight and wants to lose weight more efficiently, the person who is obese and cannot walk for exercise due to the stress it places on the joints, the fitness walker who wants to get the heart rate up, the runner who wants a low-impact but high-intensity workout outdoors, and the athlete who wants to cross train during the off-season. There is

basic Nordic walking, fitness (classic) Nordic walking, and sport (performance) Nordic walking. Teach your students Nordic walking today and for the rest of their lives they will be thankful that you gave them a sport they can keep on doing!

Summary of Benefits

- Can be performed anywhere and all year
- Increases the heart rate by 10 to 30 beats/min
- Increases caloric expenditure by 20% to 46%
- Provides the same intensity as running but is low impact
- Makes the body work harder with less perceived effort
- Provides a full-body workout outdoors
- Creates upper-body strength, especially on uphill trips
- Can be performed by any age, any fitness level, and any gender
- Requires little investment and low maintenance
- Reduces stress on the joints, especially the ankle, knee, and hip
- Improves neck and chest mobility
- Improves gait and posture
- Enhances mood
- Is more fun
- Provides social benefits when performed in groups

EQUIPMENT

You do need specially designed equipment to enjoy Nordic walking. Every sport is unique and has unique features that athletes must develop to perform at an optimal level. The good news is that the gear used for Nordic walking is low maintenance and minimal. Nordic walking requires only a pair of poles. Adding Nordic walking shoes will be quite beneficial using different surfaces like dirt and asphalt. What makes it possible to go Nordic walking anywhere on any surface is a tiny but powerful piece called the *asphalt paw.*

Nordic Walking Poles

The Nordic walking pole can be divided into three parts: the top, the middle, and the bottom (figure 12.1). Starting at the top, you have a grip and a strap. Grips are made of a variety of materials, including plastic, rubber, and cork. The shape can be curved and ergonomic, thick and comfortable, or just plain straight. Choose what feels best. There are many types of straps. Some poles are even strapless; these are designed for Nordic walkers such as the elderly who don't do any advanced techniques. Other poles come with straps that are part of the grip. Some poles have a trigger strap system that clicks in and out of the grip. The important thing about a strap is that it is adjustable and that it gives support for the hand.

The middle part of the pole is called the *shaft* and can be fully adjustable, partially adjustable, or fixed length (see figure 12.2). Common materials of the shaft are carbon fiber and aluminum. Travelers usually enjoy the fully adjustable poles, though these poles tend to be heavier and create more vibration. Choose 100% carbon over aluminum, as aluminum tends to vibrate more. The partially adjustable shafts can be used to fit vary-ing heights of Nordic walkers. Since they are adjusted in only one place at the top, they tend to vibrate less or hardly at all. Finally, the fixed-length pole fits only a specific range of heights but is hassle free—you can grab it and go without making any adjustments. Choose a pole that fits your needs and that is light and durable and vibrates as little as possible.

Adjustable poles work well for a physical education class because they can be used by more than one student. The quality adjustable poles tend to be more expensive than the fixed-length poles. However, overall you need fewer adjustable poles than fixed-length poles, and the cost between the two types evens out. Additionally, the adjustable poles take up less storage space because you need fewer of them and you can shorten them.

The bottom part of the pole has the spike tip, which is a metal piece (sometimes sharp) that makes it possible

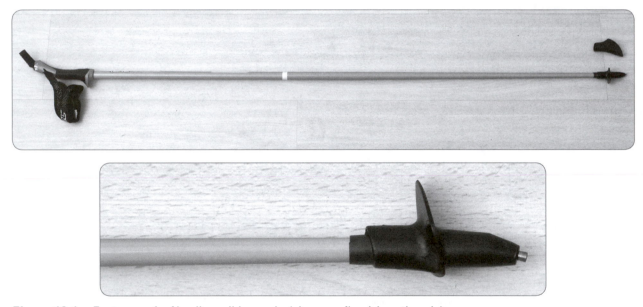

Figure 12.1   Features of a Nordic walking pole (shows a fixed-length pole).

Figure 12.2   Fully adjustable pole collapsed for traveling and extended for Nordic walking.

to walk on grass, dirt, sand, and ice. To walk on cement and asphalt, you can cover the spike tip with an asphalt paw, a little piece that looks like a shoe for the pole (see figure 12.3). It also acts as a cushion and shock absorber. Make sure the paw faces backward so you can get the best traction.

Figure 12.3 The asphalt paw makes Nordic walking possible on cement and asphalt.

TEACHING TIP

To select the correct size of pole, stand on an even surface while wearing the walking shoes you plan to use. Strap into the pole and keep the hand in neutral. Keep your elbow by your side and hold the pole vertically—parallel to your legs. The angle of the elbow should be 90° or slightly more.

Nordic Walking Shoes

Since Nordic walking is an enhancement of regular walking, a good walking shoe and a Nordic walking shoe have three features in common: a flexible front, a supportive middle, and a rounded heel (see figure 12.4). When you are walking you land with your heel, and a rounded heel facilitates this landing. After landing you continue to roll onto the rest of the foot, and so the sole must be flexible enough to allow the foot to roll and to prevent the foot from slamming into the ground, which results in painful shin splints. At the same time the middle of the shoe needs to provide good support as you transfer all your weight to that foot. At the end of the rolling action you start lifting the heel off the ground and shift your body weight to the ball of the foot before pushing off. Thus the front of the shoe needs to bend into the optimal push-off position. In addition

to having a flexible front, a supportive middle, and a rounded heel, a good Nordic walking shoe is light, is form fitted, has good traction, and is water resistant (so you can show off your Nordic spirit in the rain).

Figure 12.4 A Nordic walking shoe needs (a) to provide a good heel strike when landing, (b) to provide good support as you put all your weight on that foot, and (c) to bend in the front to provide a good push-off.

Nordic Walking Clothing

You dress for Nordic walking just like you dress for cross-country skiing: in layers. Using two poles to propel the body forward warms the upper body rather quickly. A vest allows you to move freely as well as keeps the internal organs warm. Unless it is summer and you need only one layer, you should avoid cotton. That applies to socks as well. The layer that you wear closest to your body removes moisture. The second layer keeps the body warm. The third layer protects the body from wind and rain.

> **TEACHING TIP**
> A water belt is a must to keep your hands free but the body hydrated. Make sure your water belt has a pouch that can hold emergency items such as a cell phone, money, and snacks.

BASIC SKILLS AND TECHNIQUES

Now it's time to learn this incredible sport. You can start learning indoors if doing so makes it easier for you to refer to this book. To begin practicing regular walking, all you need is a room in which you can take 5 to 10 steps. Once you add the poles, a long hallway is perfect for practicing, although a room with enough space for 10 to 15 steps also works. However, once you advance to downhill and uphill technique, you must step outdoors unless you have access to an incline indoors. Some indoor inclines built for wheelchairs could be an option for practicing as long as you give courtesy to the people who use wheelchairs and allow them to pass first.

Basic Walking

Often people do not swing their arms when walking. How many times have you seen your students walk with their hands in their pockets? Teaching them to use the arms naturally while walking will help them to prevent future back aches and stiffness. It will also help them learn Nordic walking more quickly. Figure 12.5 illustrates basic walking.

Practice to Increase Awareness of the Arm Swing

To begin basic walking, stand tall with good core activation (stomach slightly pulled in) and good posture (shoulder blades down and slightly retracted) and with the feet hip-width apart in a staggered stance (right foot in front and left foot behind). Figure 12.5 shows the correct push-off and landing positions for the feet, but for now keep both feet flat while you focus on the arm swing.

Figure 12.5 Basic walking.

- Start swinging your arms back and forth. Make sure your arms are going straight forward and backward—do not cross the arms in front of or behind your body.
- Make sure the swing is even. People have a tendency to swing more forward than backward, which causes them to miss out on the natural rotation of the trunk. If you have access to a mirror, watch yourself while you swing your arms. You should be able to see you chest twisting to some extent.
- Let your thumb lead the forward swing and your pinky finger lead the backward swing. Doing so is a sign of good posture. If you do not lead with the thumb and pinky finger, you may notice that your shoulders are rounded.
- If you don't have access to a mirror, close your eyes to experience the slight rotation of the rib cage. As you reopen your eyes, make sure your trunk, and not your arms, is providing the rotation.

Apply the Awareness to Walking

Start walking, applying your new awareness of your arms as you do so. Swing the arms as much forward as backward to get a natural trunk rotation. Feel the trunk rotate.

Practice to Increase Awareness of the Leg Swing

Next, increase your awareness of pushing off and landing with the feet and legs. Keep your right leg forward, left arm forward, and right arm back. Stand still with both feet flat (no toes up or heels up). This position may challenge your balance. If it does, stand close to something that you can grab onto if you lose your steadiness.

- Slowly lift the heel of the left (back) leg. Feel how the weight transfers to the ball of the left foot. Activate the buttocks of the left leg and stay with this feeling, noticing how the ball of the foot and the buttocks work together.
- Push off from the ball of your left foot. Move the leg forward and land with the left foot in heel strike (toes up). Stay in this new position awhile. Make sure your arms changed places and that your upper body leans slightly forward as one unit with the whole body. See if you can get a sense of having the *center* of the heel touch the ground.
- Now move between these two positions—push-off and heel strike—about 10 times.

Apply the Awareness to Walking

Start walking, applying your new awareness as you walk. Feel the trunk rotate and the push-off from the ball of the foot activate the buttocks. Feel your foot land with the center of the heel and feel yourself leaning forward. Make sure you lean slightly forward as one unit—a straight line from heel to head.

When walking with the left leg feels natural, practice standing still on the right leg 10 times (awareness) and then move into walking 15 steps or more (application). Now you are ready to integrate both sides, and for this you need a long hallway or a space in which you can keep on walking for 5 to 15 min. As you walk, apply the key pointers listed for regular walking, checking them off like a checklist. Once you master a key pointer, check it off and move on to the next item on the list. The goal is to make walking feel as natural as possible.

Key Pointers for Regular Walking

- Keep an active core.
- Use good posture (shoulder blades down and retracted, thumb leading the forward swing and pinky finger leading the backward swing).
- Use a straight arm swing (no crossing of the arms or wide arms).
- Evenly space your arm swings (swing as much forward as backward).
- Slightly rotate the rib cage (which is possible with an even arm swing).
- Push off with the ball of the foot (heel off the ground).
- Activate the buttocks.
- Land with a heel strike (center of the heel lands; toes up).
- Roll onto the rest of the foot.
- Lean forward as one unit (a straight line from heel to head).
- Meet the opposite leg with the arm.

Basic Nordic Walking

Some poles are easy to strap into, while others come with instructions. Whatever Nordic walking pole you purchase, make sure you read or get the proper strap instructions. How you strap in varies from pole to pole and changes as new systems develop.

There are three steps in learning basic Nordic walking: (1) practicing the pole rhythm exercise, (2) planting the pole, and (3) pushing the pole. These are each described in turn.

1. *Begin with the pole rhythm exercise.* After you strap into your poles, let your arms hang straight and relaxed (while your core and shoulder blades are active). Keep the poles behind your body and let the bottoms of the poles touch the ground (figure 12.6). For a moment, pretend you don't have poles in your hands. Open the hands—you won't lose the poles since you are strapped in. Now start walking and get into your basic walking technique that you just practiced. As you swing your arms, let the poles just drag on the ground. This is an excellent exercise to help you practice meeting your arms with their opposite legs. However, this is just an exercise: Dragging the poles is *not* part of the Nordic walking technique. Start with this pole rhythm exercise (in which you're dragging the poles) the first 3 to 5 times you Nordic walk.

2. *Plant the poles.* If you are not already walking at your regular speed, start increasing to that tempo. At the beginning of this step, you are still performing the pole dragging exercise to make a smoother transition into correct pole planting. Whatever you do, keep walking at a good pace. The more you think about what you are doing, the slower you walk, until your walk becomes unnatural. At this point you may already feel some

traction from the bottoms of the poles as they catch the ground. This is good. This is the cue for you to grab the grips and plant the poles (figure 12.7).

If you have not felt traction from your poles, don't worry. Keep walking at a good pace. As your forward arm swing reaches the height of your navel, grab onto the grip of the pole and plant the pole.

3. *Push the poles.* After you plant the pole, keep holding onto the grip as you keep applying pressure down and back on the pole. Push the pole back at least to your hip (figure 12.8). The farther you push the pole, the better—the more muscles you use. At the end of the pushing phase, soften your grip on the pole before swinging the pole forward to plant again.

Try the three basic steps in learning Nordic walking out for awhile. When you are ready to add more layers, you can deepen your practice by adding the following elements. Add one at a time. Some of them will just be a check in. Others will require more practice. When one element feels natural, move on to the next one. You will also get a chance to polish your technique as you read and apply the day 10 lesson for the Nordic walking unit.

- **Stop dragging the poles**. The pole rhythm exercise (see figure 12.6) that you practiced in step 1 for learning Nordic walking is just an exercise to find

Figure 12.6　Drag the poles as an exercise to get the rhythm of the poles.

Figure 12.7 Plant the poles.

Figure 12.8 Push the pole back at least to the hip.

the natural Nordic walking pole rhythm. The purpose is to walk with your arms meeting the opposite legs. However, a lot of people misunderstand and think that the exercise and hence dragging the poles is part of the technique. However, once you begin Nordic walk-

ing, make sure you do not continue to drag the poles. To experience Nordic walking without dragging the poles, try exercising on a hard surface with the spike tips exposed. You should hear only one sound as you walk, and that is the sound of planting each pole. If you drag the poles, the sound will be so awful that you will immediately begin planting the poles. If you hear only one clicking sound with each step, then you are planting the poles correctly—the poles are staying airborne during the return.

- **Meet the opposite leg with your arm.** Even if you practice regular walking and then practice dragging the poles, you may still get distracted by using the poles while walking. If you walk with the same leg and same arm, go back to dragging the poles to find the natural walking rhythm of matching your arms to the opposite legs. Watch the timing. Make sure the opposite pole lands *at the same time* that the opposite heel lands. Refer back to figures 12.6 to 12.8 for guidance.

- **Maintain your pole angle.** When you are trekking, you plant the pole vertically. When you are Nordic walking, you plant the pole in an angle. Make sure you maintain the same pole angle the whole time you are Nordic walking. If you are unsure about your pole angle, try the pole rhythm exercise again and note your pole angle when you are dragging the poles. Just keep the same angle when you stop dragging the poles and you will be fine. Refer back to figures 12.6 to 12.8.

- **Plant in a handshake position.** When you plant the pole, you can do it with the elbow either glued to the waist or freed from the waist. The latter style is called *planting in a handshake position* and is the better way to plant because it engages more muscles, including the big back muscle. When you keep your elbow glued to the waist, you work only the backs of the arms. Refer back to figure 12.7.

- **Plant the pole firmly.** If you only tap the pole to the ground as you plant it, you engage hardly any of the upper-body muscles you engaged in the upper-body muscle test (page 193 under Benefits). Instead of tapping the pole, plant it firmly to strengthen the upper body. As you apply pressure down and back on the pole, it is very easy to let go of your good posture and round your poor shoulders. Make sure you respond to the pressure by keeping the shoulder blades stabilized—slightly down and together (retracted). This way you can maintain good posture while Nordic walking.

- **Use the strap to plant the pole.** When you plant the pole, you don't want to squeeze the grip so firmly that your knuckles turn white. That is why you have the strap—you can use the strap to help transfer the power. Make sure the strap is tight but still comfortable so that using the strap to help plant the pole is possible.

- **Push the pole back to at least the hip.** You may do everything right as you Nordic walk but then fail to move your arm past the front of your thigh. Again, by not completing the push back at least to the hip, you are missing out on engaging your muscles. Try walking a little bit faster to have time to push back to the hip. Remember in regular walking that when you pushed off with the ball of the foot you activated the buttocks. This is one way to increase the speed and to keep it powerful. Refer back to figure 12.8.

- **Push back through the strap.** As mentioned earlier, when you plant the pole you can transfer power via the strap. You can continue to use the strap throughout the whole time you are pushing back. Make sure the strap is tight but comfortable so that using it to transfer power is possible.

- **Soften the grip by the hip.** As you firmly plant the pole, you engage the upper body muscles. As you push back via the strap you soften the grip to relax the muscles. This is called *squeeze and release*. Start the release by the hip. In advanced Nordic walking you push the arm back even farther and then open the hand completely at the end of the push back. In basic Nordic walking, however, you push the hand back only to the hip and then only soften your grip once there. It can be tricky to master this coordination of contracting and relaxing the grip muscles. Practice, practice, practice.

- **Keep the pole on the ground as long as possible.** If you have problems pushing the pole back to the hip, this tip will help you. Practice keeping the pole on the ground as long as possible before you return it so you can plant it again. If you are walking too fast and missing out on the pole technique, keeping the pole on the ground will help you polish your push back.

Key Pointers for Basic Nordic Walking

- Do not drag the poles (day 3 in the lesson plans).
- Meet the opposite leg with the arm (day 3).
- Maintain the pole angle (day 3).
- Plant in a handshake position (day 3).
- Plant the pole firmly (days 6 and 7).
- Plant the pole using the strap as well (day 5).
- Push back to at least the hip (day 3).
- Push back through the strap (day 5).
- Soften the grip by the hip (day 6).
- Keep the pole on the ground as long as possible (day 8).

Basic Nordic Walking Uphill and Downhill

Even though it may sound advanced to include hills your routine, walking uphill is actually a great way to build a correct Nordic walking technique. When you are walking uphill, it is almost impossible to not feel how you should be using the poles when Nordic walking. On flat ground, you can get away with just tapping the poles. When you are going uphill and slipping (not getting enough traction from the poles), however, you must plant the poles in a correct handshake position to avoid slipping with the poles. When you are just looking to improve your technique, you can begin on a small incline. Later you can move to steeper hills to get more aerobic and muscular strength benefits. The downhill Nordic walking technique is used to save your joints. If you don't have any aches and pains going downhill and are more interested in keeping your heart rate up, you can learn more-advanced downhill techniques from the recommended resources at the end of this chapter.

- As you Nordic walk uphill (figure 12.9), work the arms and legs more aggressively and lean forward as one unit. Do not bend in the waist or the upper back. Keep the core active as you lean. The steeper the hill, the more your movements are exaggerated.

- When Nordic walking downhill (figure 12.10), bend the knees, shorten the stride, and lean back ever so slightly. Adjust your body according to the grade of the hill. The steeper the hill, the more you get support from the poles and the smaller your movements are. You use less range of motion when swinging the poles, take shorter steps, and squat lower to the ground. The only thing that becomes exaggerated is the frequency of your steps and pole planting. In the beginning, going downhill may throw off the rhythm of your arms and legs. Practice until going downhill feels natural. Long strides and straight knees put too much impact on the joints (hips, knees, and ankles) as you walk downhill. Shift to short strides and soft knees to save the joints.

SAFETY CONSIDERATIONS

Be very cautious when handling the poles (with or without the spike tips exposed) around other people. Always

Figure 12.9 When you Nordic walk uphill, you naturally lean slightly forward as one unit.

Figure 12.10 When you Nordic walk downhill, adjust your body to the grade of the hill.

keep the spike tip covered with the asphalt paw when you are keeping the poles off the ground, such as when performing warm-up exercises with the poles. Crossing a stretch of asphalt with exposed tips may be noisy and you may instinctively lift the poles off the asphalt and point them backward to stop the noise. In doing this, however, you can easily poke somebody behind you. The spike tip is somewhat sharp and can hurt people. Therefore, always keep your poles vertical when they're off the ground so that the spike tip is always pointing down. When removing the asphalt paw, make sure you do it safely. Remove the paw one pole at a time. When you are removing a paw from a pole, be sure to lay the other pole down on the ground. It is easy to forget about the spike tip of the other pole when you are concentrating on getting the paw off, and if you keep the other pole in your hand you may hit somebody accidently before you know it.

When you Nordic walk with a group, make sure you keep enough distance between group members. You don't want to step on the pole of the person in front of you, as doing so may yank on that person's arm and shoulder joint. If you stay too close to somebody beside you, you may end up tripping over the other person's pole, and vice versa. Tripping may also occur if you turn too narrowly at the beginning, before you get used to walking with two poles. On uneven terrain keep an eye out for holes to avoid getting a pole stuck in one. Otherwise you may come to a sudden and unpleasant stop.

Day 3

CONCLUSION

While Nordic walking has been around since the 1990s, it is still regarded as a new fitness exercise. Especially in North America, a lot of people still do not know what Nordic walking is. Whether you may or may not be a Nordic walking pioneer at your school, it is my hope that you will enjoy learning about Nordic walking. Turn around and teach the basic skills to your students and give them this fitness activity as a gift for life.

Often it is easier to just say Nordic walking is "walking with poles." Encourage people to do the upper body muscle test to experience the reason why they would need poles. By now you already know the answer to that question—to engage the upper body muscles and to propel the body forward. Remember some of the amazing benefits from simply applying correct pole technique—burn 20% to 46% more calories, strengthen the upper body, and reduce the stress on the lower body joints. These main benefits make Nordic walking the

perfect tool in fighting the obesity epidemic in this country. Why not teach parents Nordic walking as well so the whole family can enjoy quality time together to support healthy habits across all generations!

REFERENCES

Church, T.S., Earnest, C.P., & Morss, G.M. (2002). Field testing of physiological responses associated with Nordic walking. *Research Quarterly for Exercise and Sport, 73*(3), 296-300.

Svensson, M. (2003). *Nordic walking USA basic instructor manual.* Santa Monica, CA: Author.

Svensson, M. (2009). *Outdoor adventures: Nordic walking.* Champaign, IL: Human Kinetics.

RECOMMENDED RESOURCES

Nottingham, S. (2009). *Nordic walking for total fitness.* Champaign, IL: Human Kinetics.

Svensson, M. (2003). *Nordic walking USA basic instructor manual.* Santa Monica, CA: Author.

Svensson, M. (2009). *Outdoor adventures: Nordic walking.* Champaign, IL: Human Kinetics.

Walter, C. (2009). *Nordic walking: The complete guide to health, fitness, and fun.* Long Island City, NY: Hatherleigh Press.

RECOMMENDED WEB SITES

Nordic Walking USA

www.NordicWalkingUSA.com
This Web site provides more information on the research from the Cooper Institute Study.

Nordic Walking North America

www.NordicWalkingNA.com
Become a certified Nordic walking instructor.

TEACHING TIP

Feedback on your technique. Send the author a one minute video clip of yourself Nordic walking and she'll evaluate it and give you feedback. Nordic walk along a triangle so she can see you from three angles: back, side, and front. Send your e-mail to info@NordicBody.com and please write "Evaluation of Nordic walking" in the subject line.

NORDIC WALKING UNIT PLAN

General Lesson Information

Each lesson contains the following seven elements:

1. Objectives—primary learning outcomes
2. Equipment—specific materials for each lesson
3. Introduction—fundamental concepts and skills pertaining to the lesson's focus
4. Warm-ups—walking to warm-up and a review of the previous lesson
5. Central activities—introduction of new techniques and walking workouts
6. Closure—suggested discussion and reflection items
7. Assessment—evaluation strategies for checking for understanding

The goal is to teach the basics of Nordic walking in 10 sessions that are 50 min each. This includes teaching the basics in core activation and posture to build a good foundation as well as the basics in regular walking since Nordic walking is an enhancement of regular walking.

Day 1

Focus: Building a good foundation

- Core and posture
- Regular walking
- Walking together
- Walking speed

Day 2

Focus: Structure of a cardiorespiratory workout

- Review of last lesson
- Warm-up
  - Technique
  - Add theme
  - Slowly add speed
- Endurance
- Cool-down
  - Gradual slow down
  - Static stretch

Day 3

Focus: Introducing Nordic walking poles

- Review of last lesson
- Features of a Nordic walking pole
- Reasons for pole use
- Pole safety
- Pole rhythm, pole plant, and pole push
- Building the basic Nordic walking technique

Day 4

Focus: Nordic walking uphill and downhill techniques

- Review of last lesson
- Pole rhythm (no dragging, maintain angle), pole plant (handshake), and pole push (at least to hip)
- No dragging test
- Nordic walking uphill and downhill

Day 5

Focus: Transferring power through the strap

- Review of last lesson
- Pole rhythm (no dragging, maintain angle), pole plant (handshake), and pole push (at least to hip)
- Pushing through the strap
- New surface

Day 6

Focus: Contracting and relaxing muscles

- Review of last lesson
- Pole rhythm (no dragging, maintain angle), pole plant (handshake), pole push (at least to hip), and pushing through the strap
- Squeeze and release
- New surface

Day 7

Focus: Creating maximal resistance

- Review of last lesson
- Pole rhythm (no dragging, maintain angle), pole plant (handshake), pole push (at least to hip), pushing through the strap, and squeeze (planting) and release (end of pole push)
- Powerful or tapping push
- New surface

Day 8

Focus: Duration of pole on the ground

- Review of last lesson
- Pole rhythm (no dragging, maintain angle), pole plant (handshake, powerful), pole push (at least to hip), pushing through the strap, and squeeze (planting) and release (end of pole push)
- Practice keeping the pole on the ground as long as possible
- New surface

Day 9

Focus: Different intensity walking with or without poles

- Review of last lesson
- Taking a pulse manually
- RPE
- Pole rhythm (no dragging, maintain angle), pole plant (handshake, powerful), pole push (at least to hip, pole on ground as long as possible), push through the strap, and squeeze (planting) and release (end of pole push)

- Endurance
- Review of uphill and downhill techniques
- Hill training with and without poles

Day 10

Focus: Nordic walking freestyle

- Review of last lesson
- Pole rhythm (no dragging, maintain angle), pole plant (handshake, powerful), pole push (at least to hip, pole on ground as long as possible), push through the strap, and squeeze (planting) and release (end of pole push)
- Endurance
- Creative and safe moves with the poles
- Student demonstration and teaching

chapter 13

Knot Tying

Tim P. Taylor

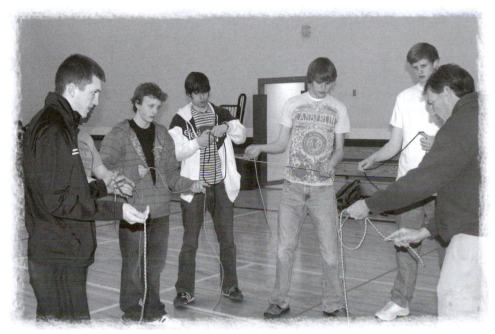

When you get to the end of your rope, tie a knot and hang on.
Franklin D. Roosevelt

This chapter discusses how knots can be used to augment on other outdoor pursuits or used as a stand-alone unit that teachers can implement in their physical education class. As a supplement to other outdoor pursuits (climbing, camping, boating, kayaking, and so on), a knot unit can be a great tool to tie your curriculum together. Many educators introduce knots at the beginning of their curriculum, knowing that over the course of a semester or year, the knots will be revisited and applied in many different scenarios.

Even if your physical education curriculum does not offer outdoor pursuits, knots make a wonderful stand-alone unit. You will be amazed at how interested, engaged, and engrossed your students will become in a simple knot unit. To help you teach a knot unit, this chapter includes

- general information about knots and knot terminology;
- important facts and safety information about knots;
- recommendations on the best type, size, and length of rope to use for knot tying; and
- instructor methodologies and teaching strategies.

While this chapter does not include step-by-step instructions on how to teach each knot, a few clicks of your mouse button will take you to a wide variety of Web sites that have visual step-by-step instructions on a spectrum of knots. The CD-ROM accompanying this chapter includes an in-depth table that covers more than 17 knots used for around-the-house applications, general usage applications, and outdoor pursuits applications. This table includes visual references for each knot, shares fun and insightful knot facts, and offers practical applications and uses for each knot.

Additionally, the CD-ROM features a handful of assessment strategies you can use to formally and informally assess your students' knowledge of the knots you teach. These assessment strategies include written, demonstrative, and critical thinking approaches to evaluating students' comprehension of knots. There's even a great game that makes knot testing fun for students!

BENEFITS OF TEACHING KNOT TYING

Knots are a fantastic tool you as a physical education instructor can use to enhance your adventure-based classroom environment. Most commonly, knots are associated with a functional purpose. Boy Scouts use knots in camping, construction workers use knots for securing heavy loads, ranchers use knots to tie off livestock, climbers use knots for safety, and sailors use knots to harness the wind. But knots can be more than a functional outcome of a task, work activity, or recreational activity.

Often overlooked is the advantage knots can provide in a physical education environment. From an objective perspective, knots can be used to harness learning through cross-lateral movement development or can be used as a method of introducing solutions to practical everyday situations. From a subjective perspective, knots can represent pride, organization, and penchant for detail. Ultimately, knots are a lesson every physical education instructor can use to enhance student learning.

Knots can be taught periodically throughout the school year or as an all-inclusive unit. When taught throughout the school year, knots can be introduced in conjunction with other outdoor pursuits as they apply to the situation. When taught as a stand-alone curriculum, 15 to 20 knots can be covered efficiently over the course of 2 to 3 weeks when games and assessments are included and an adequate amount of time is provided for students to practice and master each knot.

Knots also provide versatility for the instructor. Knots can be taught just as easily and readily indoors as outdoors. Knots are also an excellent classroom management tool to help keep students engaged (see figure 13.1). Passing out a short piece of rope to all participants at the beginning of an adventure trip can provide endless hours of involvement, challenge, and stimulation. Savvy educators will begin a day hiking trip or weeklong outdoor camping trip by providing participants with enough basic knot knowledge, skill, and challenges to keep everyone continually engaged and perplexed as the day or week progresses. By the end of the experience, students are desperately asking for more information about knots. You will quickly find that knots are a great help in supervising unstructured time or make a great culminating experience such as a final knot tying championship (see the knot games on the accompanying CD-ROM).

INTRODUCTION TO KNOTS

To begin any knot unit, all you need is a piece of rope. This rope, however, can take on many different forms. Things to consider when picking rope may include the following:

- Type of rope
- Diameter of rope
- Length of rope

Type of Rope

Most experienced physical education instructors lean toward a braided rope as opposed to a twisted rope for a classroom knot-tying curriculum. Kernmantle rope or cordage falls into the category of braided ropes (see figure 13.2). Kernmantle rope has two components: an inner core that is the meat or strength of the rope and an outer sheath that protects the core. Kernmantle rope is durable and easy to work with and can be burned when it frays to make it useful again. Since a true kernmantle climbing rope can be very expensive and much larger than you need, try using cordage, cordelette, or accessory cord.

Diameter of Rope

Rope that is smaller in diameter can take on a variety of names, such as cordage, cordelette, or accessory cord. The diameter of this smaller rope usually ranges between 0.08 in. (2 mm), which is very small, and 0.28 in. (7 mm), which is nearly the size of true climbing rope. If your budget is not an issue, 0.20 to 0.24 in. (5-6 mm) accessory cord is an excellent choice for a classroom knot-tying curriculum. If you are looking to save money, small 0.08 to 0.12 in. (2-3 mm) cordage found in a hardware store can be equally effective (although your students may find this diameter a little harder to work with; see figure 13.3). When deciding on what diameter to purchase, a greater-diameter cordage is easier for students to untie after they have pulled their knots tight. A smaller-diameter accessory cord may cost less, but it can be harder to work with, too. The smaller diameter has a tendency to become very tight as the cordage crosses around itself, and it binds very tightly, much like a shoelace does when it falls into an overhand knot and is stuck for eternity.

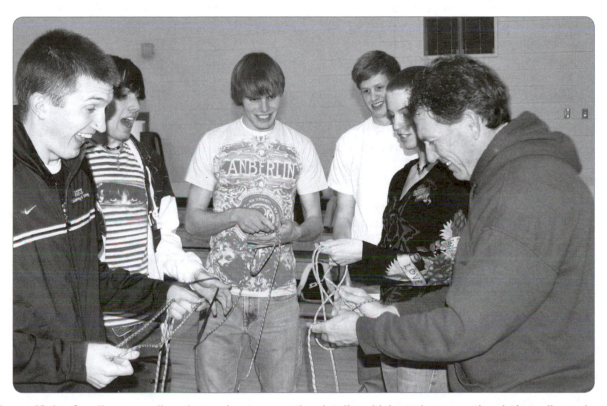

Figure 13.1   Small groups allow the teacher to cover tiny details, which students can then help to disseminate.

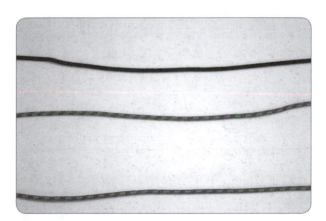

Figure 13.2   Kernmantle rope.

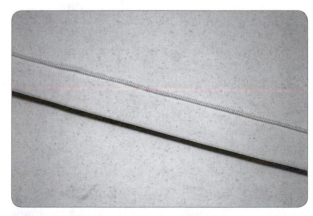

Figure 13.3   Examples of 0.12 in. (3 mm) diameter rope and 0.24 in. (6 mm) diameter rope.

Length of Rope

Fortunately, the equipment needed for a knot unit is very cost efficient, whether you buy 0.20 to 0.24 in. (5-6 mm) or 0.08 to 0.12 in. (2-3 mm) cordage. At the very minimum a cord that is approximately 4 ft (1.2 m) long is all that is needed, but slightly longer and shorter lengths are acceptable.

When you purchase cordage, most specialty climbing shops and some hardware stores will cut it to the length you desire. A more efficient and cost-effective way to purchase cordage is on the spool. Purchasing cordage on a spool allows you to cut sections to the length you desire. You can cut cordage with a pair of scissors and then burn the tip with a match to seal the end (avoid allowing the cordage to become so hot that it melts and drips while it burns, as this can be dangerous). Or you can use a rope cutter, a device that cuts the rope and seals the end of the cordage while you are cutting it.

KNOT TERMINOLOGY

Knot terminology is used to describe how a knot is tied. Knot terminology is often similar to knot names. Just as the name of a knot can vary depending on the culture or situation it is used in, knot terminology changes depending on the circumstances. Many books on knots use different terms to describe the same knot-tying motions. Many books also make reference to certain knot terms with a lot of similarities. If there is one consistency about the language of knots, it has a lot of subtle inconsistencies. For example, in the book *The Handbook of Knots,* Des Pawson (1998, 20) defines

- a *crossing turn* as "the rope is crossed to form a full circle," and
- a *loop* as "formed into a circle without being crossed over itself."

However, in the book *The Ultimate Book of Knots: More Than Two Hundred Practical and Decorative Knots,* Peter Owen (2003, 13) defines

- a *turn* as "one complete revolution of one line around another," and
- a *loop* as the "part of the line that is bent so that it comes together across itself."

Although there are some very similar terms used for the technical moves needed to tie a knot, almost every knot book you pick up will vary slightly on the definitions given for knot terminology. Since knots have such a long and rich history and have been used in such a wide variety of cultures and situations (shipping, ranching, construction, climbing, fishing, and so on), it is reasonably safe to assume that all these authors are correct in their own culture. The variances in these definitions are so slight that as long as your students know that knot descriptions can vary among cultures and as long as you inform your students before beginning the knot unit what definitions you will be using, consistency and integrity will be maintained. See the sidebar for the definitions of some of the common terms found in knot tying.

Common Terms

bight—Folding the rope back next to itself *(a)*.

working end—The end of the rope that you use to tie the knot *(b)*.

standing end—The part of the rope that hangs there and does nothing *(c)*.

loop—Put a bight on the rope and then form the shape of a loop with the rope *(d)*. Depending upon the book you read, a loop is formed by either creating the shape of a circle without the rope crossing over itself, or creating the shape of a circle by taking the rope and crossing over itself which is known as a "crossing turn."

turn, crossing turn, or crossing point—When the rope crosses across itself *(e)*.

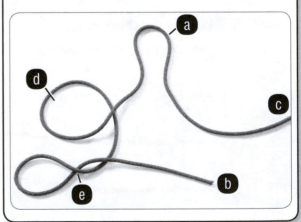

ABOUT TEACHING KNOTS

Technically, a knot forms a loop or noose, fastens two ends of the same cord, or creates a stopper at the end of a rope (Luebben, 1993). While this may be the technical description of a knot, seasoned educators know knots serve a far greater purpose than forming a loop, creating a stopper, or fastening two ends of a rope. For the elementary, middle school, or high school student, knots can be an excellent source of nonconscious learning.

Many students become fascinated with the history, challenge, and application of knots. They become so engrossed in tying knots that they do not realize they are involved in a skill that has practical applications for the rest of their lives. This nonconscious learning provides an environment for a nearly endless source of focus, concentration, challenge, eye–hand coordination, cross-lateral brain development, fortitude, tenacity, and entertainment (see figure 13.4).

Additionally, knots provide a foundation for interested learners to discover how to succeed in their own learning style, whether it is kinesthetic, active, or visual. As an instructor, remember your students learn differently, and knots seem to accentuate this point. Therefore, when teaching knots, teach in as many different styles as you can.

Instructor Methodology

You can use different learning styles to your advantage when teaching students how to tie knots. By emphasizing to students that researchers have discovered a variety of learning styles and teaching students to become aware of these different learning styles, you can help your students to identify their own learning style and become in tune with the learning style that fits them best.

Kinesthetic Learning

Kinesthetic learning is a style in which a student learns by carrying out a physical activity rather than listening to a lecture or watching a demonstration (Kinesis Institute, N.d.) For example, you might teach students kinesthetically how to tie the knot by taking hold of the learner's hands and guiding them through the movements (see figure 13.6 on page 213). When you use this approach, make sure that the student takes in one movement at a time. If the knot has a sequence of many steps, reinforce each movement before completing the entire knot. Even though it seems that many students learn knots best in a kinesthetic learning environment, many kinesthetic learners still struggle with how to tie a knot correctly because they do not grasp important details regarding hand position, spatial awareness, and hand movement when tying the knot. When this occurs you may want to try an active learning approach.

Active Learning

Active learning "derives from two basic assumptions: (1) that learning is by nature an active endeavor and (2) that different people learn in different ways" (Meyers & Jones, 1993). Whereas a kinesthetic learner jumps

Figure 13.4   Nonconscious learning.

right into the hand maneuvers to tie a knot, an active learner takes time to think things out before attempting the knot. It helps to remember a few basic assumptions associated with an active learning style. If you choose to teach to this learning style, remember to follow these principles:

- Spend less time talking.
- Provide an ample amount of time for students to be actively engaged.
- Watch for students who are not grasping the concept of tying a knot through your demonstration.
- If students are still struggling, change your approach as needed to reach all learning styles.

One example of teaching to an active learning style is to emphasize what hand is holding the accessory cord (left or right), what position the hand is in (up or down, left or right, in or out), and what direction the hand is moving in (away or toward, up or down). Many times, students will grab the cordelette in a manner that differs from what you are demonstrating or will move their hand in a direction that differs from what you are demonstrating. Or you may be right handed and the student may be left handed and wants to use the left hand instead of the right hand. Spatial ability can be extremely important in helping students with tying knots successfully (Nilges & Usnick, 2000). Facing the same direction as your students (with your back to the students) helps to emphasize left and right, over

and under, and top and bottom. For example, it is not uncommon for students to hold the rope with their hand over the rope, when it may be easier for them to start with their hand underneath the rope (see figure 13.5).

Visual Learning

It is equally important for you to cover visual learning in your approach. For visual learners, you might place the rope on the ground and break the knot into steps or parts, moving one step at a time, allowing the learners to see the knot being tied on a flat surface without having to hold the rope in their hand.

Another style that can be effective for visual learners is to have them teach the knot to you (the instructor). As you hold the cordage, allow the student to explain to you how to tie the knot. Tie the knot as they teach it to you, stopping as needed to emphasize important points.

Teaching Strategies

There are a variety of teaching strategies that you as a physical education teacher can use to teach knots successfully. The size of your class and the amount of time you have for class can guide which strategy you implement. You may also gravitate toward a strategy or teaching style that fits your own personal teaching personality and strengths, or you may use a combination of strategies to meet the needs of your students. The following sections describe suggested strategies for you to use to teach a knot unit successfully.

Figure 13.5   Facing the same direction helps students with spatial awareness as it relates to tying a knot.

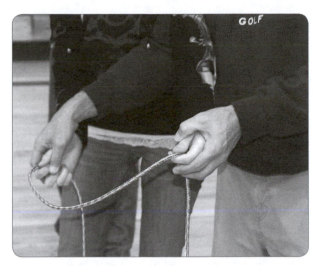

Figure 13.6   Direct, hands-on physical assistance can help students with the kinesthetic feel of tying the knot.

Direct Teaching Strategy

This teaching strategy involves direct instruction by the teacher. You may arrange your students in a semicircle and give each student a piece of accessory cord before facilitating the lesson by explaining and demonstrating how to tie the knot. When using this direct teaching strategy, there are three substrategies you can use to teach your knot unit with greater efficiency and comprehension for students.

- **First substrategy.** Always face the same direction your students are facing when teaching a knot. Turn your back to your students where everyone is facing the same direction to help augment the spatial ability students need when learning knots.

- **Second substrategy.** When teaching a knot for the first time, have the students place their cordage or rope on the ground and watch and listen to your direct instruction before attempting the knot themselves. This strategy for direct instruction is a proven method used by many physical education instructors. Research has shown that eliminating the distraction of the cordage or rope helps students grasp the concept of how to tie a knot much more quickly.

- **Third substrategy.** Make sure you present the appropriate amount of information when teaching a knot. While some students can learn a knot by watching it one time, the vast majority of students will need to watch or listen many times to grasp the understanding of how to tie the knot. Then, what becomes important to you is how much information you should teach at

a time. Most of the time, the complexity of the knot drives the answer to this question. Simpler knots can be shown in their entirety, while more complex knots should be broken down into parts. You can use the whole-part-whole methodology of teaching to your advantage when working with complex knots.

Another point to consider is the number of knots you should teach at a time. Once again, the simpler the knot, the easier it will be for students to learn. A good rule of thumb is to teach no more than three knots in a 50 min class of approximately 25 to 30 students—adjusted for the complexity of the knot and the size of the class. Always try to start the next class with a review of all the knots you have covered in previous lessons.

Reciprocal Teaching Strategy

You may choose to start a lesson by explaining and demonstrating a knot, and then turn the lesson over to the students and allow them to help teach each other for clarification and competency. Or you may choose to show the knot without any explanation and challenge the students to help each other solve the problem.

Posters

You can create an environment featuring pictures or posters of each of the knots you wish to cover. Arrange the posters in your gym or classroom in a manner that creates a station-to-station effect and have students travel to each station to learn a different knot. You may choose to set an allotted amount of time for each station or leave the timing open ended. Once students have traveled to each station, have them come back to a group setting so you can answer any questions or bring closure to the lesson.

Technology

Try creating a DVD of how knots are tied and distribute the DVD to your class. Students can then learn to tie the knots outside of the classroom environment and return for clarification or testing if desired.

FIVE THINGS TO REMEMBER ABOUT KNOTS

The following are five basic points you can emphasize when tying knots with your students. These five points make knots easier for students to apply to various situations:

- Tie it right, pull it tight.
- Knots make the rope weaker.
- Tie a knot you can untie after using it.
- Knots are known by different names.
- Never place a rope with a knot in it around a person's neck—not even as a joke.

Tie It Right, Pull It Tight

Always tie the knot correctly, double-check the knot, and then dress the knot and pull it tight. A knot that is dressed is tied in such a manner that it does not cross itself unless it is designed to do so. For example, when laid on a flat surface, a trace eight (or follow-through figure-eight) knot has both sections of the rope laying side by side the entire length of the knot (see figure 13.7).

Knots Make the Rope Weaker

Whenever you place a knot in a rope, the rope grows weaker. Some knots do a better job of retaining the rope's original strength. See the knot table (in the accompanying CD-ROM) for a list of knots and how those knots affect the original strength of the rope.

Tie a Knot You Can Untie After Using It

Many people can tie a knot, but most do not consider what happens to a knot after it has been used. This is because once the rope is loaded with weight, it pulls tighter and binds on itself. Think of a shoelace. Have you ever tied a simple overhand (thumb) knot in your shoelace only to have it pull so tight that it remained in the shoelace for life because it was not worth your time to try and untie the knot? The following are a couple of general rules to tell students when they are tying knots:

- The greater the diameter of the rope, the easier it is to untie the knot after it has been loaded.
- More turns, crossing turns, or bends in the knot usually makes it easier to untie the knot after it has been loaded.

There are always exceptions to any general rule, but overall, if you tie a barrel knot with a piece of cordage that is 0.12 in. (3 mm) in diameter and you tie the same barrel knot with a piece of cordage that is 0.28 in. (7 mm) in diameter, you will find it much easier to untie the 0.28 in. (7 mm) knot than the 0.12 in. (3 mm) knot. Remind students who are using a smaller section of cordelette (when they are practicing knots for the sake of learning how to tie the knot and not tying knots for use) that there is no need to bear down on the rope and pull it tight. They will spend more time trying to untie the knot than they did tying the knot in the first place.

Additionally, students need to practice choosing the correct knot for the correct situation. An overhand on a bight, for example, is a good solid knot that forms a loop at the end of a rope that can be placed over the end of a hitch on a truck to tow something. An eight on a bight, however, is a better choice for towing because it has an extra crossing turn that creates greater surface and contact area for the knot to be untied after it is loaded. An even better choice might be a bowline on a bight because it can be loaded with a substantial amount of weight and can be easily untied later due to the configuration of the crossing turns and bends in the knot.

Figure 13.7   A knot that is *(a)* dressed (notice how the rope lays side by side to itself) and *(b)* not dressed (notice how the rope crosses over itself).

Knots Are Known by Different Names

You should always explain to your students that knots are known by different names. The culture in which the knot is used frequently reflects the name of the knot. On ships and boats, the *reef knot* is used quite often, but in climbing, the *reef knot* is referred to as a *square knot*. An *alpine butterfly knot* is sometimes known as just a *butterfly knot*. An *overhand knot* is also called a *thumb knot*. Climbers may call it a *granny,* while around boats, ships, and dockyards it is a *lubber's knot*. The lesson here is don't ever argue when you hear a knot called by a different name.

Never Place a Rope With a Knot in It Around a Person's Neck

Knots should always be taken seriously. Instruct your students to *never,* not even in jest, place a loop with a knot in it around another person's neck. A rope with a knot can be construed as a weapon when it is used improperly.

CONCLUSION

While these 5 basic points are very useful to remember, you can also use these points as a critical thinking assessment tool to ascertain if your students are learning more than just tying the knots. Use these points to challenge students to know the different names of the knots they tie, know the culture the knot may be used in, explain why they would tie a certain knot based on the strength of the knot, or explain why they may use a certain diameter rope in a given situation.

REFERENCES

Kinesis Institute. (N.d.) Kinesthetic learning. http://kinesisinstitute.schools.officelive.com/default.aspx.

Luebben, C. (1993). *Knots for climbers.* Evergreen, CO: Chockstone.

Meyers, C., & Jones, T. (1993). *Promoting active learning: Strategies for the college classroom.* San Francisco, CA: Jossey-Bass Publishers.

Nilges, L., & Virginia Usnick, V. (2000). The role of spatial ability in physical education and mathematics. *Journal of Physical Education, Recreation and Dance, 71,* 29-33.

Owen, P. (2003). *The ultimate book of knots: More than two hundred practical and decorative knots.* Guilford, CT: Lyons Press.

Pawson, D. (1998). *The Handbook of knots.* New York: DK Publishing.

RECOMMENDED READINGS

Bigon, M., & Regazzoni, G. (1982). *The Morrow guide to knots.* New York: William Morrow.

Budworth, G. (1997). *The complete book of knots.* New York: Lyons and Burford.

Budworth, G., & Dalton, J. (2003). *The book of knots: How to tie 200 practical knots.* Evergreen, CO: Sterling.

Luebben, C. (2002). *Knots for climbers.* (2nd ed.). Evergreen, CO: Globe Pequot Press.

Owen, P. (2003). *The ultimate book of knots: More than two hundred practical and decorative knots.* Guilford, CT: Lyons Press.

Raleigh, D. (1998). *Knots and ropes for climbers.* Mechanicsburg, PA: Stackpole Books.

RECOMMENDED WEB SITES

Web Sites Demonstrating How to Tie Various Knots

www.animatedknots.com
www.ropeworks.biz
www.ehow.com/videos-on_8373_knot-tying-instructions-hitches.html#at
www.abc-of-rockclimbing.com/howto/learn_climbing_knots.asp#at
www.chockstone.org/TechTIps/F8Knots.htm

Appendix

Thomas Jefferson Middle School Trip Information and Itinerary

Class:	Physical Education, Outdoor Pursuits—Hiking
Instructor:	Jeff Davis
Dates:	12 April
Location:	Rocky Mountain National Park (RMNP)
Activities:	Day hike and outdoor skills instruction
Maps:	National Park Service map of RMNP, Trail Tracks RMNP Hiking Map
Travel time:	From Greeley, 1:30 h (approximately 55 mi, or 89 km)
Starting point:	RMNP Headquarters Visitor Center parking lot (Estes Park, Colorado)
Ending point:	Fern Lake Trailhead
Narrative:	Depart school at approximately 7 a.m. and travel west on Hwy 34 to Estes Park, turning southwest on Hwy 36 to park headquarters (7,840 ft, or 2,390 m). Proceed as a caravan through Beaver Meadows entrance ($15 U.S. fee per car). Follow signs to Cub Lake Trail, but go 1 mi (1.6 km) beyond to Fern Lake Trailhead (8,155 ft, or 2,486 m). Park at parking lot. Upon arrival, hike 2.5 mi (4 km) to Fern Falls (645 ft, or 197 m, elevation gain), proceeding to hike another 1.3 mi (2.1 km) to Fern Lake (730 ft, or 223 m, additional elevation gain). Per instructions at trailhead, plan to return to school no later than 6:30 p.m. Difficulty = *easy*. Easy = 0-1,000 ft (0-305 m) elevation gain or 0-3 mi (0-4.8 km) one way, *moderate* = 1,000-2,500 ft (305-762 m) gain or 3-6 mi (4.8-9.7 km) one way, *difficult* = more than 2,500 ft (762 m) gain or more than 6 mi (9.7 km) one way.
Total hike time:	8 h
Hazards or obstacles:	There are dangers related to automobile travel. While hiking, there is the possibility of high-altitude illnesses (increased chance of dehydration, hypothermia, severe sunburn, mountain sickness); giardiasis; animal or insect bites; route finding; loose rocks; mountain weather (thunderstorms, lightning, early snowstorms); encountering streams, lakes, and waterfalls; and human error.
Emergency contacts:	RMNP Headquarters: 970-586-1399 Estes Park Police: 970-586-4000
	Note: 911 is operational in this area.

About the Editors

Jeff Steffen, PhD, is a professor in exercise and sport science at the University of Wisconsin at La Crosse (UWL). He has worked in outdoor physical education for more than 20 years, and over that time he has developed and supervised numerous outdoor programs while having the opportunity to influence both practicing and prospective teachers. He has many publications in outdoor physical education, and has presented at conferences and workshops on outdoor topics.

Steffen is director of the UWL adventure program and the graduate physical education program, is past chair of the AAHPERD Outdoor Education Council, and has received the AAHPERD Julian Smith Lifetime Achievement Award. In his leisure time, he enjoys hunting and fishing, backcountry travel, and rock climbing and mountaineering.

Jim Stiehl, PhD, is a professor in the school of sport and exercise science at the University of Northern Colorado (UNC) in Greeley. Like Steffen, Stiehl has more than 20 years of outdoor physical education experience, as well as experience in developing and supervising outdoor programs. He has authored other outdoor titles and presented at workshops and conferences on a variety of outdoor topics.

Stiehl is director of the UNC challenge course and has served as coordinator of the UNC outdoor program. He is past chair of the AAHPERD Outdoor Education Council and has received the AAHPERD Julian Smith Lifetime Achievement Award. He enjoys hiking and backpacking, backcountry skiing and snowshoeing, and rock climbing and mountaineering.

About the Contributors

Stacy Birdsall Claus, MS, has been teaching and coaching middle school in Hood River, Oregon for a decade. Her physical education curriculum emphasizes lifetime activities such as cycling, climbing, and yoga. Birdsall Claus teaches local women mountain biking skills during summer bike camps. She is a member of OAHPERD and AAHPERD. Birdsall Claus enjoys windsurfing in the summer, telemark skiing in the winter, and riding single-track year-round. She earned her bachelor's degree in exercise science and nutrition from James Madison University, and her master's degree in physical education from Oregon State University.

Daniel L. Chase, PhD, is the project manager for Get Outdoors Nevada at the University of Nevada at Las Vegas (UNLV) Public Lands Institute. For three years at the University of Northern Colorado, he taught several outdoor education classes, including outdoor leadership, backpacking and hiking, orienteering, and rock climbing. He has also presented outdoor and adventure education topics at the American Alliance for Health, Physical Education, Recreation and Dance (AAHPERD) National Conference. Chase is an author of *Traversing Walls: 68 Activities On and Off the Wall,* a book of 68 activities geared toward challenging participants and physically preparing them to climb. He has also been involved in planning, leading, and guiding overnight and extended backpacking excursions since 2001. Chase is a member of AAHPERD and the National Intramural-Recreational Sports Association (NIRSA). He received his PhD in sport pedagogy from the University of Northern Colorado.

Kristen Csiacsek, MS, is a middle school physical education teacher. She started climbing with her family at a young age and now climbs recreationally as an adult. Csiacsek taught a college level activity course in rock climbing and bouldering, and developed and incorporated outdoor pursuits and adventure for a middle school curriculum that also includes bouldering. She belongs to the Association for Challenge Course Technology and AAHPERD. She received her master's degree in adventure education from the University of Wisconsin at La Crosse.

Steven J. Eggerichs, MS, is an adapted physical education teacher and adventure coordinator for the school district of Holmen, Wisconsin. He is a member of AAHPERD and the Wisconsin Association for Health, Physical Education, Recreation, and Dance (WAHPERD). Eggerichs received his master's degree in physical education pedagogy with a concentration in adventure education from the University of Wisconsin at La Crosse.

Ryan Hammes, MS, is a coordinator of outdoor recreation at Sonoma State University and also teaches a rock climbing course for the kinesiology department. He led a yearly anchor training course at Sonoma State University and has also led instructing and course directing for Outward Bound Wilderness in Colorado for four years. Hammes published an article titled "Orienteering with Adventure Education: New Games for the 21st Century" in *Strategies: A Journal for Physical and Sport Educators.* He is a member of the American Mountain Guides Association (AMGA) and the Association of Outdoor Recreation and Education (AORE). In 2006, Hammes received his top-rope site manager certification and in 2009, he received his single pitch instructor certification from AMGA. He also enjoyed guiding groups all over the United States in both top-roping and multipitch environments. He received his master's degree in physical education teaching with an adventure concentration from the University of Wisconsin at La Crosse.

Amy Lutz, MA, is a physical education curriculum specialist. She has over 20 years of cycling experience as a triathlete, mountain biker, endurance rider, and bicycle commuter. In 2005, she became a certified cycling instructor and has instructed physical education teachers in implementing a bicycle safety curriculum in a variety of settings. She developed and conducted two-day workshops to train more than 100 physical education teachers in implementing the curriculum with students. Lutz has also conducted numerous bicycle safety workshops and presentations at Safe Routes to School Conferences, Summer Institutes, the American Association for Physical Activity and Recreation's Out There Conference, and the American College of Sports Medicine Health and Fitness Summit. She wrote *Fit for the Future: Spokane Public Schools Bicycle Safety Curriculum,* which was developed with teachers and for teachers in a format that is practical for physical education classes. She received her master's degree in physical education from Oregon State University.

Jeff McNamee, PhD, is an associate professor at Linfield College. He has taught both elementary and middle school physical education in Wisconsin before completing his PhD from Oregon State University in 2004. McNamee has been an avid road cyclist and mountain biker for over 14 years and rides recreationally and competitively. He is the physical education program director at Linfield College and teaches courses that demonstrate how to integrate outdoor pursuits in existing physical education programs. He is the author of several journal articles and is a member of AAHPERD and the Oregon Association for Health, Physical Education, Recreation, and Dance (OAHPERD).

Michael Odberg, MS, is founder and operations director for Ascending Adventures and is also an American Canoe Association coastal kayaking instructor. He has been guiding coastal kayaking in the Apostle Islands of Lake Superior for the past 10 years, introducing hundreds of people to coastal kayaking. Odberg is also a past outdoor recreation coordinator at the College of St. Scholastica and is currently an adjunct instructor for the college. He taught physical education for 12 years at the elementary, middle school, and high school levels. He also coached high school hockey, volleyball, and golf. Odberg is active in many outdoor pursuits in his home area of Duluth, Minnesota. He received his master's degree in physical education from the University of Wisconsin at La Crosse and also instructs pedagogy of outdoor pursuits: coastal kayaking for the University of Wisconsin at La Crosse.

Ryan Olson, MS, is the ESS/adventure coordinator at the University of Wisconsin at La Crosse. He teaches rock climbing for the University of Wisconsin at La Crosse and also operates a private guide service. He is a member of the Professional Climbing Instructors Association and obtained his base managed climbing instructor certification in 2008. Olson is a certified K-12 physical education teacher. He received his master's degree in physical education teaching with an adventure concentration from the University of Wisconsin at La Crosse.

John T. Saunders, PhD, is the director of the outdoor education program and is a professor of outdoor education at Colorado Mountain College Alpine Campus.

He has been involved with teaching snow sports and travel techniques for over a decade. He has extensive mountaineering experience. For his doctoral dissertation, he wrote *Leadership for Students Program: Through Their Eyes.* He is a member of AAHPERD and the American Avalanche Association. Saunders received the Teacher of the Year award at Colorado Mountain College Alpine Campus in 2002 and 2006. He is passionate about education and promoting healthy lifestyles and believes snowshoeing is a valuable aspect of winter activity. He received his PhD from the University of Northern Colorado.

Malin Svensson, MS, is a certified international coach through the International Nordic Walking Association (INWA) and is one of only four individuals, and the first female, to obtain this prestigious certification. Also a certified personal trainer (NSCA and NASM), Svensson is founder of Nordic Walking USA and founder and owner of Nordic Body. She is a nationally ranked track and field athlete. As a fitness speaker and coach, Svensson has conducted Nordic walking seminars and presentations throughout North America, Europe, and New Zealand. She is the author of *Outdoor Adventures: Nordic Walking,* published by Human Kinetics, and has also written the *Nordic Walking Instructor Manual.* Svensson received her master's degree in physical education from Örebro University in Sweden.

Tim P. Taylor, MA, is a professor of adventure education. He created and built the first indoor ropes course for elementary students in the state of Colorado. Taylor is the former president and owner of JungleQuest, an indoor ropes course and climbing gym. He also created and designed a complete curriculum built around adventure-based activities for elementary to high school students. He published a book of safety protocols for owners of climbing gyms. Taylor received his master's degree in physical education.

Gay L. Timken, PhD, is an associate professor of physical education teacher education at Western Oregon University. Timken works with preservice and inservice teachers in the areas of curriculum, instruction, and assessment. She teaches a course for preservice teachers on outdoor and adventure education with the goal of exposing future teachers to outdoor and adventure programming, and encouraging them to think more broadly about the content of physical education and its impact on youth. She wrote a chapter titled *Teaching All Kids: Valuing Students Through Culturally Responsive* *and Inclusive Practice* in the book *Standards-Based Physical Education Curriculum Development.* Timken is a member of AAHPERD and the American Education Research Association (AERA). Timken is a converted runner who now enjoys cycling (both road and mountain) and has been riding seriously since 2001. She received her PhD in sport pedagogy at Oregon State University.

Mark H. Zmudy, PhD, is an assistant professor at the University of Minnesota-Duluth in the department of health, physical education, and recreation. He teaches adventure education and outdoor pursuits to under-graduate students working on degrees in physical education teacher education as well as recreation/outdoor education. Zmudy is an American Canoe Association certified flat-water instructor and has instructed canoeing to a wide range of students. He also worked as a physical education teacher at the elementary and middle school levels and taught canoeing in that curriculum. He is a member of AAHPERD, the Association for Challenge Course Technology, and the American Canoe Association. Zmudy received his PhD in sport pedagogy in 2007 from the University of Alabama.

CD-ROM
User Instructions

SYSTEM REQUIREMENTS

You can use this CD-ROM on either a Windows-based PC or a Macintosh computer.

Windows

- IBM PC compatible with Pentium processor
- Windows 2000/XP/Vista/7
- Adobe Reader 8.0
- Microsoft Excel
- 4x CD-ROM drive

Macintosh

- Power Mac recommended
- System 10:4 or higher
- Adobe Reader
- Microsoft Excel for MAC
- 4x CD-ROM drive

USER INSTRUCTIONS

Windows

1. Insert the *Teaching Lifetime Outdoor Pursuits* CD-ROM. (Note: The CD-ROM must be present in the drive at all times.)
2. Select the "My Computer" icon from the desktop.
3. Select the CD-ROM drive.
4. Open the file you wish to view. See the "00Start.pdf" file for a list of the contents.

Macintosh

1. Insert the *Teaching Lifetime Outdoor Pursuits* CD-ROM. (Note: The CD-ROM must be present in the drive at all times.)
2. Double-click the CD icon located on the desktop.
3. Open the file you wish to view. See the "00Start" file for a list of the contents.

For customer support, contact Technical Support:
Phone: 217-351-5076 Monday through Friday (excluding holidays) between 7:00 a.m. and 7:00 p.m. (CST).
Fax: 217-351-2674
E-mail: support@hkusa.com